8.95

D0672198

CONTINENTAL ASIA

Hokkaidō

Sea of Japan

Sado

Honshū

KOREA

Oki

Tsushima

Strait

Korea

L Biwa

Mt Fuji

Tokyō

Osaka

Inland

Shikoku

Kyūshū

PACIFIC OCEAN

Tanegashima

Japan

Ryūkyū Is

Flat land

0   250 Km

A History of
JAPAN

R. H. P. Mason
J. G. Caiger

THE FREE PRESS
A Division of Macmillan Publishing Co., Inc.
New York

THE FREE PRESS
A Division of Macmillan Publishing Co., Inc.
866 Third Avenue, New York 10022

Library of Congress Catalog Card Number: 73–13581

First published 1972
Cassell Australia Limited

Printed and bound by Times Printers, Singapore

Contents

List of Illustrations

MAPS

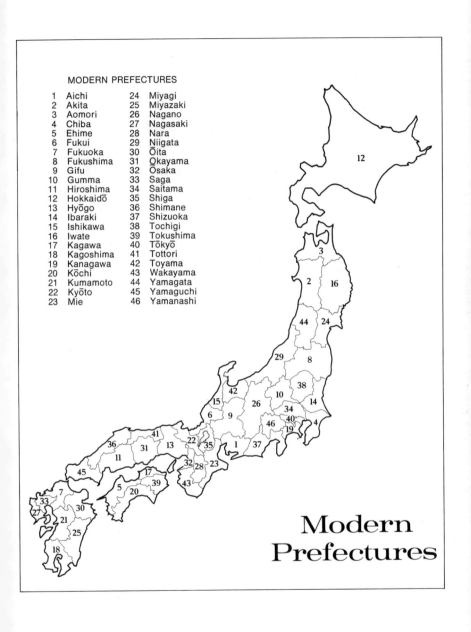

MODERN PREFECTURES

1	Aichi	24	Miyagi
2	Akita	25	Miyazaki
3	Aomori	26	Nagano
4	Chiba	27	Nagasaki
5	Ehime	28	Nara
6	Fukui	29	Niigata
7	Fukuoka	30	Ōita
8	Fukushima	31	Okayama
9	Gifu	32	Ōsaka
10	Gumma	33	Saga
11	Hiroshima	34	Saitama
12	Hokkaidō	35	Shiga
13	Hyōgo	36	Shimane
14	Ibaraki	37	Shizuoka
15	Ishikawa	38	Tochigi
16	Iwate	39	Tokushima
17	Kagawa	40	Tōkyō
18	Kagoshima	41	Tottori
19	Kanagawa	42	Toyama
20	Kōchi	43	Wakayama
21	Kumamoto	44	Yamagata
22	Kyōto	45	Yamaguchi
23	Mie	46	Yamanashi

Modern Prefectures

ACKNOWLEDGEMENTS

The authors wish to thank Professor J. D. Legge for his full and courteous assistance as general editor of the *Cassell Asian Histories*; Professor E. S. Crawcour for his encouragement; Miss Wyn Mumford for preparing the maps and line drawings; Mrs Ruth Rush for her typing; Miss Mary Hutchinson for proof reading; individuals and institutions in Japan and Australia, particularly the International Society for Educational Information in Tōkyō, for supplying photographs for the illustrations; and, for the illustration on page 86, A. L. Sadler and Charles E. Tuttle Co. Inc. and, finally, the authors and publishers listed in the bibliography for permission to reprint copyright material.

R.H.P.M.
J.G.C.

Foreword

China, Japan, India and Indonesia are, in their several ways, of tremendous importance to their neighbours and to the world at large. The progress of Communist revolution in China's vast agrarian society, the success story of Japan's industrial revolution, the efforts of India to combine the pursuit of economic development with the preservation of democratic institutions, and the problems of political stability and of population pressure in modern Indonesia, are issues of general and crucial significance. It is therefore surprising that it should have taken so long for the study of these countries to have become completely accepted as a normal part of the offerings of Australian schools and universities. The present series of volumes is designed to aid that study and, at the same time, to offer a treatment which can interest the general reader.

The authors of the four individual studies which go to make up the series have been left considerable freedom in handling their subjects as they see them, but they have accepted one common principle: they share the view that the study of any Asian country cannot be seen solely in terms of its recent history and its present situation. They recognize the persistence of tradition into the present and the way in which contemporary behaviour may reflect the long-established patterns of ancient societies. They share also the view that, quite apart from its importance in interpreting the present, the study of traditional societies is worthwhile for its own sake.

Each of these volumes therefore is concerned to place 'modern' history in the context of the longer history of the country concerned, whether it is the shape of early Asian trade and the rivalry of maritime and land-based kingdoms in the Indonesian archipelago, the artistic triumphs of the the Gupta period in India, the character of Confucian thought in China or the contribution of bureaucracy in Japan. If history must have a utilitarian purpose it is hoped that, in this way, students will be led to a more subtle and sympathetic understanding of the character of the modern countries of Asia.

J. D. Legge
Monash University

PART I

Archaic Japan

CHAPTER ONE

Environment and Early Settlement

The early Japanese, like all other peoples, wove mythological stories to explain the origin of their land. At a time in the dim, distant past, so one of these myths relates, two gods stood on the Floating Bridge of Heaven. Wondering whether there was land below, they took a jewelled spear and dipped it down into the ocean. The brine that dripped from the point of the spear formed an island. Descending to this island, the gods, one male and one female, erected a pillar and, when they had danced round it and conversed in the proper order (the male speaking first), they produced offspring: the eight main islands of Japan.

These days the Japanese turn not to the creation myths of the gods Izanagi and Izanami but to the work of archaeologists and their scientist colleagues for a rational account of their land, its formation and early settlement. Yet the old stories draw attention to the fact that the country consists of a chain of islands; and this is something which has influenced its inhabitants throughout history.

Japan took its present shape as a string of islands about 20,000 years ago. Great natural forces cut off the four largest islands of Japan and hundreds of smaller ones from the continent of Asia, leaving an arc of islands strung out over 1,500 miles. These were once linked in the south to the Korean peninsula and to China, and in the north to Siberia, leaving the Japan Sea as a huge lake. With a rise in sea level, the land-bridge in the south disappeared; later the northern land-bridge also disappeared. It was in this changing world that man began his habitation.

Until recently Japanese archaeologists thought that human occupation of the islands dated back to 5000 B.C. at the earliest, and that the first inhabitants used pottery. Now they are sure that people who did not use pottery lived in Japan long before that time, though it

3

is uncertain exactly how long. It is not known whether they crossed from Asia to the Japanese islands by means of the land-bridges or by boat. These early inhabitants of Japan are known only by their stone implements of many types: pointed knives, blade-flakes, scrapers, knife blades, hand-axes and so on, indicating by their great variety that this pre-pottery culture may have existed for tens of thousands of years.

Pottery, that durable indication of a civilizing people, was made in Japan before 10000 B.C. This date is very early indeed by world standards, and says as much for the comparatively advanced archaeological techniques that are used by Japanese today, as it does for the cultural level of the people making pottery in ancient Japan. When advanced techniques like carbon-dating are more widely used in investigating early settlement of neighbouring areas in Korea, China and Siberia, the early development of pottery in Japan may be seen in truer perspective. Nevertheless, the artistic qualities of the pottery, which changed as new uses were evolved and new decorative effects attempted, are of a high order. This pottery is named 'Jōmon' (rope-marked), and gives its name to the culture associated with it.

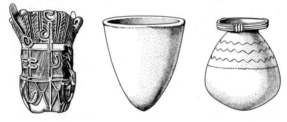

The piece in the centre, crudely shaped, thick and brittle, is a reconstruction of one of Japan's earliest pots, presumably put to a variety of uses; on the left is a Middle Jōmon pot with characteristically elaborate ornamentation; on the right is a wine container showing the simplicity typical of Yayoi pots

What we know of the way of living of Jōmon people comes from the materials found in their pit-dwellings and refuse heaps. They were gatherers, hunting and fishing; and when their control over their environment permitted, they settled for a time in camps by rivers and springs in the mountains or by the sea. The shell mounds left by the Jōmon people furnish the fullest evidence of their lives, and show us that they hunted deer, boar and many other animals with bows and arrows, and fished with harpoons and bone fish-hooks. Quite a number of skeletons of Jōmon men have been preserved in the mounds where the shells' lime has acted as a neutralizer (because of the humid climate and acidity of the soil in Japan, skeletons outside shell mounds disintegrated quickly). It is difficult to tell from the Jōmon skeletons whether these people were the ancestors of the present-day Japanese or not; nor do we know whether the Jōmon people were the ancestors of the people who produced the next and one of the greatest changes in Japanese history.

This change was the introduction of agriculture into a hospitable environment. In winter, the country's proximity to the Asian continent gives it a climate not greatly different from that of the eastern edge of Siberia, though the Siberian winds are neither as dry nor as cold after crossing the Japan Sea. In summer, with warm moist winds blowing towards the continent, Japan shows herself more clearly to be a chain of islands in the Pacific. These monsoon winds from the ocean give ample rain in summer, permitting rice to grow. Rice-growing was first established in western Japan sometime after 300 B.C., probably by immigrants from the continent driven out by disturbed conditions. At first, no doubt, the rice was grown in marshy places. Later, land in valley-bottoms and coastal plains was drained, levelled and irrigated in operations demanding communal effort. Similarly the planting, transplanting and harvesting of rice demanded co-ordinated effort by a community. The new knowledge spread very quickly from west to east, and enabled a far denser population to live in one place. Permanent villages began to appear. In this way, in Japan as elsewhere, agriculture led people to make more efficient use of their environment.

Apart from indirect evidence of rice-growing, charred grains of rice and chaff have been found in jars and imprinted on the bases of pots. These finds enable us to say that the grain originated in eastern China, though it probably came through north China and Korea. Again the pottery has given its name to the culture of its creators. The name 'Yayoi', after the district in Tōkyō where this plain, regular type of pot was first found in 1884, is used to describe the period in Japanese history when rice-growing and then metal-working, as well as the new pottery, were introduced from continental Asia.

A second great step towards a civilized life was taken by the Yayoi people when they began to use metal. Tools, weapons and mirrors made of bronze and iron were brought from the continent at first, but in time were made in Japan. Bronze articles (swords, mirrors and a bell-like object known as *dōtaku*) seem to have been used as symbols of power and for religious rituals, while iron was used by farmers and builders. An iron working-edge greatly improved the efficiency of implements used in daily work for such tasks as shaping wooden spades, rakes and hoes, and splitting the wooden slats used to reinforce paths between the rice fields. The wooden tools used in Yayoi times and preserved in the mud bear a striking resemblance to the tools used less than a century ago. It is only recently, in the twentieth century, that the load borne by human labour has been lightened by the use of machines, with profound social effects. Such changes in present-day Japan are similar to the transformations in the Yayoi period, which seem to have set a general pattern of social organization and to have regulated social behaviour for the mass of the Japanese people for two millennia.

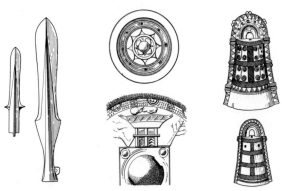

This flat bronze sword and halberd of local make were patterned on continental examples. The complete mirror shown here is of Chinese origin, but the lower drawing shows the central part of a later mirror, made in Japan, decorated with a raised storehouse of the Yayoi period. The bronze bells, of peculiarly Japanese design, exemplify the level of sophistication reached by the Japanese in the Yayoi period

Despite all these developments the Japanese were still far from being as civilized as the Chinese. In the sense that they had no written script, they were still a prehistoric people before about 400 A.D.[1] However, Chinese writings, almost certainly based on travellers' reports, provide a picture of life. The passage that follows is taken from a third century A.D. Chinese history that included a section on the land of Wa (Japan).

[1] Their spoken language probably resembled the continental Asian language group called Altaic, of which the westernmost member is Turkish, with words that suggest links with south-east Asia.

The social customs [of the Wa] are not lewd. The men wear a band of cloth around their heads, exposing the top. Their clothing is fastened around the body with little sewing. The women wear their hair in loops. Their clothing is like an unlined coverlet and is worn by slipping the head through an opening in the center. [The people] cultivate grains, rice, hemp, and mulberry trees for sericulture. They spin and weave and produce fine linen and silk fabrics. There are no oxen, horses, tigers, leopards, sheep, or magpies. Their weapons are spears, shields, and wooden bows made with short lower part and long upper part; and their bamboo arrows are sometimes tipped with iron or bone. . . .

The land of Wa is warm and mild [in climate]. In winter as in summer the people live on vegetables and go about bare-footed. Their houses have rooms; father and mother, older and younger, sleep separately. They smear their bodies with pink and scarlet, just as the Chinese use powder. They serve meat on bamboo and wooden trays, helping themselves with their fingers. When a person dies, they prepare a single coffin, without an outer one. They cover the graves with sand to make a mound. When death occurs, mourning is observed for more than ten days, during which period they do not eat meat. The head mourners wail and lament, while friends sing, dance, and drink liquor. When the funeral is over, all members of the whole family go into the water to cleanse themselves in a bath of purification.

When they go on voyages across the sea to visit China, they always select a man who does not arrange his hair, does not rid himself of fleas, lets his clothing [get as] dirty as it will, does not eat meat, and does not approach women. This man behaves like a mourner and is known as the fortune keeper. When the voyage turns out propitious, they all lavish on him slaves and other valuables. In case there is disease or mishap, they kill him, saying that he was not scrupulous in his duties.[2]

Such an account shows that Japan was clearly a part of the rice-growing, metal-working civilization of East Asia, but not yet a highly developed part, the Japanese being still a long way from achieving that degree of unity which already at times made China a powerful and centralized empire. Yet in time, and in its own way, Japan achieved a degree of unification that is remarkable both in political and cultural terms. The earliest phase of this development was not recorded in writing until centuries had passed, but the archaeologist is recovering more and more detail about the beginnings of Japan as

[2] Tsunoda and Goodrich, *Japan in the Chinese Dynastic Histories—Later Han Through Ming Dynasties*, pp. 10–11.

a civilized State. In 1965 on a construction site near Ōsaka airport, a Yayoi period village was unearthed which showed that a few of its people had been treated in a privileged way both when alive and dead. This find has caused some excitement because such distinction is seen as a step in the important process of social selection that creates a few families who wield conspicuously greater power in agricultural communities. Later, from the third to the sixth centuries A.D., the evidence for social differentiation and growing political unity is far richer.

CHAPTER TWO

Yamato

Japanese legends give a remarkably specific answer to the question, 'When did the Japanese State begin to emerge?': Jimmu ascended the throne as the first emperor of Japan on 11 February (the first day of spring) in 660 B.C. at his palace in the Yamato region.

The makers of legends may speak in certainties, but modern historians present us with the hesitant statement that a start was made towards building a centre of political power in the Yamato region probably in the late third or early fourth century A.D. They regard the date 660 B.C. as about a thousand years too early.

The Beginnings of Political Unity

How do modern historians work out the problem of dating the beginnings of political unity? They subject the earliest Japanese histories, full of legendary material, to critical examination and try to explain what they find. Historians have not rejected 660 B.C. because it is an arbitrary date conjured out of the imagination of men in ancient times, but because rational calculation indicates that it is based on premises which we cannot accept. The learned men who first settled on this date were aware of the Chinese notion of time cycles. These cycles lasted sixty years, and the fifty-eighth year of each cycle was said to bring with it some remarkable change. The year 601 A.D. was the fifty-eighth year of one of these cycles, and in fact momentous changes were taking place at the time. The Chinese believed that in the fifty-eighth year of every twenty-first cycle of sixty years, that is to say once every 1,260 years, an event of even greater importance took place. Counting back one great cycle of 1,260 years from 601 A.D., the date for the accession of the first emperor to the throne, an event of surpassing importance, was determined as 660 B.C.

Modern historians have built up a credible alternative to 660 B.C.

9

not by rejecting legends and early stories as nonsense, but by examining early Japanese histories, even earlier Chinese accounts dating from 25 A.D., and a rich and growing store of archaeological finds. It is the Chinese histories that give the earliest contemporary accounts of political life in Japan.

The Chinese reported that, in the mid third century, the Japanese lived not in a single State but in more than one hundred small communities. The State which most interested the Chinese was one ruled by a queen.

> The country formerly had a man as ruler. For some seventy or eighty years after that there were disturbances and warfare. Thereupon the people agreed upon a woman for their ruler. Her name was Pimiko. She occupied herself with magic and sorcery, bewitching the people. Though mature in age, she remained unmarried. She had a younger brother who assisted her in ruling the country. After she became the ruler, there were few who saw her. She had one thousand women as attendants, but only one man. He served her food and drink and acted as a medium of communication. She resided in a palace surrounded by towers and stockades, with armed guards in a state of constant vigilance.[1]

Queen Pimiko is best described as a female shaman or high priestess, combining religious and political power. She was the ruler of a state called Yamatai. Was Yamatai, as the Chinese thought, the political centre of the whole country? This is doubtful.

If the Chinese account is followed faithfully, Yamatai can only be placed well to the south of Japan, in the Pacific Ocean. If, however, an adjustment is made to the distances mentioned, then Yamatai can be located on the west coast of the island of Kyūshū. If an adjustment is made to the direction but not the distance, then Yamatai can be located in the central area of Japan in the region known as Yamato, where Japanese tradition and archaeological evidence agree that some political unification existed. Argument about the true location of Yamatai has continued for centuries and still continues.

The Chinese records, then, do not describe with absolute certainty the Court in Yamato, which is the place celebrated in legend and accepted by modern historians as the birthplace of the Japanese State. They do suggest strongly that Japan was not yet a single political unit in the period from 221 to 265 A.D. of which the Chinese scholar was writing. Unfortunately, the Chinese were not in constant

[1] Tsunoda and Goodrich, *Japan in the Chinese Dynastic Histories*, p. 13.

touch with events in Japan, so that all the subsequent changes in the concentration of power were not reported in writing by contemporaries but recorded four or five centuries later in Japan for the imperial family. These native records establish a great centre of political power in the Yamato region and record the spread of Yamato influence elsewhere. But the account is imprecise and frequently erroneous; the modern Japanese archaeologist's task has been to supply more accurate information, above all on the question of dates.

Control of the eastern provinces was rather slowly established. Yamato influence was first felt in the western part of the country, extending as far as Mimana in southern Korea. Even this was a sizeable area, and the Yamato rulers left impressive monuments to their territorial power in the form of their own burial mounds. At first, at the end of the third or beginning of the fourth century, mounds were comparatively small and built into natural hills. By the fifth century the power of the Yamato rulers had increased, judging by the scale of the greatest of their resting places. These graves still stand on the plains like small hills. They were surrounded by moats and had a distinctive 'key-hole' shape. Too big to be seen properly from the ground, only aerial photographs do justice to these structures, which are as bulky as the pyramids, though not as high. The greatest of them, the tomb of the Emperor Nintoku, situated in modern Ōsaka prefecture, occupies an area of eighty acres and is 2,695 feet long including its moats. It is said to have taken twenty years to complete. Such was the enormous power of one Yamato ruler to mobilize men to work for him.

The practice of building tombs in the style of the Yamato rulers soon spread as local rulers followed the fashion set by the most powerful men in the land. In all, perhaps twenty thousand of these burial mounds survive throughout Japan, with a greater number in more advanced areas, that is, areas in close touch with the Yamato Court. The tombs of the Yamato rulers show by their size that their builders were able to command the greatest supply of labour in the country, but outlying rulers of local areas could also construct sizeable graves. In the area called Kibi, west from Yamato along the Inland Sea, 140 huge 'key-hole' tombs of local chieftains have been found.[2] The largest is a mound 90 feet high and over 1,100 feet long. On a reasonable estimate it would have taken a thousand men four years to

---

[2] The details are taken from Hall, *Government and Local Power in Japan 500–1700—A Study Based on Bizen Province*. This is an excellent survey of local history set in a national context.

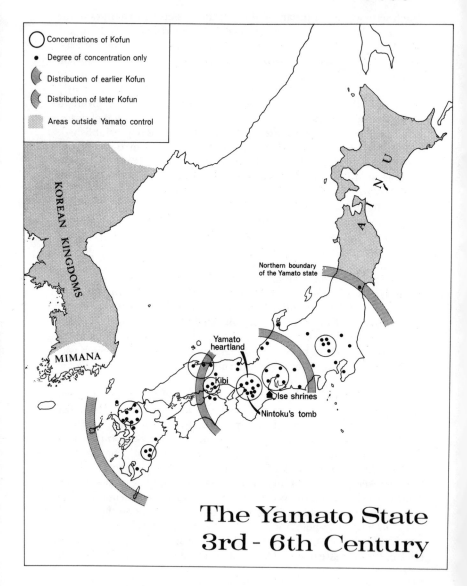

Concentrations of Kofun

Degree of concentration only

Distribution of earlier Kofun

Distribution of later Kofun

Areas outside Yamato control

KOREAN KINGDOMS

E Z O

MIMANA

Northern boundary
of the Yamato state

Yamato
heartland

Kibi

Ise shrines

Nintoku's tomb

The Yamato State
3rd - 6th Century

complete the mound itself, not including the burial chambers and decorations. Such tasks required a considerable degree of control by the ruling *élite* over a mass of labourers, and mark the beginning of political authority by men who can only be described as rulers.

Large 'keyhole'-shaped tombs with their moats now lie scattered in fields close to residential areas near Osaka. The largest, that of Emperor Ojin, measures 415 metres in length and 35 metres in height. The scale of smaller tombs is shown by one in a group on the Kantō plain, far to the east of the heartland of tomb-culture

In their external decoration, the burial mounds were from the beginning distinctively Japanese. On their sloping sides pottery workers set up unglazed clay cylinders of a reddish-brown colour, known as *haniwa*. They are several feet high, for they were made to be seen by worshippers and passers-by from a considerable distance, at least from across the moats surrounding the mounds. Set into the ground in rows, the *haniwa* are thought to have been fences to mark out the hallowed burial ground and, when moulded at the top in the form of houses, to have provided a home for the spirit of the dead chieftain.

Found in Kyushu, the *haniwa* boat is a reminder of the importance of contact with the continent during the period of tomb-building. The house represents one style favoured by powerful families. The horse, a common animal representation among *haniwa*, was highly prized by the ruling *élite*

At first, *haniwa* were simply cylinders. Later they were decorated with elaborate representations, not only of houses but of objects in everyday life: horses, which were especially prized, and other domesticated animals, boats, ceremonial sunshades, warriors' equipment (shields and quivers, archers' wrist protectors, armour and helmets). Human representations include female shamans in ritual attire such as they might have worn when presiding at funeral celebrations, fully armed warriors, peasants, and dancing figures of men and women. Since they were portrayed in detail, it is possible to learn something about the way of life of the people in Yamato times as well as about the aesthetic sense of *haniwa* creators and their patrons.

Haniwa were made by a group of craftsmen whose hereditary occupation was working in clay. There were a number of specialized groups called *be* in the community, most of them concerned with rice-growing. Others provided such varied goods and services as war materials, woven fabric, fish, and military service. The *be* were subordinate to the ruling families or *uji*, which were kinship groups linked by blood, not by common occupation.

More than a hundred years after the first burial mounds were built in the late third or early fourth century, a remarkable change occurred in the articles buried with the dead chieftains, which distinguished them even more dramatically than before from the mass of the people. The chieftains, it seems, had acquired luxurious tastes and had taken up habits similar to those of warriors on the continent of Asia as a result of the inclusion of north Kyūshū in the Yamato State and the Yamato military advance across the sea into Korea some time in the fourth century. These developments brought the Yamato *élite* into close touch with life on the continent, and the contents of the later chieftains' graves include the equipment and trappings of a privileged, horse-riding aristocracy: iron armour and swords, horse-masks, gilt-bronze shoes, gold and silver ornaments and crowns. This display of wealth is a reminder that while the rice farmer and the fisherman lived simply and naturally off the resources immediately available to them, it was otherwise with the more civilized part of the population. Their taste was formed by continental Asian influences.

The greatest chieftains or *uji* leaders lived at the Yamato Court, where their effective power was often greater than that of the Yamato ruler himself. One reason was that *uji* leaders had direct control over large areas of productive land and the people who worked it. Another important reason was that when the Yamato ruler died, the chieftains shared in choosing his successor from among the members of the ruling family. Thus, under the Yamato State Japan was not yet a single political unit but a complex of groups—*uji* and *be*—which were partly territorial and partly occupational. Nevertheless the imperial family in Yamato was growing in influence, as evidenced most clearly by their tombs.

The authority of the sovereign in the Yamato State depended to some extent on military might, and the traditional Japanese accounts describe the conquest and cunningly contrived subjugation of the

Japanese islands by the Yamato Court. A network of family connections through marriage enabled the sovereign to exert authority over powerful chieftains in other parts of the country. In time these blood relationships were turned into something more impersonal, resembling more closely the link between a ruler and his officials. The wealth of the imperial family was also an important factor in the rise of the Yamato Court, drawn as it was from various parts of the country where imperial *be* of all kinds were situated. Especially important were the imperial *be* composed of skilled foreign immigrants. These foreign artisans seem to have been sent as tribute by Korean rulers, and the very fact that kings across the sea recognized the claims of the Yamato dynasty bolstered its authority within the country.

The authority of the sovereign, though supported by religious, military, familial, economic and diplomatic sources of strength, was still not sufficient for the Yamato Court to govern the whole country effectively. Nevertheless, the men at the Yamato Court, with the sovereign at their head, were better practised than their fellow chieftains in the art of exerting control over far-flung parts of the country. Despite the rudimentary nature of the Yamato administration, it was much more advanced than the leadership of the small communities of the Yayoi period. As the Yamato Court became more sophisticated, it appreciated the more advanced techniques of government evolved in China. The time was not far off when it would deliberately adopt Chinese governmental institutions to bring the country more securely under the control of the emperor.

Government and Religion

The first emperor of Japan did not ascend the throne in 660 B.C., but Japan's imperial institution is still the world's oldest hereditary office. It has been passed down through the members of one family, seemingly without any break through adoption or usurpation since archaic times. Religious beliefs have helped to perpetuate it.

The head of the imperial family in Yamato, from whom the present emperor is descended, claimed direct descent from the sun goddess (Amaterasu Ōmikami) and was thought to possess the unique ability to call on her powers. For an agricultural people the role of the emperor as direct intercessor with the sun goddess was most important. The very word for 'government' in ancient Japan was *matsurigoto* meaning 'the business of worship'. It is the sacred character of the office that has helped to preserve the imperial institution through many centuries and various turbulent times. Although government (control of taxation, armed forces, and so on) may have fallen under the control of one great family or another, the sacred role of the emperor has never been usurped.

The term *kami* is important in trying to understand why the imperial institution has survived. The most famous attempt at explaining what is meant by *kami* was made in the eighteenth century by the great scholar Motoori Norinaga.

> I do not yet understand the meaning of the term, *kami*. Speaking in general, however, it may be said that *kami* signifies, in the first place, the deities of heaven and earth that appear in the ancient records and also the spirits of the shrines where they are worshipped.
>
> It is hardly necessary to say that it includes human beings. It also includes such objects as birds, beasts, trees, plants, seas, mountains, and so forth. In ancient usage, anything whatsoever which was outside the ordinary, which possessed superior power or which was awe-inspiring was called *kami*. Eminence here does not refer merely to the superiority of nobility, goodness or meritorious deeds. Evil and mysterious things, if they are extraordinary and dreadful, are called *kami*. It is needless to say that among human beings who are called *kami* the successive generations of sacred emperors are all included. The fact that emperors are also called distant *kami* is because from the standpoint of common people, they are far-separated, majestic and worthy of reverence. In a lesser degree we find, in the present as well as in ancient times, human beings who are *kami*. Although they may not be accepted throughout the whole country, yet in each province, each village, and each family there are human beings who are *kami*, each one according to his own proper position. The *kami* of the divine age were for the most part human beings of that time and, because the people of that time were all *kami*, it is called the Age of the Gods (*kami*).[3]

Kami no michi (the Ways of the Gods), or Shinto, as this animistic religion is called, has no founder and no bible. To gain an understanding of Shinto in archaic times it is necessary to study later written records of its buildings, ceremonies and prayers and to examine the places where worship has been conducted down the centuries. In its most ancient form the religion is thought to have emphasized ritual purity, a cleansing of pollution stemming from disease and death, from bleeding and anti-social acts. Worship expressing hope (at the

---

[3] Holtom, *The National Faith of Japan*, pp. 23–4.

time of rice-planting for example) and gratitude (at the completion of the harvest) was designed to attract supernatural protection. Sacred areas where worship was performed were marked off; straw ropes hung with strips of paper were strung round special trees and rocks or hung across *torii*, the ceremonial entrances to sacred places. In ancient times, if there was a special building to house the *kami*, it was a simple structure, even a temporary one, but in time the shrine became permanent and complex. Extra buildings were added: buildings for worship, for reciting prayers and for purification, as well as stages for ceremonial dances. Today there are tens of thousands of shrines throughout Japan, and several of great distinction, among them the shrines of Ise.

The simplicity of the buildings at Ise belies the skill of the carpenter in working wood and enhancing its innate beauty. In their use of plain wood and thatch and their natural setting among tall trees the shrines form the greatest examples of an ancient tradition of taste still surviving. These buildings, of national importance because the sun goddess is enshrined in the greatest of them, have been preserved by the practice of periodic rebuilding, in a style resembling the granaries of the archaic period. The present buildings, where the reigning emperor has paid his respects from time to time, date from 1953. They are the fifty-ninth in the series of structures erected since the late seventh century A.D., and there were buildings of a presumably simpler style from centuries before that time. The sites for new buildings, to appear in the early 1970s, stand empty beside the present ones, now weathered to a mellow grey. The continuity of worship in buildings regularly renewed is impressive, and all the more so when it is realized that the aristocratic rulers of Japan became highly sophisticated in other ways—especially in their adoption of Buddhism.

PART II

Ancient Japan

CHAPTER THREE

The Creation of a Unified State

Isolation from the Asian continent, which gave the Japanese security from attack by foreign peoples, provided the chance for a distinctive civilization to evolve in Japan. It also had the effect of making the Japanese more self-conscious in their dealings with foreign cultures, more willing to borrow deliberately when the need became apparent. The creation by the Japanese of a unified State under an emperor served by bureaucrats was just such an undertaking—the result of conscious borrowing of Chinese ideas and practices by the court in Yamato, which had already begun to assert a measure of control over the whole country.

It is possible to learn something of the details of the creation of a unified State during the sixth, seventh and eighth centuries because the Japanese had already adopted yet another skill of Chinese origin, the art of writing. Rather than archaeology and Chinese accounts, therefore, the main source of information for the late sixth and the seventh centuries is a history of Japan called the *Nihon shoki*, submitted to the sovereign by officials in 720 A.D. As an official history, the *Nihon shoki* concentrates on the role of the imperial line and its bureaucratic servants. It practically ignores the rice-farmers and fisher-folk and so of necessity have later historians, for history is not the story of everything that happened in the past but only of the knowable past. Yet the official record for these years is anything but uneventful, since it is essentially an account of how a few men transformed the Yamato State into a centralized empire.

The Soga Victory

In 552 A.D., according to the *Nihon shoki*, the king of one of the small kingdoms in Korea appealed to the Yamato Court for troops to use

21

against his enemies in Korea. He sent a copper and gold image of Buddha, some religious flags and umbrellas, and volumes of sacred Buddhist writings. In an accompanying letter he warmly commended Buddhism, saying, 'This doctrine is amongst all doctrines the most excellent. But it is hard to explain, and hard to comprehend'. The Yamato ruler's response was diplomatic. 'Never from former days until now have we had the opportunity of listening to so wonderful a doctrine. We are unable, however, to decide of ourselves.'[1] When he asked his ministers, their responses varied. The head of an important *uji* called the Soga recommended acceptance of the gifts but the *uji* leaders of the powerful Mononobe and Nakatomi declared that 'If just at this time we were to worship in their stead foreign Deities, it may be feared that we should incur the wrath of our National Gods'.[2] The emperor compromised and gave the image of Buddha to the head of the Soga *uji* so that he could worship it privately. Not long afterwards many people died in an epidemic, giving the Mononobe and Nakatomi *uji* the chance to claim that the plague was connected with the new religion. The emperor sided with them, and officials threw the image of Buddha into a canal and burned the temple where it had been housed.

The conflict over the official approval of Buddhist worship continued until 587 A.D. This time the Soga won decisively. The supporters of Buddhism led by the Soga destroyed the Mononobe who had insistently cried, 'Why should we reverence strange deities, and turn our backs upon the gods of our country?'[3] The Soga leader had vowed before the final attack to build a temple and encourage Buddhism if his prayer to the Buddhist gods for protection was answered. He fulfilled his vow by building the Hōkōji, the Temple of the Rise of Truth, and Buddhism began to spread.

What has this story to do with the making of a centralized State? At the time the dispute may have seemed no more than a wrangle between factions at court but, seen in perspective, the military victory of the Soga in 587 A.D. is of great historical importance.

The Soga was a new family, a branch of the imperial line, which rose to eminence quite late. Its chieftains did not base their authority on the claim that they were descended from the mythological *kami* of high antiquity. Rather, they served at court as treasurers, collecting and storing and paying out goods produced by people directly under

[1] W. G. Aston's translation of the *Nihongi—Chronicles of Japan from the Earliest Times to A.D. 697*, Part II, p. 66. The *Nihon shoki* is also called the *Nihongi*.
[2] *Nihongi*, Part II, p. 67.
[3] *Nihongi*, Part II, p. 110.

the authority of the Yamato rulers. These goods included rice from land recently developed by the imperial house, and the products of immigrant Chinese and Korean craftsmen. None of these workers and craftsmen owed their allegiance to the head of the Soga *uji* as a *kami*, but they were subject to his authority as a bureaucrat, acting in the name of the sovereign.

The victory of the Soga over the Mononobe in 587 A.D. can be seen as the victory of the new men, the bureaucrats, over figures of traditional authority. The imperial family recognized the Mononobe claim that they were descended from a *kami* who flew down from heaven riding in a 'heavenly-rock-boat' and performed a singular act of loyalty to the first legendary emperor, Jimmu, very early in his reign. The Mononobe, bound together in worship of the founder of their *uji*, traditionally supplied weapons to the court. They gained a strong degree of independent authority by virtue of their length of service and divine descent. The Mononobe naturally feared that respect due to divine descent would be discounted when the authority of the *kami* was challenged by Buddhist teaching; but in fact Buddhism did not wreck the political order by suddenly destroying respect for the *kami*. Buddhism and Shinto were to find ways of coexisting. Nevertheless after 587 A.D. the native cult was overshadowed, as the sovereigns and their Soga ministers openly patronized the new religion which helped their power to grow at the expense of that of the semi-independent *uji*. In this way, Buddhism aided the centralization of political authority.

Prince Shōtoku

Buddhism, though a religion of peace and favoured by powerful men, did not still the turmoil at the Yamato court. In the same month that the Soga leader, Umako (born ?–died 626) completed the worship hall and covered gallery of the Hōkōji Temple, he was conspiring to assassinate the emperor. This he did and set his own nominee, his niece, on the throne. Umako was anxious to keep control at court not by usurping the throne for himself but by dominating an acceptable titular ruler, or in plain terms by being the power behind the throne. Umako went further and nominated as heir apparent and regent for the new empress a young man of great promise who was remarkable for his understanding of, and enthusiasm for, Buddhism. His name was Shōtoku, and he was descended from both the imperial and the Soga families.

Prince Shōtoku (574–622) is the Prince Charming of Japanese

history. So many remarkable gifts have been ascribed to him that it is difficult to believe that he was once a real man. The *Nihon shoki* says that he was able to speak as soon as he was born; that when he grew up he could attend to the petitions of ten men at once and in his wisdom could decide them all without error; and that he knew beforehand what was going to happen. When Prince Shōtoku died after a regency of thirty years, the well-born and the common people, young and old, all lamented his death: 'The sun and moon have lost their brightness; heaven and earth have crumbled to ruin: henceforward, in whom shall we put our trust?'[4]

We know very little about what Prince Shōtoku had done to deserve such veneration. He founded a Buddhist temple that now ranks as the oldest in Japan. In his time as regent, a system of grades for court officials on the Chinese pattern was introduced that cut across the old native Japanese system of inherited office; also the Chinese-style calendar mentioned at the beginning of Chapter Two was adopted. These same years saw the despatch of the first official envoy from the ruler of a united Japan to the Chinese court. This man, and other ambassadors and scholars who followed him, brought back knowledge of Chinese government that was put to good use in the years ahead. In short, the prince was responsible for closer, peaceful contact with China and the deliberate adoption of several civilized Chinese practices.

Prince Shōtoku is venerated not so much for what he did as for what he stood for. He seems to have been the first Japanese to proclaim principles intended to support properly a centralized State under imperial rule. These principles were borrowed from Chinese Confucian doctrine and are expressed in full in the so-called constitution of Prince Shōtoku. In broad terms, this document, in seventeen articles, says that people should accept imperial rule in order to achieve social harmony.[5]

Prince Shōtoku also symbolized Japan's early efforts to come to grips with Buddhism, both in his role as a student and as a teacher of its doctrines. The Buddhist religion, as contained in a body of writings called Sutras, was already highly developed by the time it came to Japan through China.

According to its fundamental doctrine, all living beings, animals as well as men, are doomed to successive lives in an endless and hateful

---

[4] *Nihongi*, Part II, p. 148.

[5] This document is found in *Nihongi*, Part II, pp. 129–133 or, in adapted form, in Tsunoda, *Sources of the Japanese Tradition*, pp. 50–53.

cycle of existence. The state in which any being is reborn on a particular occasion depends on past deeds and the intention behind them (karma). A person will either rise to a happier state of existence or sink to a more miserable one according to his accumulation of karma. However, this is really a secondary consideration because, for the Buddhist, existence at all times and under all circumstances is inherently evil. To live is to suffer. Therefore the great aim of the believer is to break the cycle of rebirth and so be free from suffering for ever. Suffering has its cause in a craving for existence and pleasure which can be suppressed by moral conduct, mental discipline and wisdom. It is possible then for a person to break the cycle of existence and cease to be reborn by eliminating selfish desire.

Even this short explanation shows how far Buddhism went beyond the native Japanese religion of the time in attempting to explain the nature of existence. In Prince Shōtoku's day, salvation was regarded as a matter of personal effort on the part of monks and nuns. Each monk was concerned about accumulating his own meritorious karma through study shut away from the world in a monastery. It was Shōtoku's patronage of monasteries, as well as his personal piety and studies, that earned him a high place in the history of Japanese Buddhism.

The prince was to die before he saw his Confucian and Buddhist principles put into practice. Harmony was not greatly valued by the Soga leaders, who were less prudent after Umako's death. Umako had been content to operate quietly behind the throne. His son and grandson not only decided which member of the imperial family should occupy the throne, but also gave every appearance of planning to usurp it for themselves and their descendants. This would have destroyed the imperial family and violated the fundamental principle of Japanese imperial succession, which was that the emperor or empress must be descended from the sun goddess because only such descendants could communicate with her.

In the year 645, opponents of the Soga leaders struck back. The final coup was preceded by careful preparations that included a famous meeting at a football game between the two leading anti-Soga aristocrats, the head of the Nakatomi clan, named Kamatari (614–669), and a young imperial prince, Naka-no-Ōe (626–671). The final scene of the Soga era was played out in front of the empress herself at court when the leading Soga strongman was wounded in a sudden attack. After the empress had retired in great distress, he was killed.

The victors in this coup took advantage of their sudden rise to power to announce within a surprisingly short time reforms that followed the general principles of Shōtoku's constitution.

The Taika Reform

To celebrate the change ushered in by the death of the Soga leaders, the chief conspirators, who had now become the crown prince and the chief minister, gave the era a name, *Taika*, meaning 'Great Change'. They intended this name to signify not so much a change in their personal fortunes as the transformation they hoped to bring about in the government of the country.

Although the name Taika suggests a sudden change, the work of Naka-no-Ōe and Nakatomi Kamatari was not a new beginning in the process of centralization; the forebears of the recently assassinated Soga had played a leading part in this process, ironically enough, as bureaucratic servants of the imperial clan. Nor did the reformers transform Japan into a centralized State at one stroke. The changes outlined in their reform edicts were not realized for decades. But Kamatari and his youthful associate have been justly celebrated as the first men to try to embody Prince Shōtoku's principles in practical form, using Chinese precedents so as to make a fully centralized imperial State out of the loosely associated *uji*.

On new year's day 646 they promulgated a reform edict of four articles to strengthen the political power of the sovereign. Article One declared that land and people formerly controlled by the *uji* were to be placed under imperial administration.[6] Article Two decreed that a capital city be built as the centre of a system of government which was to reach out into the country at large. Article Three ordered the compilation of population and taxation registers and land laws. Article Four introduced a new system of taxation.

This new year's day edict was a statement of broad principle that reformers spent the next fifty years putting into practice. The effective embodiment of these principles was the Taihō administrative and penal code, promulgated in the years 701-2. Despite the need to adapt the principles to the existing political and social situation, the underlying purpose of the Taika Reform was not neglected. This was

[6] When a particular case concerning control over some *be* came up later in 646, the crown prince made the following general statement: 'In Heaven there are not two suns: in a country there are not two rulers. It is therefore the Emperor alone who is supreme over all the Empire, and who has a right to the services of the myriad people.' *Nihongi*, Part II, p. 217.

the creation of a centralized imperial State, which would be ruled directly by the emperor in accordance with a system of written law and with the help of bureaucratic officials whom he himself had appointed to office and could dismiss whenever he pleased.

These officials were largely drawn from the old aristocratic class. However, the basis of aristocratic power had altered significantly. Whereas before 645 the old *uji* families had controlled their *be*, after 645 the imperial State stepped in. It took taxes in the form of goods and services directly from the people, and distributed part of the tax, in its own name, as payment to those aristocrats who acted as officials. In trying to achieve greater control of the country by the emperor, the reformers chose to regard all people as his subjects but to treat them differently according to their rank as determined by birth. Consequently, although the Taika Reform was a political revolution, and although it altered the social status of the masses from a condition of serfdom as members of the *be* to one of free subjects as leaseholders from the State, the upper class in no way considered the Reform to contain an element of social revolution.

The reasons for this seem to have been as follows. Firstly, any outright attack on the hereditary principle might have endangered the sovereign claims of the imperial dynasty itself. Secondly, the reformers had come to power as a result of what was no more than a palace revolution, and had to carry out their programme with limited popular support and even more limited military strength. In effect the Taika Reform was a far-sighted policy enforced from above by a small number of the ruling *élite* under extremely hazardous conditions. They could not afford to antagonize the established aristocracy and so they seem to have created a principle of compensation. The authority and social status which the *uji* leaders lost with the abolition of the *be* and estates were largely restored to them in the form of a monopoly over the new bureaucratic posts.[7] An intriguing element of the Reform should be pointed out. Taika period Japan is a singular example of a society attempting to set up a centralized imperial form of government without a strong element of armed force and preliminary conquest.

The Taihō Code probably operated more effectively after 710 when

[7] Even the powerful Emperor Temmu (reigned 673–686), who exercised personal leadership, insisted that officials should above all else be suitably well-born. He issued a decree in 682, saying, 'Let the lineage and character of all candidates for office be always inquired into before a selection is made. No one whose lineage is insufficient is eligible for appointment, even though his character, conduct and capacity may be unexceptionable.' (Adapted from *Nihongi*, Part II, p. 357.)

a capital was built at Nara in the Yamato region.[8] It provided for a Department of Worship and a Department of State. Despite the growing interest in Buddhism, the Department of Worship was concerned with Shinto only: the supervision of the principal shrines and rites (enthronements, and services of purification and thanksgiving). This body took precedence over the Department of State but its functions were restricted. The Department of State, with its many ministries, was concerned with the material needs of the court and the general administration of the country.

The highest posts were reserved for the high nobility. Men had to be of noble rank to hold the newly created office of governor of a province, of which there were later sixty-six. These men, the senior officials in the countryside, were from the capital and their ancestors had lived at court for generations. The old local aristocracy, who had not left the provinces, operated at a lower level in the new scheme of things. They were put in charge of the districts that made up each province and were under the control of the imperial governor. There were more than five hundred of these districts. Both groups of traditional power-holders, the clan leaders and the local aristocrats, now occupied a different position in the government of the country, functioning as servants of the emperor. No longer were they absolute masters of territory and people.

Nevertheless, as agents of the central government, officials at the provincial and district levels continued to be in control of the manpower of the country—the only kind of power which could physically move mountains in those days or open up new rice-lands, repair roads and build palaces. The mass of the people were peasant cultivators. The officials kept track of the population through a regular census, which was meant to be taken every six years. Census records enabled the officials to collect taxes from the peasants as well as to allocate rice-fields to them. The amount of land a peasant household received depended on its size. The peasants could use this land but could not dispose of it privately, as in theory all land belonged to the ruler.[9]

[8] Up to this time the capital had been moved from time to time. Only the barest traces of some former capitals now remain. The capital called Fujiwara where the Taihō Code was drawn up is now marked by a clump of trees. Nara remained the capital until 784.

[9] The regular pattern of this system of uniform land division can be seen in aerial photographs of parts of the country in close touch with the capital. The system was probably not extended to outlying parts of the empire for several centuries, but in some areas uniform land division may well have predated the Taika Reform.

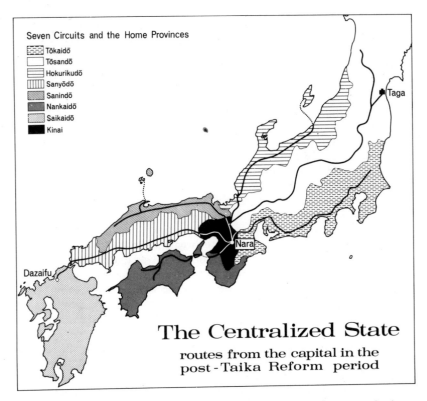

Seven Circuits and the Home Provinces
- Tōkaidō
- Tōsandō
- Hokurikudō
- Sanyōdō
- Sanindō
- Nankaidō
- Saikaidō
- Kinai

Taga

Nara

Dazaifu

The Centralized State

routes from the capital in the
post - Taika Reform period

The land itself was not intended to yield the bulk of the tax, for it was assessed at the low rate of between three and five per cent of the yield. Heavy taxes of other kinds were levied on the male population. Labour was required by the provincial and central administrations for public works, but this could be converted into its equivalent value in cloth. Products of the region: cotton cloth, hemp, salt, earthenware vessels, timber, vegetables or fish, were payable to the government. Military service was also required and seems to have caused great distress. One third of the male inhabitants of each province between the ages of 20 and 59 were supposed to spend one year at the capital and three years on the frontiers. While they were on active service they were expected to provide their own equipment and provisions. This aspect of the reforms was not a great success because its severity encouraged people to desert their land to avoid being conscripted.

The government in Nara, once it was established, used its army to gain control over more of Japan proper. In the extreme south of Kyūshū partially assimilated communities (variously known as the Kumaso or Hayabito) were brought under control. In the north of Honshū, however, the Ainu people held out more strongly. Renowned as fierce fighting men, in 776 they stormed the main government fort at Taga, massacred the garrison, and invaded the settled regions to the south from which they had been expelled. In these attacks the Ainu were almost certainly assisted by dissident Japanese who were already inhabiting the frontier regions in considerable numbers.

The central government also maintained an army to guard the north coast of Kyūshū, facing Korea, against the possibility of Chinese or Korean attack. This was in sharp contrast to times past, when China had been weak and divided and the Japanese actively involved in power struggles in Korea. However, in the sixth century the Yamato State had found itself too weak to intervene any longer in Korea; and even later, when conditions improved under Soga Umako and Shōtoku, Japan was powerless to act because a reunited China was relatively much stronger. A disastrous defeat in Korea in 662 finally persuaded the Japanese to adopt a defensive policy for good.

Buddhism and the Centralized Imperial State

Although the authority of the centralized State was accepted in far-flung parts of Japan, it was in the capital itself that its power could be seen to the best advantage. The attempt to build a city with the proportions of a Chinese capital was an ambitious one in the year 710. In fact Nara never seems to have been as large as its designers planned. For all that it fell short of its Chinese model, the building of the new capital must have helped to promote the unity of the country.

The building of a temple called the Tōdaiji, in Nara, was a national undertaking that gives an idea of the resources that the centralized State could muster in the 730s and 740s. It was the chief temple in a system covering every province, that was meant to focus the attention of the people on the welfare of the State and the supremacy of the imperial house. It occupied sixteen city blocks; its twin pagodas were over 300 feet high; and its Buddha Hall, larger then than it is now, is still one of the largest wooden buildings in the world. All this was inspired by the piety and shrewdness of the Emperor Shōmu (reigned 724–749), which can best be seen in the story of the casting of a huge bronze image of the Buddha for the Tōdaiji. In 737 an epidemic of smallpox caused great consternation in Nara, carrying off four grandsons of Kamatari among many others. It was to propitiate the gods that Shōmu undertook to erect the image. In the words of his declaration:

> . . . We wish to make the utmost use of the nation's resources of metal in the casting of this image, and also to level off the high hill on which the great edifice is to be raised, so that the entire land may be joined with Us in the fellowship of Buddhism and enjoy in common the advantages which this undertaking affords to the attainment of Buddhahood.
>
> It is We who possess the wealth of the land; it is We who possess all power in the land. With this wealth and power at Our command, We have resolved to create this venerable object of worship. The task would appear to be an easy one, and yet a lack of sufficient forethought on Our part might result in the people's being put to great trouble in vain, for the Buddha's heart would never be touched if, in the process, calumny, and bitterness were provoked which led unwittingly to crime and sin.
>
> Therefore all who join in the fellowship of this undertaking must be sincerely pious in order to obtain its great blessings, and they must daily pay homage to Lochana Buddha, so that with constant devotion each may proceed to the creation of Lochana Buddha. If there are some desirous of helping in the construction of this image, though they have no more to offer than a twig or handful of dirt, they should be permitted to do so. The provincial and county authorities are not to disturb and harass the people by making arbitrary demands on them in the name of this project. This is to be proclaimed far and wide so that all may understand Our intentions in the matter.[10]

The cooperation of the mass of the people in this enterprise seems to have been secured by a priest named Gyōgi (668–749), the most outstanding of a number of priestly advisers to the emperor. Many remarkable works are associated with the name of Gyōgi: the building of alms-houses, the construction of irrigation works and harbours and the planting of trees. Priests were after all probably the best educated group in society, in terms of technical as well as philosophical knowledge. Moreover, because the highest posts in the bureaucracy were monopolized by the hereditary aristocracy, the priesthood was the only way in which an able person from the lower classes could rise to

---

[10] Taken from the court chronicle, the *Shoku Nihongi*, that continued from where the *Nihon shoki* (*Nihongi*) left off in 697. The translation can be found in *Sources of the Japanese Tradition*, pp. 106–7.

prominence. An intelligent and forceful ruler such as Shōmu was not slow to make use of such men.

In the case of the Tōdaiji Buddha, the emperor and Gyōgi were successful within a remarkably short time. The completed figure must have deeply impressed the gathering, which included priests from India and China, as they participated in the solemn service of dedication in 752.[11]

The Nara period also saw the beginnings of the spread of Buddhism from the court to the provinces. As mentioned earlier, the Tōdaiji was intended as the centre of a nation-wide system of temples with a government-sponsored temple in each province. The local aristocracy, undoubtedly impressed by what they saw or heard about the Buddhist temples patronized by the court, built temples on their own initiative in the country. In Kibi, for example, the area where so many grave mounds were once built, the remains—mainly tiles and foundation stones—of no fewer than forty-two eighth century temples have been found. Powerful local families stopped building the traditional burial mounds after the middle of the seventh century, when they adopted the Buddhist practice of cremation which the court was trying to enforce. The effort that had gone into the building of mounds after the style of Yamato was now used for the erection of Buddhist temples in the manner of Nara.

This idea of emulation is an important one and, in the case of areas like Kibi, seems to have been operating since the days of the Yamato State. The wonderfully sophisticated buildings, statues and paintings of Buddhism must have intensified the long-established tendency for the political centre of the country to increase its power through cultural as well as political and military means.

Not all the effects of the enthusiasm for Buddhism were beneficial. The greatest single political scandal of the eighth century concerned a love-affair between the Empress Shōtoku and a Buddhist priest, Dōkyō (?–772). Shōtoku was the reputedly pious daughter of Shōmu and first came to the throne in 749. In 758 she was obliged to abdicate, but re-ascended the throne in 764, after she and Dōkyō had brought about the banishment of her successor, who shortly afterwards died in suspicious circumstances. A few years later Dōkyō reached the summit of his power when it was proposed that the

[11] About a hundred years later the Buddha's head was toppled by an earthquake; subsequent earthquakes and fires (with the typhoon, the three scourges of traditional Japan) helped to destroy the original, so that scarcely anything now remains of the eighth century statue after repairs. Even so the present image is supposed to weigh 452 tons and towers more than 50 feet above the tourist.

empress should pass on the throne to him. A Shinto oracle affirming the principle that the distinction between ruler and ruled should be strictly observed saved the day; and when the empress died in 770, Dōkyō was banished. A strong prejudice against having women on the throne dates from this incident, as does a general fear of politically ambitious monks aroused in the minds of officials.

Conclusion

This chapter has emphasized the achievements of the reformers in bringing to maturity a truly centralized imperial State. It has not fully acknowledged the debt owed by the reformers to Chinese administrative and legal precedents, as introduced to Japan by ambassadors, priests and scholars returning from China. By 645 China had reached one of the most impressive periods in its history under the T'ang dynasty. Some writers stress Japan's role as a pupil of T'ang China.

From the point of view of such writers the Taika Reform was 'an experiment doomed to failure'[12] because Japan did not conform rigidly to contemporary Chinese ideas and practice of government. However, Japanese history should be studied primarily from the point of view of Japanese development. Though the idea of a centralized imperial State subsequently lost ground in Japan, the political aspects of the Reform laid the foundations of later administrative systems. On the cultural side, the situation is much clearer. Buddhism and other aspects of culture, once absorbed, continued to flourish in Japan as elements of a distinctively Japanese civilization.

---

[12] Hall, *Japanese History, New Dimensions of Approach and Understanding*, p. 27. Hall himself sees shortcomings in this point of view.

CHAPTER FOUR

Culture in the Nara Period

Despite its insular character, Japan had for centuries been in contact with the civilization centred on China, but only from Prince Shōtoku's time did the Japanese court consciously and habitually borrow from the continent the knowledge that could be used to heighten its power and glory. For generations after Shōtoku's death in 622, Japan's courtiers regarded themselves as the pupils of their continental neighbours.

Buddhist temples were particularly important as centres of the new learning. As many as forty are supposed to have been built in Shōtoku's time. None is more important than the Hōryūji. It was constructed on a Korean model, based in turn on the plan of Chinese palaces enclosed by walls, and incorporated a pagoda, developed from a structure of Indian origin. The pillars of the enclosing cloisters, convex in the middle, drew on techniques of entasis which had originated in classical Greece. The Hōryūji as it stood complete in 607 was foreign in form.

Later, probably in 670, the Hōryūji was burnt down and then rebuilt. It still stands today, celebrated as the fountainhead of Japanese Buddhist architecture, and the oldest surviving complex of wooden buildings in Japan. The rebuilders departed from the original Korean model. The main hall, containing images of worship, and a pagoda to house sacred relics, were set beside each other and not in a line from the entrance. The lecture hall, for the reading of scriptures, was retained as were the cloisters enclosing the main buildings, to maintain the impression of religious life as something apart from the world. The Hōryūji remained monumental, not relying in any way on the use of natural settings that has distinguished Japanese religious architecture.

Thanks to the piety of successive generations, people like Prince

34

Shōtoku's wife, the Emperor Shōmu and his wife and mother-in-law, presented the Hōryūji with precious gifts. Within a year of the prince's death the Hōryūji received a set of three life-sized bronze images, each with a face in his likeness. These images, made in Japan after a Chinese style, survive to this day as further reminders of the debt owed by Japan to continental civilization.

Material Culture

Like Prince Shōtoku, Emperor Shōmu sent official embassies not only to pay respect to the emperor of China, but also to learn and to bring back writings and articles of the highest quality. The court in Nara profited from the advances made by China. Not even in China has the imprint of Chinese material culture of this period been preserved as distinctly as in Japan. Something of the life of the Japanese court in the eighth century can still be glimpsed by examining the treasures preserved for twelve hundred years in a simple wooden building called the Shōsōin, situated near the Tōdaiji in Nara.

On the death of Emperor Shōmu in 756, his equally pious empress, Kōmyō, dedicated to the Great Buddha of the Tōdaiji the objects used by the emperor during his lifetime, praying for the peace of his spirit. To these were added objects employed in the dedication ceremonies of the Great Buddha, like the huge brush used to bring the image to life by painting in the pupils of the eyes and so investing it with spiritual power.

Some of the treasures originally kept in the Shōsōin have disappeared, but much of the furniture, ceramics, paper, weapons and rare glass from the continent of Asia survives in remarkably good condition. There remain some medicines given by Empress Kōmyō for the healing of sickness among the people; these were almost all imported from China, and some originally came from south-east Asia, India and Persia. Literally thousands of pieces of textiles illustrate not only Japanese techniques but methods of weaving, dyeing and embroidery as practised throughout continental Asia. Of the many musical instruments from the whole of the civilized world that looked to China, the most famous is a five-stringed lute, the only one of its kind still preserved. The lute is supposed to have originated in India and to have come to Japan by way of central Asia and China. The rich decoration on the lute must have appeared superbly exotic to the Nara Court; the makers used mother-of-pearl, tortoise shell and agate, and delineated a figure playing the lute while riding on a camel. with a palm tree above. The Shōsōin also contains strikingly dramatic masks,

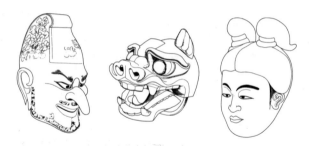

Each of the *gigaku* dance masks from the Shōsōin treasure house is made of wooden sections and painted. They represent the character Suiko-O, 'an intoxicated king of foreigners' (Persians), a lion and a girl

lively reminders of dances performed at the Tōdaiji dedication ceremony. Such masks belong to a tradition established earlier in south China and central Asia. A finely made *go* board, for playing a game something like chess, shows that pastimes popular in China also had a place in Japan. It is said that a distinguished scholar named Kibi no Makibi (695–775) introduced the game to the Emperor Shōmu's court on his return from China. It is still played on boards like that in the Shōsōin.

Another building in the Tōdaiji complex, the Hokkedō (or Sangatsudō), houses some of the finest Buddhist statues from this period. In contrast to the masks in the Shōsōin, which show great freedom of expression, these statues have been made according to set rules as objects of worship. They are made of clay, wood and lacquer. The principal figure, of hemp and lacquer[1], is complex, nearly twelve feet high, with eight arms holding a lotus, a staff and rope. It is crowned by a superb jewelled head-piece, with a solid silver image of Buddha set in the front. A third eye, a large black pearl, is set in the forehead of the image. For all its strangeness, it stands for a fine ideal: the limitless benevolence of the Lord of Mercy dangling the cord of salvation to draw men to the shore of enlightenment.

On each side of the central image stands a simple pair of attendants worked in clay. These are even more highly regarded than the main

[1] The juice extracted from the lacquer tree hardens when exposed to air, making a durable surface that resists heat, damp and insects, and can be coloured and polished. In the construction of hollow lacquer statues, like that of the Lord of Mercy, layers of hemp were moulded on a clay model and the layers cemented with liquid lacquer. When the outer casing had dried, the clay model was removed.

figure as works of art. Though in other branches of civilization the Japanese took some time to reach the level of their mainland mentors, in sculpture they seem to have quickly mastered the techniques and gone on to achieve artistic excellence. Eighth century Japan produced some of the finest sculpture of all time, showing traces of styles which must have had their origin in Alexander's invasion of India.

Writings

Immigrant artisans had their counterpart in the immigrant scholars who introduced the best that continental civilization could offer in written form: the Buddhist sacred scriptures, Chinese works on government, history and philosophy, and Chinese literary works. Native Japanese had to be taught to read and write in Chinese before this treasury of higher civilization was open to them.

Even Prince Shōtoku had been the pupil of foreign Buddhist scholars. At that time and for many years afterwards, the main Japanese effort went not into interpreting the scriptures but into copying them from Chinese manuscripts (themselves translations of of Indian texts), distributing them, and, presumably, into understanding what they said. As temples were founded all over the country the demand for Buddhist works grew, and attempts were made to copy all the Buddhist scriptures.

The most widely distributed work was probably the Sutra of the Sovereign Kings of the Golden Light Ray. A copy was sent to each provincial temple by order of Emperor Shōmu, for this Sutra showed most clearly what should be the ideal relationship between Buddhism and the government of a country. The extract that follows describes the visit to the Buddha of four guardian spirits known as the Deva Kings.

Then the Four Deva Kings, their right shoulders bared from their robes in respect, arose from their seats and, with their right knees touching the ground and their palms joined in humility, thus addressed Buddha:

'Most Revered One! When, in some future time, this *Sūtra of the Golden Light* is transmitted to every part of a kingdom—to its cities, towns and villages, its mountains, forests and fields—if the king of the land listens with his whole heart to these writings, praises them, and makes offerings on their behalf, and if moreover he supplies this sūtra to the four classes of believers, protects them and keeps all harm from them, we Deva Kings, in recognition of his deeds, will protect that king and his people, give them peace

and freedom from suffering, prolong their lives and fill them
with glory. . . .'

Then Buddha declared to the Four Deva Kings:

'Fitting is it indeed that you Four Kings should thus defend
the holy writings. In the past I practiced bitter austerities. . . .
Then, when I attained supreme enlightenment and realized in
myself universal wisdom, I taught this law. If any king upholds
this sūtra and makes offerings in its behalf, I will purify him of
suffering and illness, and bring him peace of mind. I will protect
his cities, towns and villages, and scatter his enemies. I will make
all strife among the rulers of men to cease forever. . . .

In this way the nations of the world shall live in peace and
prosperity, the peoples shall flourish, the earth shall be fertile,
the climate temperate, and the seasons shall follow in the proper
order. The sun, moon, and the constellations of stars shall continue
their regular progress unhindered. The wind and rain shall come
in good season. All treasures shall be abundant. No meanness
shall be found in human hearts, but all shall practice almsgiving
and cultivate the ten good works. When the end of life comes,
many shall be born in Heaven and increase the celestial multi-
tudes.'[2]

Japanese students of Buddhism were largely overshadowed by
foreign teachers until the end of the Nara period in 784. On the other
hand, outstanding Japanese students of Chinese ideas on government
—a quite separate branch of study—took a leading role in court life
even before Nara became the capital. The experts who advised
Naka-no-Ōe and Kamatari in 645 when they instituted the Taika
Reform were Japanese with twenty-five years' experience in China.
By the reign of Emperor Shōmu, the machinery of government had
become relatively sophisticated and needed educated administrators
to run it properly.

A university in Nara provided education in the Chinese Confucian
tradition. That is to say, it was an education designed to enhance the
power and prestige of the centralized imperial State and its officials,
but at the same time one which emphasized the moral obligation of
rulers to govern benevolently as well as the duty of subjects to be loyal
to their rulers. Examinations at the university were intended to test
knowledge of the Confucian classics[3] or statutes based on Confucian
principles, and the ability to apply these principles to practical
problems.

[2] Tsunoda, *Sources of the Japanese Tradition*, pp. 100–101.
[3] The basic texts were the *Classic of Filial Piety* and *The Analects of Confucius*.

Japanese students at the university probably studied with less zeal than their Chinese counterparts. While examinations in China theoretically gave everyone a chance to rise in society, in Japan the university was virtually closed to all but the sons of courtiers. This was because a young man had to hold court rank before he could be appointed to an official post. In effect, all but the very dullest aristocratic sons were assured of bureaucratic office without having to make an effort at the university. Young men from the provinces seldom passed the university's examinations. A brilliant exception to this was Kibi no Makibi, previously mentioned, from the Kibi area in the provinces. He was sent to China to study at the age of twenty-four. In 735, having spent twenty years abroad, he returned and Shōmu appointed him head of the national university to guide the Confucian studies of future bureaucrats.

After the Japanese took up the serious study of the classics of Chinese philosophy, history and literature around the beginning of the seventh century, there was an understandable delay before they produced their own works of merit. Educated Japanese of the Nara period did not emulate the Chinese in writing philosophical works, but they did write histories and poetry of high quality.

The first proper national history is the *Nihon shoki*.[4] By the year 720 when it was submitted to the throne, Japanese scholars were steeped in Chinese culture, which included a notable tradition of history writing. This is reflected in the language of the *Nihon shoki* which is Chinese throughout. In addition to this, the courtiers who compiled it occasionally went so far as to describe events recorded in the official Chinese histories as if they had happened in Japan. Extensive quotations indicate that the authors also used official Korean histories, and there is evidence that for the later part of the book they had available Japanese documents and records to supplement oral traditions. It is clear that by the late seventh century the Japanese had fully absorbed the general east Asian view that the writing of history was a proper thing for imperial bureaucracies to undertake. However, the book undoubtedly has another specific purpose, judging from its mythological beginnings and its constant concern with matters of ancestry. It can be readily deduced that the *Nihon shoki* was written to confirm the claims of the imperial line to legitimate

---

[4] See p. 21 above. Some earlier national records were destroyed by mischance in 645, and the Nara period had already seen the completion of the *Kojiki* (*Record of Ancient Matters*) in 712. The latter book was not sufficiently sophisticated to be regarded as an official national history.

authority. Because of this, and because Japan had never had a change of dynasty, it differed in structure from the more famous Chinese dynastic histories. The *Nihon shoki* was written as a national history in annalistic form, beginning with the 'age of the gods' and continuing with chapters taking their titles from sovereigns of the unbroken imperial line down to the death of Empress Jitō in 697.

The book's contents covered a great variety of subjects of concern to the court. Events were recorded simply as events, under dated entries in the order in which they were supposed to have happened, and regardless of logical arrangement, let alone analysis. For example, the eleventh month of the year 680, in the reign of Emperor Temmu, has the following entries:

eleventh month, 1st day: There was an eclipse of the sun.

3rd day: There was a brightness in the East from the hour of the Dog to the hour of the Rat (Note: 8 p.m. to midnight; an aurora?).

4th day: Nineteen men of [the Korean Kingdom of] Koryö returned to their own country. These were condolence envoys who came over on the occasion of the mourning for the late Okamoto Empress. They had been detained and had not yet taken their departure.

7th day: The Emperor issued an edict to the officials, saying: 'If any one knows of any means of benefiting the state or of increasing the welfare of the people, let him appear in Court and make a statement in person. If what he says is reasonable, his ideas will be adopted and embodied in regulations.'

10th day: There was thunder in the West.

12th day: The Empress-consort was unwell. [The Emperor], having made a vow on her behalf, began the erection of the Temple of Yakushiji, [dedicated to the Buddha of Healing] and made one hundred persons enter religion as priests. In consequence of this she recovered her health. On this day an amnesty was granted.

16th day: There was an eclipse of the moon. The Imperial Prince Kusakabe was sent to pay a visit of inquiry to the Priest Yemiō. On the following day Priest Yemiō died, and the three Imperial Princes were sent to make a visit of condolence.

24th day: [The Korean Kingdom of] Silla sent Kim Ya-phil, of Sason rank, and Kim Wön-seung, of Tè-nama rank, to offer tribute. Three student interpreters arrived in the suite of Ya-phil.

26th day: The Emperor took ill. For this reason

one hundred persons were made to enter religion as priests, and he presently recovered.

        30th day: Bramblings covered the sky, flying from south-east to north-west.[5]

The Japanese wrote poetry as well as history in the Chinese language. It is not surprising that some verses in the first anthology of Chinese poetry by Japanese, the *Kaifūsō*, 'give the effect rather of copy-book exercises than of true poetry', as one commentator has remarked.[6] This anthology appeared in the 750s. The same decade also saw the production of the first great anthology of Japanese verse. The latter is anything but crudely imitative, although it shows signs of Chinese theories of poetry. Known as the *Manyōshū*, the collection contains about 4,500 poems.

The *Manyōshū* is Japanese in the vital sense that the language in which it was written was Japanese, a language quite different from Chinese in its structure. But since the Japanese had not yet evolved a script of their own, the verses were written in Chinese characters. Some of the characters were used, as in China, to convey meaning; but others were used in a different way—to give an idea of the sounds that made up the Japanese words. The result is that while the *Manyōshū* looks Chinese, it is really Japanese written down in the only script its compilers knew.

> Oh, Yasumiko I have won!
> Mine is she whom all men,
> They say, have sought in vain.
> Yasumiko I have won![7]
>
>   * * *
>
> I, Ōkura, will leave now;
> My children may be crying,
> And that mother of theirs, too,
> May be waiting for me![8]

The writer of the first poem, composed on the occasion of his marriage, was none other than Kamatari, the architect of the Taika Reform. The writer of the second, an important official, composed the poem on leaving a banquet. The writing of poetry was a proper and fashionable

[5] *Nihongi*, Part II, pp. 348–9.

[6] Keene (editor), *Anthology of Japanese Literature from the Earliest Era to the Mid-nineteenth Century*, p. 59.

[7] The Nippon Gakujutsu Shinkōkai, *The Manyōshū—One Thousand Poems*, p. 13.

[8] Ibid, p. 198.

activity for the nobility, but was by no means restricted to this class.

Although most of its poems are short, the *Manyōshū* contains some of the best longer verse in Japanese.

In the sea of Iwami,
By the cape of Kara,
There amid the stones under sea
Grows the deep-sea *miru* weed;
There along the rocky strand
Grows the sleek sea-tangle.

Like the swaying sea-tangle,
Unresisting would she lie beside me—
My wife whom I love with a love
Deep as the *miru*-growing ocean.
But few are the nights
We two have lain together.

Away I have come, parting from her
Even as the creeping vines do part.
My heart aches within me;
I turn back to gaze—
But because of the yellow leaves
Of Watari Hill,
Flying and fluttering in the air,
I cannot see plainly
My wife waving her sleeve to me.
Now as the moon, sailing through the cloud rift
Above the mountain of Yakami,
Disappears, leaving me full of regret,
So vanishes my love out of sight;
Now sinks at last the sun,
Coursing down the western sky.

I thought myself a strong man,
But the sleeves of my garment
Are wetted through with tears.

* * *

My black steed
Galloping fast,
Away have I come,
Leaving under distant skies
The dwelling-place of my love.

Oh, yellow leaves
Falling on the autumn hill,

> Cease a while
> To fly and flutter in the air
> That I may see my love's dwelling-place![9]

Natural imagery and deep human feeling are drawn together in many poems of parting: husband from wife, lover from lover, and soldier son from parents, wife and children.

Verses were composed in more formal tone but with no less skill for official occasions, to speed guests on their way. The following poem was written for the farewell banquet in honour of the ambassador to Pohai, a kingdom in southern Manchuria, and others at the residence of the chief minister (*dajōdaijin*) in the year 758.

> The wind and waves sinking low
> Over the blue plains of the sea,
> Swift will be your ship
> Without hindrance,
> As you go and as you come home.[10]

Poems by emperors, empresses and aristocrats are balanced by those attributed to humble subjects: soldiers sent off to Kyūshū to guard Japan against attack from across the sea, and anonymous men and women.

> How I regret it now—
> In the flurry of departure,
> As of the waterfowl taking to flight,
> I came away without speaking a word
> To my father and my mother.[11]
>   written by Udobe Ushimaro, a guard.

> If you so heed your mother,
> All is lost—never could you and I
> Fulfil our love![12]
>   Anonymous

---

[9] Ibid., pp. 33–4.
[10] Ibid., p. 180.
[11] Ibid., p. 252.
[12] Ibid., p. 298.

CHAPTER FIVE

Government in the
Heian Period

The Heian era is divided from the Nara period by the court's transfer in the closing years of the eighth century to a new capital at Kyōto.[1] This city remained the effective centre of government until the late twelfth century. While the institutions of the imperial State remained formally intact during these four centuries, in the sense that they were not swept aside by revolution, the political history of this long period did pass through three distinct stages.

At first, strong emperors used the established bureaucratic machinery to administer the country. This was a continuation of Nara-style administration and lasted until about 850. Subsequently there was a period of two centuries during which the Fujiwara family dominated the court and governed through puppet emperors. Inevitably, this meant that administration paid more attention to narrow Fujiwara family concerns than to broad national interests. Finally, after a change of ruler in 1068, the imperial family regained its political independence from the Fujiwara, but continued having puppets on the throne. This was the age of rule by retired (cloistered) emperors, and lasted approximately one hundred years.

Beneath these political changes lay two important trends which affected society in general. These were the gradual replacement of public allotment lands by hereditary private estates (known as *shōen*), and the tendency for the family or clan to take precedence over the post-Taika State in political thinking and action. To put matters in another way, the Heian period saw a considerable domestication of imported civilization.

As a result of these developments, the Heian period, which had begun with a centrally administered and imperial government,

[1] The old name for Kyōto was Heian-kyō (Capital of Peace and Ease), and it is from this name that historians have derived the term 'Heian period'.

44

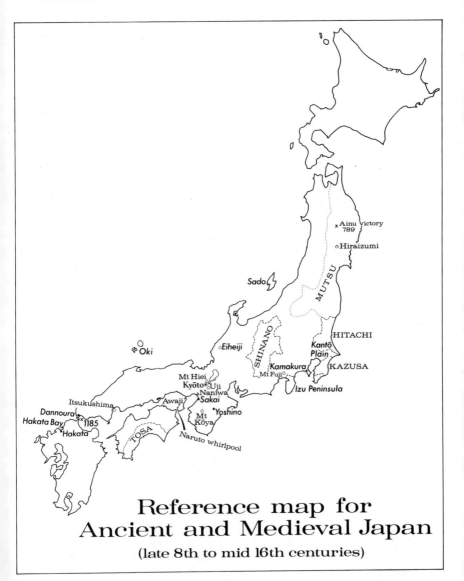

Reference map for Ancient and Medieval Japan

(late 8th to mid 16th centuries)

ended with the throne's power being balanced by other forces both at court and in the provinces. Japan remained united, but during this age evolved its own distinctive pattern of political and social life. The term 'familial State' most aptly expresses the institutions and ideas which underlay this development.

Emperor Kammu and his Successors, 781–850

The Emperor Kammu, who had been born in 737, came to the throne in 781 politically experienced and still enjoying the full vigour of manhood. Three years later he ordered that a new capital be built at Nagaoka, about twenty miles north-west of Nara. In 794 he moved the centre of government for the second time, a few miles to where the present city of Kyōto stands.

The reasons for leaving Nara are not clear. The most likely single reason was a general wish on the part of the government to avoid monastic intrigues of the type perpetrated by Dōkyō under Empress Shōtoku. With Buddhism entrenched at Nara, the court justifiably feared the emergence of another supremely ambitious monk. Economic conditions may have also played a part in the decision to build a new capital. It is conceivable that having the capital city in one place for nearly a century reduced the productivity of surrounding fields and forests. At any rate, special grants of land to monks and courtiers must have reduced the portion of their yield available to the government as tax. Behind such problems of urban provisioning and government revenue presumably lay a bigger one of transportation. Certainly while Nara lacked water communications, the Kyōto district could easily draw supplies from an extensive area by shipping goods from the north-east across Lake Biwa, and from the south-west along the Yodo River which flowed into the Inland Sea.

Unlike 'former capitals' of Yamato State times, Nara did not disappear with the court's departure. Though reduced in size and status, it survived as a religious and commercial centre. (In the last hundred years, it has regained some administrative functions as a prefectural capital, and embarked on a new career as an international tourist attraction). Inevitably, though, the 'southern capital' as it came to be called, has been eclipsed by Kyōto since 794. Another Chinese- (or Melbourne-) style metropolis, Kyōto was planned on a grid pattern with wide avenues crossing each other at right angles. Between these avenues, and parallel with them, ran narrower lanes. Wooded hills enclose the city to the east, north and west; and it originally lay between the Kamo and Katsura rivers. Kyōto, too, has had changes of fortune during its twelve centuries of existence, but it has never been merely a large town. With its distinctive charm, large population and general busyness it has remained one of the world's perennial cities.

The great task of moving his capital testifies to Kammu's energy as a ruler. In fact, he is usually considered the strongest of all Japanese sovereigns. The effective personal rule which was a key element in the Chinese system of imperial government adopted by the Japanese suited Kammu's character and abilities, and it is logical that the trend of the period 781–850 should have been towards strengthening the regime. This trend had begun under Kammu's predecessor in the Nara period and continued under his three sons (Heijō, reigned 806–9; Saga, reigned 809–23; Junna, reigned 823–33), but it owed most to Kammu himself. Clearly, the imperial family still had the will to rule and, when one considers the great expense of a double shift of capital, the economic resources to do so. It is still far too early to talk of any breakdown of the Taika system of centralized monarchy.

In fact, administrative innovations of the time were expressly designed to increase the emperor's authority over the cumbersome machinery of State. Thus, there evolved about 810 an important bureau known as the household treasury office (*kurando-dokoro*), a small, coordinating body of trusted advisers directly responsible to the emperor and with whose help he could regulate the government. At the same time, there appeared the metropolitan police office, which gradually assumed in the provinces as well as the capital many of the peace-keeping duties hitherto entrusted to the ministry of justice. The police office too, operated in close conjunction with the throne. In these ways the central administration was streamlined. At the same time, provincial affairs were closely supervised. Japan in the ninth century was more unified than it had ever been, in terms of effective administration.

A striking example of the throne's resilience and power during this period was the successful pacification of the Ainu and other dissidents on the north-east frontier after a series of reverses. In 789 the imperial commander, Ki no Kosami, suffered a disastrous defeat in the far north of Honshū. Kammu, who had equipped Ki with a force of 52,000 horse and foot soldiers, had him recalled to Kyōto and temporarily disgraced. The government then made strenuous preparations for a new campaign. In 794 an army under the leadership of Ōtomo Otomaro and Sakanoue Tamuramaro (758–811) routed the enemy. Ōtomo, who had been given the high-sounding title of barbarian-quelling-great-general (*sei-i-tai-shōgun*), returned to the capital in triumph and handed back his sword of office. Tamuramaro stayed behind in the north-east to consolidate this initial victory by building guard posts and ensuring permanent defence of the frontier. The court supported his efforts by resettling prisoners in the west and encouraging Japanese farmers to migrate eastwards. By 820, the Ainu and their associates could no longer resist in force; and by the close of the century, the imperial frontier was the northern tip of Honshū. Hokkaidō, the last real homeland of the Ainu, was to remain outside effective Japanese control until the nineteenth century.

Rule by the Fujiwara, 850–1068

If the early Heian period saw a further growth in the territorial jurisdiction of the empire, the latter part of the ninth century witnessed a sudden check to the personal authority of its emperors. The main sign of change was the rise to power of a great court family—the Fujiwara. The Fujiwara traced their descent from Kamatari, the principal person behind the Taika Reform. In the Nara and early Heian periods, members of this family held high posts in the bureaucracy and were prominent advisers to the throne. After 850, as a result of close marriage ties with the imperial family and the low calibre of actual occupants of the throne, they acquired virtually dictatorial control over the court. These developments illustrate the struggles revolving around family interests which were the essence of politics in the unified State, and it is worth looking more closely at methods used by the Fujiwara to create and keep their supremacy.

Family ties conferred political power. It had become customary for imperial princes to marry Fujiwara ladies. The following table shows the strong position this gave to heads of the Fujiwara family once ex-Emperors Saga and Junna died. After their deaths, Fujiwara Yoshifusa intrigued to have Montoku put on the throne and not Tsunesada; he then took the formal title of regent in the reign of the young Emperor Seiwa.

Fujiwara Yoshifusa (804–872) was: Brother-in-law of Nimmyō
                                              Father-in-law of Montoku
                                              Grandfather and Great-uncle of Seiwa
                                              Great-grandfather and
                                              Grandfather of Yōzei

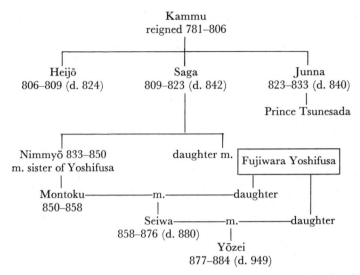

Yoshifusa and his successors were powerful enough to decide who should be emperor, and to have themselves appointed regent (*sesshō*) for a youthful ruler. When an emperor reached an age to rule in his own right, his regent would take the alternative title of *kampaku* (mayor of the palace) and continue to direct affairs. The Fujiwara saw to it that further marriages would perpetuate their power. Reigning emperors had to marry daughters or sisters of the Fujiwara chief, and often could be persuaded to abdicate as soon as these unions produced sons. This marriage policy could be operated all the more easily because it was customary for high-ranking persons to have several wives, and because there was no clear law that the eldest son should automatically succeed to the throne. Skilfully enforced, it kept the Fujiwara supreme for two not inglorious centuries.

The crucial nature of Fujiwara family status and connections is important for this period not only as the basis of the Fujiwara ascendancy, but also because it typifies what was happening in government and society generally. Increasingly, families or groupings modelled on the family eclipsed the State as effective units of Japanese social, political and economic organization.

The weakening of imperial power was gradual, but it can be said to have started about 850. It should not be equated with a sudden collapse of the political and social order. On the contrary, the country continued to be reasonably well governed. Moreover, for the next three centuries the metropolitan *élite* (i.e., court nobles and senior clergy), which had gained most from the Taika system of imperial bureaucracy, retained its dominant position. Similarly, in the provinces, the class of local (district) administrators underwent changes in organization, but did not lose any of·its authority or accompanying privileges. In short, the familistic system which came to the fore after 850 worked well enough to preserve national peace and order, and to allow for spectacular cultural achievements.

Why was the State eclipsed in Japan? One reason perhaps was that it was not completely necessary. Unlike China, Japan had no frontiers to defend after 850, and no aspiration for foreign conquest. Unlike Chinese society, Japanese society had never experienced real social revolution, and even at its time of greatest change, power had always been linked to heredity.[2] Consequently its *élite* did not require a State-orientated bureaucracy based on merit rather than birth to distinguish it from the masses and to regulate relationships within it. Japan was a far smaller and less populous country than China, and its everyday economy was localized and of subsistence level. These factors alone would have been sufficient to diminish the role of the State. For example, no large-scale irrigation works or canals needed to be maintained by a national bureaucracy.

Apart from their relationship with the imperial family, the Fujiwara exemplified the trend towards familism in the high degree of cohesion prevailing within their own clan. The leading Fujiwara nobleman in any generation, as well as holding the public and national office of regent (*sesshō* or *kampaku*), had in addition the private and clan post of head of the family (*uji no chōja*). As head, he could coordinate the family's policies and control its sub-divisions, because he was entrusted with the administration of the clan's corporate property and the distribution of income from it among family members. Like other important families, the Fujiwara created a very effective clan or house government to manage their corporate affairs. Religious as well as financial bonds united these aristocratic clans: the Fujiwara founded temples or patronized shrines which then acquired special importance for their kinsmen and descendants. 'Inevitably, there were occasional rivalries among the topmost group of Fujiwara grandees, but for a long time these were never permitted to go so far as to undermine the family's collective strength.

Natural ability was an important element in the Fujiwara success. As has been said, the family had a reputation as competent

[2] See p. 27.

Buddhist art and temple architecture from the seventh century A.D.: the Hōryūji, fountainhead of Buddhist architecture in Japan; and *Miroku-Bosatsu* a small wooden statue in meditative pose. Shinto: a glimpse of the Inner Shrine at Ise built in an archaic style, drawing on older Yayoi traditions

The Tōdaiji and its eighth-century treasures: the hall of the Great Buddha seen now in the smaller form as rebuilt in medieval times—detail from Sōgaku-Bosatsu on the bronze lantern in front of the hall—clay and dry-lacquer statues in the Hokkedō, that are expressions of Buddhist teachings

administrators and advisers before 850. The first three regents, Yoshifusa (804–72), Mototsune (836–91) and Tokihira (871–909),[3] carried on this tradition, paying special attention to such key offices as the *kurando-dokoro* and the metropolitan police office. The Fujiwara regents also proved themselves adept at the less creditable business of removing anybody who stood in the way of their personal advance.

A marked decline in governmental efficiency occurred after about 930. Tadahira (880–949), the regent after Tokihira, was not so able; and the deaths of ex-Emperor Uda in 931 and Emperor Daigo in 930 were a further blow because these two sovereigns had come near to being statesmen in their own right. The court was threatened by a serious rebellion in the eastern provinces led by Taira Masakado, a disgruntled provincial landowner who claimed that the sun goddess had appointed him emperor, and who waged intermittent war against the Kyōto authorities from 935 to 940. At the same time, shipping on the Inland Sea was harried by a well organized pirate fleet of 1,500 vessels. The leader of these marauders was Fujiwara Sumitomo, a nobleman who had been sent to the area in 936 to suppress piracy. Sumitomo lasted as a pirate until 941. Meanwhile, Kyōto itself was frequently plundered by robbers, and was often the scene of monastic disorders.

Eventually, with the help of groups still amenable to its instructions the court got itself out of these difficulties, and the regime was greatly strengthened with the rise to power towards the end of the tenth century of two exceptional men: Fujiwara Kaneie (929–90) and Fujiwara Michinaga (966–1027). Broadly speaking, conditions still favoured the existing system of government. The Ainu problem had long since been disposed of, and after 850 communication with China was slight. As a result, there were no external threats and no external stimuli to major institutional reform. Furthermore, the ratio of resources to population seems to have been generally satisfactory; and most nobles and provincial leaders remained loyal.

After 930, the government had to seek to control the country not so much by direct administration through its established and public departments as by informal manipulation of important families and religious foundations, whose independence had greatly increased. In

---

[3] Tokihira was never actually appointed *sesshō* or *kampaku*, but exercised authority as virtual regent and was unassailable after the exile of Sugawara Michizane in 901. The retired Emperor Uda, though resentful of Fujiwara influence, evidently thought he was the most capable of his successor's ministers.

doing this, the later regents gained considerable advantage from the well developed system of court ranks and the by now often titular official appointments. These they freely used to reward and punish, for more than just social kudos was at stake: as will be seen, a court family's material welfare still depended on the holding of rank and official position. Land rights in general, together with religious affairs, were another great field where the Fujiwara could, and did, exercise a virtually limitless patronage.

Fujiwara splendour reached its peak under Michinaga, who was in power from 996 to 1027, years also remarkable for literary and cultural brilliance. Michinaga handled his own and the national fortunes with a sometimes ruthless finesse. He contrived to have four of his daughters made imperial consorts, while the fifth daughter also married the son of a reigning emperor. Within his clan, Michinaga's leadership, once established, went unchallenged; and he kept the country at peace by following nicely judged policies of conciliation and coercion towards other powerful elements in Kyōto and the provinces. He died in 1027, disappointed by misfortune in his immediate family circle but in no way diminished in his personal or political stature.

His achievements and the strength of character which produced them are celebrated in a number of ancient works. One of these records a poem Michinaga wrote in 1017 on the occasion of a banquet to mark the marriage of his fourth daughter, Takeko, to Emperor Go-Ichijō. In it, he compares his own and his family's success to the perfection of the full moon which had just risen above the festive scene.

> This world I do believe
> Is mine,
> When I consider that
> Nothing broken is
> From the fullness of the moon.[4]

Beneath the mortal glory of one individual lay the lasting power of Fujiwara family wealth. This wealth was almost entirely in the form of hereditary private estates known as *shōen*. *Shōen* are so complex and significant that they will be discussed separately in the next section. The private estates of the Fujiwara were larger than those of any other single family or religious sect. Their greater wealth made the

[4] See also Reischauer and Yamagiwa, *Translations from Early Japanese Literature*, p. 273.

Fujiwara stronger than any rivals and so sustained their authority at court and in the country.

The Development of Shōen

The Heian period as a whole saw a steady growth in the number of *shōen*, and the power of great families and temples came to be based more and more on their holdings of these estates. Changes in the way land was controlled, together with persistent familism, led eventually to the breakdown of the bureaucratic system of centralized monarchy and to the emergence of feudalism in Japan. It had been a principle of the Taika Reform that all agricultural land should be subject to taxation by the State and be held on something like a leasehold basis. The growth of private estates represented a slow departure from this principle.

Ultimately, the term *shōen* meant simply a large rural estate enjoying financial and administrative privileges. At first, however, it seems to have been used for a monastery and the surrounding land on which monks grew rice and other crops for their livelihood. Buildings and agricultural land were presented by the Crown to religious orders; and when making such gifts, the monarchy would also as a matter of course transfer some of the land's taxation rights to the monks. In an economy which was still largely 'natural', i.e. did not have much use for money, this was the only practical way for the court to provide for religious foundations such as the Tōdaiji, without which civilization could not have flourished.

Similarly, the absence of a money economy obliged the court to 'pay' many of its members and serving officials with tracts of tax-exempt rice-land. Persons enjoying hereditary court rank received and passed on to their heirs 'rank-land', the extent of which depended on their exact status within the aristocracy. In addition, courtiers holding positions in the government were allocated 'office-land' in accordance with the seniority of their appointments. This 'office-land' was not strictly speaking hereditary; but as the most prestigious court families came to monopolize the most important governmental posts, an appropriate allowance of such land did in practice tend to become a permanent family asset.

Everything said so far has been concerned with the creation of *shōen* so to speak 'from the top down', as a result of a conscious act of will on the part of the emperor and his advisers. Other examples of this type of grant were special privileges for newly opened rice-land, and estates given to members of the imperial family (gift-land) or especially distinguished officials (merit-land). *Shōen*, however, also evolved 'from the bottom up', by what is known technically as commendation. This was a process which expanded rapidly once under way and was extremely hard for the government to control.

Peasant cultivators, especially in the turbulent east, often found it suited them to give or 'commend' their holdings to a powerful local body enjoying tax immunity and possessing armed force for use against bandits and in times of civil strife. In other words, the small-scale farmer would try to have his land included in some established neighbouring *shōen* ,whose privileges were legally secure because they had been explicitly granted by the government. When entering into an arrangement of this sort the farmer would agree to pay a portion of his harvests as a kind of rent or due. In return for this formal transfer of rights and payment of regular dues, he and his descendants shared in the financial benefits and greater security of the *shōen*.

One provincial *shōen* proprietor might accept holdings on these terms from many local farmers; and in turn he himself frequently commended his entire holding and interests to a highly placed group such as the Fujiwara in Kyōto. The latter, known as the *honke* ('grand proprietor'), was expected to guard its dependants from interference by even senior local government officials. *Honke* families or institutions (e.g. great temples) received a portion of the production of lands placed under their protection; and these dues came to form the mainstay of aristocratic and senior clergy incomes.

Land titles, as such, did not change hands. What were transferred and parcelled out were shares in the produce of land. Theoretical rights of final ownership remained with the Crown; rights of actual cultivation were left to the peasant who continued to occupy his ancestral holding. Produce rights (*shiki*) were of their nature readily divisible. Given a reasonably large amount to begin with, one can go on dividing the produce of a farm a good number of times. Moreover, *shiki* could be freely bought and sold and, under the prevailing legal system, they could be inherited by women as well as men. So the *shōen-shiki* system was very flexible. As a result, it was possible for a Kyōto magnate to derive his income from a hundred different sources in widely separated provinces.

Most *shōen* originally had only partial tax immunity, being excused the labour and 'other products' taxes, but not the rice-tax. Complete exemption was obviously in the proprietors' interests, and most of them strove to obtain it. The next step was for the proprietor to succeed in getting administrative as well as fiscal immunity from the Crown. In its ultimate form this meant that proprietors could govern the cultivators on their estates with their own regulations, and the help of their own *shōen* officials: stewards, managers, bailiffs, and so forth. Direct imperial jurisdiction no longer held sway in such administratively exempt *shōen*, and imperial officials no longer had any business within them.

This erosion of the central government's financial and administrative authority clearly challenged the two great associated Taika principles of: 'universal' monarchy in full and direct control of all its subjects in all parts of the realm; and a transcendent State to be administered by a central bureaucracy and paid for by public taxes. Fujiwara domination after 850 can only have hastened the process of undermining these principles. No matter how conscientious the Fujiwara leaders may have been in their public office as regents for the throne, in their private capacity as heads of the most influential and wealthy family they had a vital stake in the development of the *shōen-shiki* system.

It is important, however, not to over-estimate the subversive consequences of *shōen* before the twelfth century. In the first place, their growth was gradual in terms of time, and very uneven in terms of geographical distribution, taking place most quickly and most fully in the areas furthest from Kyōto. Secondly, in the ninth and tenth centuries, *shōen* rights were either directly granted by the Crown or, where they had emerged 'spontaneously' through commendation, were legally sanctioned after the event by the appropriate authorities. In other words, *shōen* evolved within—not outside—the Taihō legal code with its principles of direct and active imperial rule.

Rule by Cloistered Emperors (Insei), 1068–1156

In 1068 family circumstance dealt the Fujiwara a blow from which they never really recovered. There came to the throne an emperor, Go-Sanjō, who was not born of a Fujiwara mother and who was determined to rule in his own right. The new monarch was over thirty years old when he succeeded, and he had been carefully educated by anti-Fujiwara groups at court. The Fujiwara regent and his brother, sensing trouble, retired to one of their villas outside Kyōto.

Go-Sanjō's first stroke of policy was a direct attack on *shōen*. He set up a record office (*kirokusho*) to examine documents relating to *shōen*, including those held by the Fujiwara. Many of these documents proved to be faulty or forged, and soon the emperor announced the confiscation of all *shōen* granted after 1045. He and his advisers seem to have been determined to do the right thing, but to do it in a hurry. Before they had completed their investigation of *shōen*, they moved on to the equally crucial matter of provincial governorships. Governors had long since been appointed by the Fujiwara to suit their own convenience and as part of their vast network of political patronage. Now the man on the throne made clear his intention to go back to the system of appointment by the emperor for four year periods only. Without such close control over provincial governorships, centralized government could not work properly and the emperor could not hope to exert his authority. The Fujiwara agreed to Go-Sanjō's proposals with one exception. For purely family reasons they wished the governorship of Yamato province to be left in the hands of the man who held it, because he was arranging for extensive repairs to one of the great Fujiwara family temples in that region.

The breach between emperor and Fujiwara over the Yamato governorship widened to a point where the latter threatened to boycott the court altogether. Go-Sanjō then made some concessions, because he feared a complete failure of administration should the Fujiwara withdraw their skills and services. This setback must have made him realize that his opponents' strength was due to their traditional claim to all the most important court titles and appointments. He now sought to outflank the Fujiwara opposition by setting up a new centre of government outside the court.

In 1072, Go-Sanjō abdicated to become a monk, but arranged the succession to the throne in such a way that he could continue to influence affairs from behind the scenes. The Fujiwara were caught by the ex-emperor in the very same web they had spun for so many of his predecessors. They continued to monopolize all the senior positions in the formal apparatus of imperial administration, and their family head continued to be regent for a puppet emperor. But the puppet was no longer theirs to manipulate. Real power had passed from the reigning emperor's mother's relatives (the Fujiwara) to his father or other members of the imperial family who had preceded him on the throne. These former emperors found the stratagem of formal retirement into a monastery (or cloister) very useful. It freed them from the excessive ceremonial of kingship, and allowed them to choose whom they pleased as confidential advisers and trusted agents.

Go-Sanjō himself did not do more than foreshadow the system of cloistered government. He died in 1073. However, his son

(Shirakawa) and his great-grandson (Toba) were sufficiently long-lived and sufficiently able as politicians to make it work in their favour.

	Succeeded	Abdicated	Died
Go-Sanjō	1068	1072	1073
Shirakawa	1072	1086	1129
Toba	1107	1123	1156

As senior retired emperors, Shirakawa between 1086 and 1129 and Toba between 1129 and 1156 were the effective rulers of the country.

Cloistered government (*Insei*) is best thought of as a brilliant holding operation. It is true that under the retired emperors the court enjoyed an Indian summer of political tranquility and cultural lavishness, as both Shirakawa and Toba were good administrators and generous patrons of religion and the arts. Nevertheless the actual sovereign remained without any real power; and though the imperial family had freed itself from the Fujiwara yoke it had done so at a price. It could no longer hope to impose its authority through the public offices of a centralized and aggressively monarchical State, and seemed to have been reduced to simply a great family competing for power with other great families.

The fact that Shirakawa and Toba competed successfully should not obscure the underlying weakness of their situation. To pay for their style of life and administration, they had to convert into *shōen* large tracts of land still administered by, and paying taxes to, the imperial government. Also, cloister rule lent itself to factionalism and devious politicking on a really grand scale. There could well be several retired emperors in addition to the reigning one, but only the senior retired emperor had any authority. The hidden rivalries and resentments this caused quickly burst out after Toba died in 1156.

Conclusion

Although during the Heian period an important and irreversible economic change in land rights was taking place, it did not lead to the immediate displacement of the political and social *élite* centred on Kyōto. Old privileges continued, and initially change was confined to the institutional means of delivering the bulk of surplus production to the governing class.

Thus, the two great institutional developments of the period—familism and *shōen*—grew up in the shadow of the Taika system rather than on its ruins. The twofold nature of Fujiwara power, symbolized by the double office of regent and head of the family, in itself illustrates this. Even the imperial family retained a strong economic base because of the large area of land still registered as taxable public domain, and because it could and did create *shōen* in its own interests. The cloistered emperors, with these economic resources and their special position at the religious and political head of society, were able to compete on rather more than equal terms with other elements of the metropolitan *élite*. What did lose force drastically was the idea of a transcendent State to which all *élite* groups were subordinate and which had been embodied in the person and authority of such a ruler as Emperor Kammu.

CHAPTER SIX

Heian Literature

Literature was taken very seriously by the Heian court. This attitude developed at the beginning of the period under Kammu's three successors, all of whom had scholastic and literary interests as well as administrative ability. In those early days, anyone interested in fine writing needed a knowledge of Chinese and—to a lesser extent—Buddhism, as Japanese culture was still very much subject to direct influences from the mainland. Therefore there was a close association between literature and learning.

This association led, in turn, to literature being closely connected with public administration on the one hand, and private conduct on the other. The Confucian and Buddhist texts were the courtier's manuals for good government, and knowledge of them opened the way to official advancement. At the same time, these books gave their readers guidance on matters of general behaviour. They were the basis of personal and family, as well as political, morality. Thus, scholarship, public promotion and private ethics were all involved in literary studies, and it is not surprising that literature should have been so highly regarded, although, of course, it was also pursued for its own sake.

As in the Nara period, writing was overwhelmingly upper-class and metropolitan in tone, because only aristocrats and priests were literate, and for a time it remained largely Chinese in language as well as inspiration, owing to the continuing difficulty of writing Japanese when using only Chinese characters. This situation altered radically about the year 900 with the development of a phonetic system which made it possible to write readily intelligible Japanese.[1] The invention of phonetic letters allowed the composition of enduring Japanese-language prose works from the tenth century onwards. Nevertheless, Chinese continued for some time as the main language for business

[1] This writing system, known as *kana*, is syllabic and consists of alphabet-like symbols for the sounds of the Japanese language. See also p. 41.

and official documents, philosophical treatises and so forth, partly because of tradition but also because it had a fuller and more precise vocabulary suited to such purposes.

Heian literature as a whole, therefore, has two very different streams. One consists of writings in the Chinese language and ideographic script, and is associated with men. The other is made up of works written in Japanese with considerable recourse to the native phonetic script, and is associated with women. The latter is far more important in terms of literary merit, although it should be noted in passing that the Heian period Chinese writings are a rich and largely unexplored source of historical information. Why did men tend to use Chinese and women Japanese? And how did Japanese women come to write so superbly?

It is often argued that men considered it beneath them to write in Japanese. Questions of dignity and education may have had some significance but this explanation is not satisfactory since some men did write in Japanese, especially verse; and some women studied Chinese. The divergence can perhaps best be explained by differences in the occupations of men and women and by the suitability of the two languages for different purposes. Men, accustomed to coping with the everyday affairs of government, their estates and their households in comparatively concise and concrete Chinese, doubtless found it easier to compose memoirs, family testaments and private records of public events in that tongue. By contrast, the life of introspection and sociable leisure led by women at court and at home encouraged them to write and circulate among themselves compositions in Japanese. Japanese, after all, was their mother tongue, and its tenth century form, however vague and limited it might have been in some respects, had a marvellous potential for communicating subtle emotion. This potential the court ladies taught themselves to exploit. Last but not least, the splendid flowering of feminine literary talent in the Heian period was made possible by the extraordinary degree of social and intellectual freedom enjoyed by women of the upper class.

Japanese-language literature of the late ninth to early twelfth centuries covers a wide range. The main categories are: verse; travel diaries; mixed verse and prose sketches or episodes; private journals of court and domestic life; tales and novels; and somewhat imaginative accounts of historical personages. Printing techniques were known, but were not used outside Buddhist circles, so all these books were hand-written and circulated in a few manuscripts. As a result, what is thought of today as Heian literature is only the small surviving proportion of the period's total literary output. Prose works, in particular, have disappeared.

Poetry

A great deal of poetry, however, has been preserved. The government gave it special encouragement, and from early in the tenth century the court issued a series of imperial (i.e. official) collections of Japanese poems. The most important of these is the first, the *Kokinshū* (*Poems Ancient and Modern*), completed about 905. The *Kokinshū* has a total of 1,111 poems, divided into twenty books. The seasons or nature constitute the theme of the first six books; love accounts for another five. Other topics are parting, travel, laments, and auspicious occasions. A small group of courtier poets, under the direction of Ki no Tsurayuki (?–946), was responsible for collecting and editing the poems.

Although the *Kokinshū* contains some old poems, the majority of poets represented were still alive at the time of compilation. One result of this is that whereas the *Manyōshū* is noted for its relatively large number of long poems, most *Kokinshū* verses are short poems or *tanka*. This was a refined form which had five lines arranged in 5, 7, 5, 7, 7 syllables. It was favoured by ninth century poets, and so great was the prestige of the first imperial anthology that *tanka* became the standard form of classical Japanese poetry.

Not only in the form of its poems, but also in their authorship and underlying spirit, the *Kokinshū* stands as a monument to the general attitudes of the age that produced it. It includes some notable pieces by women, and the studied elegance, wit and technical skill which characterize the collection are hallmarks of a cultivated society with a good knowledge of Chinese literary traditions. Several of these traits appear in the following poem, which is one of the many contributed by Tsurayuki himself.

Sakurabana	In the eddies
Chirinuru kaze no	Of the wind
Nagori ni wa	That scattered the cherry blossoms
Mizu naki sora ni	Waves indeed rose
Nami zo tachikeru	In a waterless sky.

Here, strict form is combined with a pleasing succession of sounds. Furthermore, there is a brilliant picture in terms of sea and sky of fallen blossom being blown up and down in the wind.

Even when nature was their theme, Heian poets usually saw it through the eyes of inveterate city-dwellers who were mainly concerned with the private emotional satisfaction of social relations. Heian society was definitely urban, not rustic; and its poetry was man-centred, not god- or nature-centred. One *tanka* by Ono no Komachi, a famous ninth century beauty and poetess whose triumphs must have aroused much envy, expresses this clearly. Komachi's idea is that there is no hatred so bad as self-hatred, and she wrote:

Utsutsu ni wa	In reality,
Sa mo koso arame	It may well have to be;
Yume ni sae	But even in my dreams
Hitome wo moru to	To see myself shrink from others' eyes
Miru ga wabishisa	Is truly sad.

The two following *Kokinshū* poems are probably fairly early works, as their authorship was no longer known at the beginning of the tenth century. Each in its own way is an example of Heian poetry at its best, with technique used to enhance genuine feeling rather than simply for its own sake, and although they both rely on nature to some extent, the feeling they evoke is directed more toward some other person:

Aki no ta no	Can I forget you—
Ho no ue wo terasu	Even for the time it takes
Inazuma no	A flash of lightning
Hikari no ma ni mo	To shine across
Ware ya wasururu.	The autumn fields of corn?
Honobono to	My thoughts are with a ship
Akashi no ura no	That slips island-hid
Asagiri ni	Dimly, dimly
Shimagakureyuku	Through the morning mist
Fune wo shi zo omou.	On Akashi bay.

Early Prose and Uta-monogatari

Apart from his great reputation as a poet and anthologist, Ki no Tsurayuki is also remembered as the probable author of a notable early Heian Japanese-language prose work entitled *Tosa Nikki* (*The Tosa Diary*). Tosa was a province in southern Shikoku where Tsurayuki was sent as governor in 925, and the diary is an account of the return journey to Kyōto he and his household made around 930. The book opens with the formalities of handing over to the incoming governor and various leave-taking parties. But it is mainly a day by day record of the voyage home around Shikoku, past Awaji island to Naniwa (Ōsaka), and then by river to the outskirts of the capital. The trip was made in an open boat propelled by oars with the occasional help of a sail. It lasted six or seven weeks and was marred by storms, sea-sickness, and the fearsome Awa (Naruto) whirlpool. Worst of all, however, was the constant danger of piracy. Tsurayuki apparently had been severe with the local pirates during his term of office, and they had sworn vengeance. In keeping with nautical convention the world over, the 'pilot' or captain of the boat was in complete charge. He seems to have been a somewhat uncouth fellow, but at one stage he and his oarsmen tried to cheer the demoralized passengers by singing sailors' songs. Unfortunately, Tsurayuki saw fit to record only a few lines of these, but enough to show that they, too, belong to a general and recognizable seafaring tradition.

The party eventually reached Kyōto unharmed, and the Tosa Diary gives a sad picture of the dilapidated condition of Tsurayuki's house and garden, despite their having been left in what was hoped would be the good care of a neighbour. 'Whenever we sent him news or instructions, we sent small presents as well. However, tonight we have no intention of showing any displeasure. Wretched though the place looks, we shall thank him for his trouble.'[2] The journal ends on a note of grief for a girl child who had died in Tosa, a recurrent undertone of the work as a whole.

The *Tosa Nikki* is of great human and literary interest; but it also sheds light on political and social aspects of the period. It shows, for instance, that the system of regularly despatching high-born aristocrats to act as provincial governors for four or five years still operated in the mid-tenth century, and it contains much information on such matters as the location of ports, navigational methods, and religious customs.

Broadly speaking, the same is true of another early Heian book, the *Ise Monogatari* (*Tales of Ise*). Though its appeal is primarily literary, it transmits something of the actual conditions and fashionable attitudes of the time. Neither the date nor the authorship of the *Tales of Ise* is precisely known. It was probably written in the first half of the tenth century, and it is certainly based on the emotional life and poetry of Ariwara no Narihira (825–80). Narihira was a grandson of Emperor Heijō. He served the court as a guards officer and was frequently sent to the provinces as an official messenger. While his public life was not

[2] Translation by G. W. Sargent, in Keene, *Anthology of Japanese Literature*, p. 91.

particularly distinguished, he achieved great fame for his unusually passionate poetry and his numerous, though not always successful, love affairs. At one point the *Ise Monogatari* says of him: 'as a general rule, we care for some and do not care for others, but this man made no such distinctions'. Some of the stories and poems that go to make up the book have no connection with Narihira at all, and it has been suggested that the author's purpose was not so much to write a romantic biography as to depict an 'ideal type' of courtier. If this is is true, the ideal is a sensitive or feeling man.

In form, the *Ise Monogatari* consists of one hundred and twenty-five sections or episodes, each of which is a mixture of verse and prose (*uta-monogatari*). The prose plays a subordinate role and tends to be rather flat and unimaginative, but it is an integral part of the work because without it many of the poems could not be properly understood. It does have the virtue of saying much in very few words, and from time to time provides a touch of sardonic humour. Despite the book's fragmentary nature, the concentration on one person (Narihira) binds together the various episodes, and the structure and wording of any one section sufficiently resemble the others to give a strong element of stylistic unity.

The following episode (XCIX) is not only typical of the Tales, but also indicates social conventions of the day. Most poems of the Heian period, though private and subjective in content, were public and social in that they were composed for a specific occasion. The occasion could be a formal poetry contest, or, as here, it could be the first encounter of prospective lovers: verse exchanges were often the only way of furthering a romance in polite society. The real significance of these poems is the question of inequality of rank. Presumably, Narihira was of much lower status than the lady and initially felt that this difference made his suit hopeless.

Once, on a day when there was an archery contest on the riding-ground of the Right division of the Palace guards, a carriage was drawn up on the opposite side of the riding-ground with a woman's face faintly visible through its curtains. Therefore Narihira wrote this poem and sent it to her.

> Having fallen in love
> With someone I can't see properly
> Surely I shall fret in vain
> All day long.

She replied:
>   To seek acquaintance,
>   Or not to seek acquaintance—
>   Why do we make such vain distinctions?
>   Love alone
>   Should be our guide.

Later, he got to know who she was.[3]

The *Tosa Nikki* was written chiefly in prose and is a travelogue; the *Ise Monogatari* relies chiefly on poetry and is, if anything, an essay in feeling. Despite these differences in literary form and purpose, the two books share a quality of robustness. Partly this is because they both pay attention to the provinces and the experiences of aristocrats outside the capital. Tsurayuki's account ends with his arrival back in Kyōto; Narihira often travelled far from the city as a courier or else for pleasure, and many of the *Ise Monogatari's* episodes have a provincial setting. Though compiled by courtiers for courtiers, the literary records of both men preserve a sense of court *and* country. The two worlds are clearly separate, but are in regular official and non-official contact with each other.

Court Diaries (*nikki*)

By way of contrast, the Heian *nikki* or *Court Diaries*, virtually ignore the provinces. They concentrate on sheltered lives in the capital, and are autobiographical. The author in each case is a woman, and the 'diary' is not so much a day by day narrative of her whole life as a description of her most memorable experiences. Such experiences gave rise to feelings which she felt obliged to put down in writing—thus the *nikki* have a strongly personal and confessional tone. Yet there is evidence that the *nikki* were not just private notebooks. They seem to have circulated among a small group of interested readers, and were perhaps altered after critical discussion. Therefore they may be products of Heian 'salon society' as well as personal introspection.

The oldest and longest of the Court Diaries is the *Kagerō Nikki*, which dates from about 975. The name of the woman who wrote it is not known, but she married Fujiwara Kaneie who was the father of Michinaga and was himself regent for the period 986–90. Kaneie had a number of wives and mistresses, and though he had a son by his union with the writer of the *Kagerō Nikki*, he consistently neglected her. She bitterly resented this, and the diary is essentially an account

[3] Adapted from Vos, *A Study of the Ise-Monogatari*, Vol. I, p. 255.

of Kaneie's courtship of her in 954 and their subsequent deeply
unhappy marriage. It breaks off rather dramatically on the evening of
the last day of 974 with the noise of someone pounding on her gate.
Perhaps it was Kaneie paying yet another short call; but by that time
they had more or less finally parted and she had become more
reconciled to her situation.

The dominant mood of the *Kagerō Nikki* is self-pity, spiced with a
spitefully jealous and sometimes petty fury at Kaneie's conduct. The
journal also reveals a wholly commendable concern on the part of its
writer for her son (Michitsuna), and a genuine reliance on Buddhism
as a source of consolation. Indeed, the authoress seldom, if ever,
attended court, and for years seems to have only left the curtained
seclusion of her own mansion to visit temples in the district around
Kyōto. She would stay at these temples for days at a time, praying and
brooding.

A lot of the interest of the *Kagerō Nikki* comes from the full self-
portrait it gives of the woman who wrote it. But it is perhaps even more
remarkable as a revealing, and often moving, study of marital incom-
patability. Although regarded by some as a conscious attack on the
Heian marriage system, there is not much evidence for this view. In
fact—and in terms of the system—the 'mother of Michitsuna' was not
badly treated. She was not Kaneie's principal wife; and his other
households as well as the duties involved in his high political position
necessitated frequent separations. He took care to keep her in a style
befitting her station and did much for the boy, Michitsuna. The real
problem seems to have been that the author was far too moody and
possessive for the role to which Heian conventions, to say nothing of
Kaneie's attitude, assigned her. She admits as much when she writes
that 'life for the most part was not uncomfortable; it was simply that
the Prince's [i.e. Kaneie's] behaviour left me chronically dissatisfied'.[4]

A similar sort of life, but a much gentler disposition, has left its
record in the *Sarashina Nikki*. This memoir spans the years 1008–1059,
and was written by a daughter of Sugawara Takasue. The Sugawara
had been a very illustrious family, but Fujiwara animosity had
reduced them to depending on provincial appointments as a means
of maintaining themselves. The *Sarashina Nikki* begins with the year
1022, when Takasue's term as governor of the eastern province of
Kazusa came to an end and he and his children returned to Kyōto.
Although the future authoress was only thirteen or so at the time, the

[4] Seidensticker (translator), *The Gossamer Years—The Diary of a Noblewoman of Heian Japan*, p. 39.

The Tale of Genji: inspiration for artists and writers. The scene here from a post-war play, presented on the stage of the *kabuki* theatre in 1970, shows Prince Genji and his young son in lightly falling snow, moments after the child's mother has announced her decision to become a nun

Gagaku musician: drum

Gagaku musician: flute

Shishin-den or Audience Hall, Imperial Palace, Kyōto

The Phoenix Hall, the Byōdōin

journey made an abiding impression on her. As she re-creates it for her 'diary', one can feel how distasteful the remoter provinces had become even for people of her class who might expect to spend a good half of their lives there.

The trouble was not so much the boredom of life in outlying regions as difficulties getting to and from them. The route from Kazusa to Kyōto was entirely overland. For the daughter of an eleventh century governor who had to travel in state in a litter, it meant two or three months of being jogged up and down and frequent nights in the open. Such travel must have been unpleasant, though on one occasion when lodged in a hut along the way the party was entertained by three local singers whose voices enthralled them. Apart from the hardships of the journey, the girl had an additional reason for wanting to get to Kyōto as quickly as possible. She explains that while growing up in Kazusa she had loved listening to works of fiction written at the court, longed to read these books for herself, and in general had a head full of romantic dreams about what lay in store for her in the bright capital.

These hopes were never completely realized. Takasue failed to obtain a new appointment for some time, and straitened financial circumstances forced the family to live quietly. The girl occupied herself with reading everything she could lay hands on, and took to visiting temples. Her father, to whom she was deeply attached, was eventually sent to Hitachi as assistant governor, but she remained behind with her 'old-fashioned' mother. In about 1036, her parents went into semi-religious retirement. A few years later she was serving at court—reluctantly at first, and always too shy to be at ease. A chance encounter or two with a handsome and talented young man led to nothing: 'his personality was very good and he was not as men usually are, but time passed without there being anything more between us'.

It was during these years (c. 1040–5) at court, however, that she did in fact marry. Her husband, Tachibana Toshimichi, also held posts in the provinces. He seems to have been a kind and tolerant person, and the marriage was happy. The authoress now divided her time between looking after her family and making leisurely excursions to temples in the Kyōto-Nara area. In 1057, Toshimichi was made governor of Shinano province, but came back to Kyōto the following year and died. His widow was clearly desolated by this, and the diary ends with her living more or less as a recluse. She corresponds intermittently with old friends, thinks even more about religion and the change-ability of fortune, and turns with a practised hand to the writing of the *Sarashina Nikki*. Her book lacks the emotional intensity of the *Kagerō Nikki*, its predominant feeling being resignation rather than anger. It is interesting as a personal record, however, and for its insights into the situation of the class of minor nobles upon whom the real work of provincial administration had by then fallen.

A notable member of this class was Murasaki Shikibu, who lived between 970 and 1040. Her journal, *Murasaki Shikibu Nikki*, is precious for its gleanings about the early life of a great writer, but it concentrates on only two years, 1008–10. During this period, Murasaki was in the service of Empress Akiko, who seems to have been the favourite daughter of Fujiwara Michinaga. Murasaki gives a vivid picture of life in this imperial household. Its high point is the birth of a boy to Akiko, in 1008 and at Michinaga's own mansion, after a particularly difficult labour. Michinaga himself was a frequent visitor to the women's apartments. The infant prince was important to him politically, yet one senses that he was also emotionally involved in the birth as a father and grandfather. Murasaki reports that he obligingly laughed off everybody's embarrassment when the baby did 'an unreasonable thing' and wet his clothes, and there are other scenes of him playing with his grandchildren.

Two Heian Masterpieces—Makura no Sōshi and Genji Monogatari

The *Makura no Sōshi*, or *Pillow Book*, of Sei Shōnagon (965–?) resembles the *nikki* in that it is a sort of private memoir, but it differs notably in structure and general character. This is because Sei Shōnagon did not set out to write an autobiography. Her intention was to record something of what she saw, heard and did during ten years of service at court in the 990s, together with her own reflections on these experiences. She also went in for listing things or activities which she considered particularly admirable, regrettable, embarrassing and so on. This method of presenting her views on life is very effective in her hands. The whole work is an assortment of anecdotes, reflections and pithy observations, with no attempt at arranging the various sections according to strict chronology. Its form makes the *Pillow Book* (so called because the authoress is supposed to have kept her writing materials handily by her pillow so that she could jot down notes at any time of the day or night) the first example of the *zuihitsu* or 'miscellany' in Japanese literature. Many celebrated works have been composed in this form since the Heian period, and it continues to be the basis of much Japanese creative writing today.

Virtually nothing is known of Sei Shōnagon herself apart from a few abusive comments in Murasaki Shikibu's diary, and what can be learnt from the *Pillow Book*, which is an ample and entertaining source of information about the lady who wrote it. It is obvious that she was very learned—even Murasaki admitted that—being able to write in Chinese as well as Japanese. Her scholarship had made her familiar with Buddhist texts which she could quote when appropriate, but her general attitude towards Buddhism was mischievously irreverent to say the least. Enemies called her conceited and eccentric. She never bothered to answer these accusations, just as she never suffered either fools or the common people gladly. Yet what was condemned as conceit in Heian society might easily pass for merely high spirits in other places and at other times.

Sei Shōnagon's distinctive personality shines through her book. Unlike many of her more timid and doleful colleagues among the ladies-in-waiting, she thoroughly enjoyed the free and open life at court, and she was determined to give no man best. These worldly and feminist characteristics give the *Pillow Book* a hard and amusing edge which the *nikki*, written by women more often than not dissatisfied with themselves and life, tend to lack. In many ways, Sei Shōnagon is less congenial as a person than these other ladies, but it is these very imperfections which make her book one of the most memorable ever written.

The outstanding attributes of Sei Shōnagon's book are wit and sensibility. Frequently the wittiness cannot be readily appreciated without a knowledge of Heian Japanese and its cultural background. However, another vein of her humour comes from skilful manipulation of the commonplace or unexpected to create a feeling of paradox, as when she concludes her section on birds with the following notes on the *hototogisu* or cuckoo:

> The poets describe the *hototogisu* as lurking in the *u no hana* and the orange tree; and there is something so alluring about the picture of this bird half hidden by the blossoms that one is almost overcome with envy. During the short summer nights in the rainy season one sometimes wakes up and lies in bed hoping to be the first person to hear the *hototogisu*. Suddenly towards dawn its song breaks the silence; one is charmed, indeed one is quite intoxicated. But alas, when the Sixth Month comes, the *hototogisu* is silent. I really need say no more about my feelings for this bird. And I do not love the *hototogisu* alone; anything that cries out at night delights me—except babies.[5]

[5] Morris (translator and editor), *The Pillow Book of Sei Shōnagon*, p. 49.

Her wit is frequently satire or caricature, as in the following extracts on religion and one of the court chamberlains, Minamoto no Masahiro:

> A preacher ought to be good-looking. For, if we are properly to understand his worthy sentiments, we must keep our eyes on him while he speaks; should we look away, we may forget to listen. Accordingly, an ugly preacher may well be the source of sin. . . .[6]

> One day when he thought he was alone in the Table Room, neither of the First Secretaries having reported for duty, Masahiro took a dish of beans that was lying there and went behind the Little Screen. Suddenly someone pulled aside the screen—and there was Masahiro, stealthily munching away at the beans. Everyone who saw him was convulsed with laughter.[7]

Sei Shōnagon's sensibility enables her to capture freshly and for ever a particular mood or scene with a few strokes of her writing brush:

> In the fifth month I love driving out to some mountain village. The pools that lie across the road look like patches of green grass; but while the carriage slowly pushes its way right through them, one sees that there is only a scum of some strange, thin weed, with clear, bright water underneath. Though it is quite shallow, great spurts fly up as our horsemen gallop across, making a lovely sight. Then, where the road runs between hedges, a leafy bough will sometimes dart in at the carriage window; but however quickly one snatches at it, one is always too late.[8]

> An attractive woman, whose hair tumbles loosely over her forehead, has received a letter in the dark. Evidently she is too impatient to wait for a lamp; instead she takes some fire-tongs, and, lifting a piece of burning charcoal from the brazier, laboriously reads by its pale light. It is a charming scene.[9]

While the *Pillow Book* was being written, Murasaki Shikibu was engaged in writing the monumental *Tale of Genji* (*Genji Monogatari*). Legend has obscured the truth about the composition of this great work, but entries in Murasaki's diary for 1008 make it clear that she

[6] Ibid., p. 33.
[7] Ibid., p. 122.
[8] Waley (translator), *The Pillow Book of Sei Shōnagon*, pp. 127–8.
[9] Morris, Op. Cit., pp. 241–2.

had already written the earlier sections, and there is a strong indication in *Sarashina Nikki* that she had completed it by 1022. Apart from this literary evidence, the *Tale of Genji* itself suggests a lifetime's labour. It runs to some 630,000 words in a slightly incomplete English translation. In its main theme—the intimate human relationships of a man between youth and middle age—there is a depth of understanding which could only come from somebody of mature years. The same is true of the book's insights into such matters as court politics, national affairs, plebeian and provincial existence, and the art of fiction. Incidentally, these are topics concerning which the *Pillow Book*, a more superficial work for all its liveliness, is generally silent.

Like so many literary figures of her time, Murasaki is hardly more than a shadow across the pages of what she wrote. She was probably born in the 970s and may have lived on until the 1030s. Her father, Fujiwara Tametoki, was a cultured official who provided his daughter with a good education in Chinese and Japanese literature, and with a suitable husband who seems to have shared her taste for books. The latter died suddenly in 1001; and it was probably after being widowed that Murasaki started writing.

Murasaki may have been shy and pensive, but she must have mixed with all types of people and her writer's instinct allowed her to understand their behaviour and characters. By the standards of her time, she was prim and prudish. Her diary confirms that this was her reputation, but the overwhelming impression created by the diary and the *Tale of Genji* is of a person who knew enough of life to imagine the rest, and who on the whole preferred the role of inspired observer to unthinking participant.

Genji Monogatari is a long romantic novel, revolving round the life and loves of a fictional hero, Prince Hikaru Genji (Genji the Shining One). The fifty-four chapters or books are more closely related to each other than appears at first sight; and there can be little doubt that Murasaki had an idea of the whole from the beginning. The last chapters describe the life led by Genji's descendants after his death.

Genji was of exalted rank, being the son of an emperor, and the web of relationships his creator spins around him covers the whole range of Heian society, from the imperial family to the common people. Though the novel's romantic main theme is Genji's experiences with women, his subsidiary relationships with men are no less skilfully portrayed. Genji voyages an emotional universe, gradually discovering in women and himself all the complexity of human personality. His journeying never ends, but it transforms him from a light-hearted adventurer to a seeker after some kind of truth. Murasaki's real concern is a man's relationship to woman not only as lover—constant or casual—but also as son, father, husband, and friend or protector. And always she handles this subject with just the right mixture of romantic idealism and unblinkered realism.

The other great theme of *Genji Monogatari* is that of the impermanence of things. Women and change are brought together in the account of Genji's relationship with a lady also named Murasaki, who grew up as his ward and later became his second wife. Almost too late, Genji realizes that she is the one person who, despite his continuing proneness to philander, could satisfy his craving for a full and durable companionship.

> Coming from the presence of younger women . . . Genji always expected that Murasaki would appear to him . . . a little bit jaded, a trifle seared and worn. Moreover, he had lived with her so long, knew her, as he supposed, so well by heart, that, even had age not touched her charms, it would scarcely be strange if they no longer had power to excite him. But as a matter of fact it was just these younger women who failed to provide any element of surprise, whereas Murasaki was continually astounding him . . . her whole person ever more radiant this year than last year, today than yesterday.[10]

Not long after this, Murasaki sickened and died. Genji lived on increasingly disconsolate, and at length prepared to make a complete break from a world where he could no longer find even a transient pleasure.

Quite apart from its content, the Tale of Genji is significant as perhaps the first mature novel ever written. Earlier 'novels' had too closely resembled fairy tales, or else were realistic but had no feeling for the complexity and capacity for development of their characters.[11]

[10] Waley (translator), *The Tale of Genji—A Novel in Six Parts by Lady Murasaki*, p. 634.

[11] It is possible, of course, but on the whole unlikely, that some now unknown earlier Heian work reached Murasaki's level of achievement. Similarly, in the West, a masterpiece written in classical times may have failed to survive; but a story like Apuleius' *Golden Ass*, though told with great skill and humour, hardly meets the requirements for 'maturity' given here.

Murasaki Shikibu's book, though imaginative fiction, is both descriptively and psychologically true to life. It deals with society as it was and people as they are. This remarkable woman had independently developed the novel as a true literary form, and in passages like the following seems to have realized the magnitude of her achievement:

> But I have a theory of my own about what this art of the novel is, and how it came into being. To begin with, it does not simply consist in the author's telling a story about the adventures of some other person. On the contrary, it happens because the storyteller's own experience of men and things, whether for good or ill—not only what he has passed through himself, but even events which he has only witnessed or been told of—has moved him to an emotion so passionate that he can no longer keep it shut up in his heart. Again and again something in his own life or that around him will seem to the writer so important that he cannot bear to let it pass into oblivion.[12]

[12] *The Tale of Genji*, p. 501.

CHAPTER SEVEN

Religion in the Heian Period

Religion in the Heian period was dominated by two Buddhist sects, Tendai and Shingon. Both of them belonged to the Mahayana (Great Vehicle) branch of Buddhism originating in India, and both of them were imported from China by the Japanese court at the beginning of the ninth century. In their new surroundings, the sects came to terms with the change from the centralized monarchy of early Heian times to aristocratic familism. Together they spread throughout the countryside, absorbing Shinto in the process, and became a fruitful source of artistic inspiration.

Tendai Buddhism

The founder of Tendai in Japan was Saichō (767–822, alias Dengyō Daishi), a sincere and intelligent monk, who was dissatisfied with the doctrines and worldliness of the Nara sects. Saichō came to the notice of Emperor Kammu, who showed him various favours before giving him leave to travel to China for further study. Saichō was overseas from 804 to 805, spending most of the time at a monastery situated on Mt T'ien-t'ai. This visit confirmed what he had already felt about the essential rightness of the T'ien-t'ai (in Japanese, Tendai) teachings. These teachings had given rise to a separate sect in China, and on his return to Japan Saichō devoted the rest of his life to establishing them in an independent school of Buddhism in his own country also.

As headquarters of the new sect, Saichō chose Mt Hiei (Hieizan) on the edge of Kyōto. This was the area to which he had retired for private meditation in 788 after a quarrel with the Nara monks. Hieizan was destined to be the greatest Buddhist centre in Japan, with about three thousand buildings on its slopes and a total population of some twenty thousand monks at the time of its destruction in 1571. In his own lifetime, however, Saichō's efforts were hampered by the enmity of the existing Nara sects, and the rivalry of the equally new and alluring Shingon teaching.

In favouring monks like Saichō, Kammu doubtless intended to strengthen the State's control over ecclesiastical affairs. Apart from any immediate checks to the political power of the Nara monks, the move to a new capital marked a fresh start in religion as well as politics. In Nara, the monks had taught the higher arts of civilization and government to the dynasty and its ruling *élite*. In Kyōto, the imperial house and bureaucracy were to be the sponsors rather than pupils of Buddhism.

Saichō himself enthusiastically argued that religion should not only submit to the political authorities but actively help them in their task of administration. A patriot at heart, he held that monks should be ready to put their learning and special skills at the disposal of the national community. Partly to enable them to do this, he insisted that his followers study, as he himself had done, all the various teachings of Buddhism. As a result, Tendai came to be the most scholarly of the sects and Hieizan the seat of Japanese higher learning.

These two principles, of partnership with the state, and stress on education, are illustrated by some of the rules Saichō framed for his pupils.

REGULATIONS FOR STUDENTS OF THE MOUNTAIN SCHOOL

Students . . . shall be appointed to positions in keeping with their achievements after twelve years' training and study. Those who are capable in both action and speech shall remain permanently on the mountain as leaders of the order: these are the treasure of the nation. Those who are capable in speech but not in action shall be teachers of the nation, and those capable in action but not in speech shall be the functionaries of the nation.

Teachers and functionaries of the nation shall be appointed with official licenses as Transmitters of Doctrine and National Lecturers . . . They shall also serve in such undertakings which benefit the nation and people as the repair of ponds and canals, the reclamation of uncultivated land, the reparation of landslides, the construction of bridges and ships, the planting of trees . . . the sowing of hemp and grasses, and the digging of wells and irrigation ditches. They shall also study the Sutras, and cultivate their minds, but shall not engage in private agriculture or trading.[1]

[1] Adapted from Tsunoda, *Sources of the Japanese Tradition*, pp. 132–3.

Two lay intendants will be appointed to this Tendai monastery to supervise it alternately, and to keep out robbers, liquor and women. Thus the Buddhist Law will be upheld and the nation safeguarded.[2]

Yet Tendai was never simply a branch of the public service which happened to be organized as a religion. The document quoted makes it clear that while its monks had a duty to the world, they were not to be of the world. Neither Saichō nor the later leaders of the sect doubted that a monk's fundamental business remained what it always had been: self-guidance through study and moral discipline to a state of spiritual enlightenment where he would cease to be reborn (nirvana). They agreed, too, with the older sects in thinking that this individualistic vocation could best be fulfilled in a monastery. There, the seeker after truth would find books and instructors as well as the bare necessities of food, shelter and clothing.

Where Tendai did differ from the Nara sects was in its actual doctrine. It was the first fully Mahayana (Great Vehicle) teaching in Japan and, with Shingon, eclipsed the older Hinayana (Small Vehicle) teaching found at Nara. In other words, since about the end of the tenth century, Japanese Buddhism has been very largely one or other school of Mahayana.

Mahayana Buddhism developed in India and China over the period 100–600 A.D. Having many branches and much subtle philosophy, it is a vast and complicated field of study. Speaking very generally, however, one can say that both Tendai and Shingon retained the Hinayana concepts of rebirth (karma), monasticism, and self-effort. Man was fated to suffer in existence for so long as he remained attached to an illusory, sinful world and to his own selfish desires. The only way he could escape was to listen to the Buddhist message, enter a monastery, and once there learn to rid himself of any sense of attachment. To this stock of basic ideas the Mahayana Buddhists added some equally important dogmas of their own.

One of these was the *bodhisattva* ideal. *Bodhisattvas* were a class of exceptional beings who had acquired sufficient merit to enter nirvana, but had given up this reward in the interests of helping others along the path to enlightenment. The role of *bodhisattvas* in Mahayana Buddhism is similar to that of saints in Christianity. It was believed that a *bodhisattva* would increase the spiritual purity and welfare of those who prayed to him. This idea is known technically as the

[2] Ibid., p. 135.

doctrine of the 'transfer of merit', and was quite contrary to the strict Hinayana insistence on the monk's achieving nirvana through his own determination and without any outside help. As a religious ideal, the *bodhisattva* stood for compassion and service to others rather than for self—and according to Mahayana, selfish—perfection.

Tendai Buddhism incorporated this theory of *bodhisattvas* in its general philosophical system. Illustrious figures like Saichō came to be regarded as *bodhisattvas* after their deaths, and the sect's emphasis on ecclesiastical participation in political administration could well have been a reflection of the *bodhisattva* ideal, However, *bodhisattvas* in general did not figure very largely in Heian religion, which in its monastic form at any rate remained committed to the idea of enlightenment through personal discipline.

Of far greater importance to religion in the Heian period was the Mahayana teaching about the eternal and universal Buddha. It taught that the historical Buddha (Gautama) was a temporary and relatively unimportant manifestation of the cosmic (i.e. eternal and universal) Buddha. The relationship between the historical and cosmic Buddhas is rather similar to that in Christian thought between God the historical Jesus Christ and God the everlasting and invisible Father. It was this concentration on the Buddha as an abstract force, above or behind all things and at the same time in all things, that allowed Mahayana to develop many of its special characteristics.

Not only Gautama but all other deities and sages could be considered manifestations of the cosmic Buddha, even if until then they had been associated with non-Buddhist systems such as Shinto or Confucianism. This comprehensive point of view obviously helped Buddhism to fuse with Shinto, and it is recorded that Saichō sought the blessing of the local Shinto god (or King of the Mountain) as well as of the Buddha, when he first took up residence on Hieizan.

Mahayana comprehensiveness was not confined to its attitude towards other beliefs. The doctrine of the cosmic Buddha meant that everybody and everything contained an element of him, however small. In other words, all mankind and other forms of life would eventually develop their inherent Buddha-nature. Nobody was too bad to be saved. This idea of the essential unity of existence weakened the rigid Hinayana distinction between monks and laity, and ran directly counter to the beliefs of certain Hinayana sects that some classes of humans were completely beyond redemption. Such a view was held by the powerful Hossō sect in Nara to which Saichō's main antagonists belonged.

The Tendai ideas discussed so far may be summarized as follows. Firstly, there was the *bodhisattva* ideal of compassion and service. Secondly, there was a benevolent attitude towards other forms of religion, including other forms of Buddhism. Thirdly, there was a belief in the eventual salvation of all beings. Fourthly, there was the idea that all life, and not just human life, was basically the same; that is, an idea of underlying unity of existence. The second, third, and fourth of these principles have no counterpart in Christianity, with its doctrines of heresy, heaven and hell, and mankind as a separate creation, and their influence was extremely important in the development of traditional Japanese culture with its—by Western standards—easy-going outlook on religion on the one hand, and semi-religious regard for nature on the other.

This teaching was based on the Lotus Sutra, one of the great scriptures of Mahayana Buddhism. The Lotus Sutra claims to be a final sermon preached by Gautama shortly before he entered nirvana. In reality, it was composed long after Gautama's death, and is a magnificent declaration of Mahayana theories about the cosmic nature of the Buddha, and his super-abundant saving power. Something of its spirit can be caught from the following extracts:

> . . . .
> It is like unto a great cloud
> Rising above the world,
> Covering all things everywhere,
> A gracious cloud full of moisture;
> Lightning-flames flash and dazzle,
> Voice of thunder vibrates afar,
> Bringing joy and ease to all.
> . . . .
> In like manner also the Buddha
> Appears here in the World,
> Like unto a great cloud
> Universally covering all things;
> . . . .
> Hearken well with your mind,
> Come you here to me,
> Behold the Peerless Honoured One!
> I am the World-honoured,
> Who cannot be equalled.
> To give rest to every creature,
> I appear in the world,
> And, to the hosts of the living,

Preach the pure Law, sweet as dew;
The one and only Law
Of deliverance and Nirvana.
With one transcendent voice
I proclaim this truth,
Ever taking the Great-Vehicle
As my subject.
Upon all I ever look
Everywhere impartially,
Without distinction of persons,
Or mind of love or hate.
I have no predilections
Nor any limitations;
Ever to all beings
I preach the Law equally;
As I preach to one person,
So I preach to all.[3]

Shingon Buddhism

Shingon Buddhism resembled Tendai in the general circumstances of its foundation and development. It was introduced into Japan by Kūkai (774–835, alias Kōbō Daishi). In his youth, Kūkai had received the Confucian training suitable for an official career but, growing disenchanted with such a prospect, became a Buddhist monk and studied assiduously. He, too, was sent to China by Emperor Kammu in 804, and returned to Japan in 806, a convert to the Shingon (True Word) school of Buddhism. It is possible that he did not spend all his time overseas in the Chinese capital of Ch'ang-an, but travelled to the far south of China where it borders on India. Like Saichō, the rest of Kūkai's life after returning home was largely taken up with religious writings and the establishment of his teaching in an independent sect. For his headquarters he selected Mt Kōya (Kōyasan), a mountain some distance to the south of Kyōto.

Kūkai's popular fame is not due only to his activities as a scholar and religious leader. He was acclaimed in his own time as a poet, painter, and calligrapher, and since then has been credited with the invention of one of the phonetic (*kana*) scripts. He is supposed to have thought of phonetic, as opposed to ideographic, writing when he came across examples of Indian scripts in his travels. Although his real character is obscured by later legend, Kūkai undoubtedly was talented and versatile, and a brilliant representative of many of the

[3] Soothill, *The Lotus of the Wonderful Law*, pp. 125–8.

attitudes and interests of the early Heian period. His religious views led him to place much less stress than Saichō had done on a church-state partnership in general administration, but he was a true son of his age in accepting both the rightness and feasibility of court rule; and his artistic and literary talents won him the favour of Emperor Saga.

The combination of unworldly and worldly strains in his personality comes through in a poem Kūkai is reputed to have composed as his deathbed verse, given here in slightly free translation.

Iro wa nioedo	The colours which were once so beautiful
Chirinuru wo	Have faded.
Waga yo tare zo	Who in our world
Tsune naran	Will last forever?
Ui no okuyama	To-day, I cross
Kyō koete	Life's furthermost mountain.
Asaki yume miji	There shall be no more shallow dreaming,
Ei mo sezu	No more drunkenness.

Shingon was Mahayana Buddhism with a strong mixture of Tibetan or Tantric[4] emphasis on such things as magical spells and mystic union with the deities. Like Saichō, Kūkai arranged all the existing Buddhist sects in an order of merit, an approach known as the doctrine of progressive revelation. Below Hinayana, he found room for Taoism,[5] then Confucianism, and finally 'animal-like existence'. Tendai ranked third from the top position, which naturally enough was reserved for Shingon. Kūkai labelled all forms of Buddhism other than Shingon as exoteric or 'public' teachings, and said that they could be freely studied and discussed. He insisted, however, that Shingon itself was esoteric or 'private', and could be taught only to those who entered a Shingon monastery, agreeing with the principle of monasticism as the essential final step in a person's spiritual training.

Within his monastery the Shingon initiate spent much time reciting *mantras* (sacred words or incantations), and practising *mudras* (sacred gestures). He also studied *mandalas* (sacred pictures) which represented in diagrammatic form the boundless power and presence of the cosmic Buddha. The object of these pious exercises, like that of the Indian yoga they resembled, was to bring the monk into a state of

[4] The third great division of Buddhism, with Hinayana and Mahayana.
[5] A native Chinese belief in nature, magic, and a private search for the truth, condemned as anti-social by Confucianists.

ecstatic union with the cosmic Buddha. In other words, Shingon held out the promise of full realization of one's Buddha-nature *in this lifetime*.

Shingon relied just as much as Tendai on the idea of a cosmic Buddha, but went even further than Tendai in affirming the value of this present life. Tendai taught that full enlightenment would come only after all earthly existences were completed. Shingon, on the other hand, claimed that a person with proper insight and training could achieve his spiritual aim of enlightenment in this present life. Whereas Tendai considered the material world a partial (and so imperfect) reflection of an ideal world, Shingon held that the world of things was completely identical with the spiritual world. In other words, the cosmic Buddha was just as perfectly within the universe as he was outside it.

This development marked an important transition from the idea of escape from existence (nirvana) to the idea of enlightenment while still in existence (*satori*) as the supreme objective of religious endeavour. Kūkai at one point argued for instantaneous Buddhahood in these vigorous terms:

> According to exoteric doctrines, enlightenment occurs only after three existences; the esoteric doctrines declare that there are sixteen chances of enlightenment in this life. In speed and excellence the two doctrines differ as much as Buddha with his supernatural powers and a lame donkey. You who reverence the good, let this fact be clear in your minds![6]

Kūkai's outstanding talent as an artist, and his idea of *satori* or union with the cosmic Buddha in this life, help to explain the great importance which Japanese Shingon placed on sacred art. It was the business of such art to portray both the awesome and the genial sides of experience, because 'good' and 'bad', 'pleasant' and 'unpleasant' were all equally important as attributes of the cosmic Buddha. Shingon art is made memorable by this inspiration. Moreover, it identified *satori* with the elation or heightened awareness imparted by a masterpiece of art.

Religion and Society

Shingon enjoyed immense popularity in Heian Japan. Its emphasis on art appealed to the well developed aesthetic sense of the nobles,

[6] Tsunoda, *Sources of the Japanese Tradition*, p. 147.

who also enjoyed the lavish rituals associated with its sacred words and gestures. Even the Tendai communities on Hieizan were deeply influenced, taking over its images and ceremonial. For most of the Heian period the two sects were intermingled.

Despite this, Tendai always retained a distinctive bias towards scholarship and an intellectual, rather than emotional, approach; it also continued to have somewhat closer links than Shingon with the court as an administrative body. Moreover, in judging the relative spiritual progress of people who were not monks, Tendai relied on the existing class structure. Those born in fortunate circumstances were reaping the rewards of special merit in previous lives and could look forward to even greater blessings in lives to come. In short, though all beings were destined to be saved eventually, aristocrats were superior to the common people in religion as in everything else. It is easy to see that such teaching would flourish in Heian Japan, which was a predominantly aristocratic society.

As religions of the aristocracy and its government, the two sects were thought of as protectors of court and State. They performed special rituals at times of political uncertainty arising from such things as the accession of a new emperor, provincial rebellion or natural disaster. Buddhism had had this protective role since Nara times, but the Heian sects' links with the court led them to full participation in society and government quite apart from abnormal occasions.

For Buddhists as well as everybody else, direct contact with China dwindled though it never lapsed. This was an extraordinary change from the time when Japanese Buddhism had been little more than a branch of mainland Buddhism. Now—in the Heian period—it became far more mature, and took on a distinctively Japanese or national character. Religion, like politics and literature, was increasingly domesticated.

This meant that Heian Buddhism conformed to the prevailing pattern of group privilege and local independence within a broad framework of national unity. The sects were deeply involved in the development of *shōen*, and, as elements in the metropolitan *élite*, they ranked with the great aristocratic families. Like the latter, they remained separate and to some extent competing units, deriving their ultimate authority from close association with the court. At the same time, they gained greatly from the weakening of centralized government, which enabled them to amass huge incomes from *shiki* rights, and to enjoy a large measure of political independence.

However, Buddhism did not just passively accommodate itself to prevailing secular trends; it was a positive influence in its own right. Japanese politics under the Fujiwara and cloistered emperors were remarkably free from bloodshed and cruelty, and this was at least partly due to Buddhist emphasis on the sanctity of life. During the Heian period Buddhism also ceased to be an exclusively aristocratic religion. Spreading among the common people, it carried with it— as always—arts, crafts and opportunities for learning. So, in the long run, Heian Buddhism helped enormously to close the great techno- logical and cultural gap that had divided the provinces from the court since the days of the Taika Reform.

Buddhism in any form had always been a missionary religion. Mahayana Buddhism was not only anxious to make converts, but was eager to absorb local religions. In Heian times, Shinto shrines throughout the country were taken over by Buddhist priests. The deities for whom the shrines had originally been built were now esteemed as minor manifestations of the cosmic Buddha, and time- honoured village festivals and other community rites continued under Buddhist sponsorship. This amalgamation of Buddhism and Shinto (called *Ryōbu Shintō* or Two-fold Shinto) was the dominant form of religion in Japan from the eleventh century to the mid- nineteenth century. Even after the forcible separation of the two faiths for political reasons in the 1870s, the amalgam has lived on among the people.

A passage in the eleventh century *Sarashina Nikki* tells how the writer's mother paid a priest to see her young daughter's future in a dream. The priest's dream seemed so nonsensical to the girl that at first she ignored it. She could not stop thinking about it, however, and somebody advised her to pray to the 'Heavenly-Shining Great Deity'. She confessed that she did not know who this deity was; only by asking a friend did she learn for the first time of the sun goddess, chief of all the Shinto deities and mythical ancestress of the imperial family. This is striking evidence of the degree to which Buddhism had supplanted Shinto by the close of the tenth century. The incident also gives some indication of the great part played in Heian religion by dreams and superstition. Shingon secret teaching on the spell-like power of *mudras* and *mantras* could buttress a magical as well as a mystical view of the world, and the ritualism favoured by both it and Tendai heightened this effect.

Particularly strong was a belief in evil spirits. Heian literature contains instances of jealous women wreaking vengeance by having their spirits take possession of their rivals, often with fatal results. Sickness was attributed to evil spirits which had entered into the body of the sick person. Medicine, then, was largely a matter of prayer; and Buddhist priests were in attendance at times of great moment in an individual's life—child-birth, grave illness and so on. In its belief in the supernatural powers of evil spirits, traditional religion in Japan as elsewhere tried to give an explanation of untoward events, and with prayer and incantation tried to provide a remedy.

The literature of the Heian period also reveals that there existed a purer kind of religious insight and experience. To cite but one example: the *Sanuki no Suke no Nikki* describes the seriously ill Emperor Horikawa joining in the recitation of scriptures read by monks for his recovery. Horikawa speaks the verses from memory. Both he and the priests come to realize that his condition is fatal. No longer do they seek to ward off catastrophe by magical incantation, but look for consolation in the face of death. The whole scene is one of deeply felt faith.

CHAPTER EIGHT

Architecture and Art in the Heian Period

Mainland influences in architecture and art continued into the Heian period; but after 800 a more creative process produced distinctively Japanese styles. The later Heian period also saw the beginnings of an emphasis in culture on the provinces and commoners, and a movement away from complete dependence on religion as a source of inspiration. As a result, architecture and art were not exclusively tied to the religious and court life at Kyōto, though they bore the imprint of Buddhist ideas and aristocratic taste throughout the period.

Architecture

The buildings used for official ceremonies at the court naturally tended to follow the monumental, symmetrical style brought over from China in the preceding era. A good example of this public-secular type of building is the *Daigoku-den* (Hall of State) where coronations and other important court functions were held. This building, as reconstructed on a smaller scale in the nineteenth century at the Heian Shrine in Kyōto, is almost purely Chinese with its stone and marble floor, tiled roof, and brilliant red colouring. By way of contrast another palace hall, the *Shishin-den* (or Audience Hall), although suitably monumental, shows the more Japanese traits of simplicity and economy of building materials. It is built almost entirely of wood from the floor up and has cypress-bark shingles, not tiles, on the roof. Since it was first erected, the *Shishin-den* has suffered the fate common to Japanese wooden architecture of having been frequently burnt. The present hall dates from the mid-nineteenth century, but is faithful to the design of the original.

None of the villas and palaces which the Kyōto aristocrats put up as their private residences have survived. However, a good idea of

A reconstruction from literary sources of a nobleman's mansion in the Heian period

what they looked like can be obtained from the pictures and literature of the period, and from some surviving religious buildings. The basic plan originated in China, but was modified by creating lighter structures of wood, several feet off the ground and roofed with bark instead of tiles. The mansions were essentially a number of separate living quarters connected by open galleries. The separate apartments were assigned to various members of the household, which could be quite large if the noble had several wives. Within each apartment people ate, slept and carried on their tasks all in the same room and on the floor, just as they do in a modern Japanese-style house.

The rooms looked out onto the garden which filled the spaces between the buildings. As the 'walls' of the house were really removable shutters, the garden could constantly be seen from within the rooms. Indeed, one of the chief features of the private residential style (known in Japanese as *shinden-zukuri*) lay in the close inter-relation of house and garden. The garden contained small artificial hills, and was planted with trees and flowering shrubs. It duplicated nature on a small scale, and in a way which satisfied the Kyōto noble-man, whose tastes were those of a city-dweller.[1] Usually a stream was directed to flow under the house and through the garden. The nobles sometimes amused themselves by sitting along the banks of the stream and floating down to one another cups bearing *sake* (rice-wine) or poems. The Heian mansions must have been draughty and uncomfortable, especially in winter. But no doubt they were quite pleasant and airy in the humid heat of summer; and whatever their practical drawbacks, aesthetically they were a charming and elegant blend of Chinese formality and domestic informality.

A justly famous sacred building is the Byōdōin at Uji, just outside Kyōto. It derives some of its fame from the fact that it is the only Heian edifice in the Kyōto district to have lasted through the centuries unharmed. Although for most of its long history the Byōdōin has been a Buddhist temple, the site was first used by one of the Fujiwara regents, Yorimichi (990–1072), for a private villa. In 1052 Yorimichi donated the grounds to religion, and started the construction of the present main structure, which is known as the Phoenix Hall from the pair of golden birds on its roof. Much of the building's beauty comes from this tiled roof, whose sweeping curves resemble a bird in flight. Two galleries, ending in two small pavilions, are designed to balance and set off the hall, and to provide support for

[1] There may be a parallel between this and what was said of the *Kokinshū* poet's attitude towards nature on p. 62.

the elaborate roof. The building and garden, in true Heian style, perfectly complement each other; and the Phoenix Hall is all the more beautiful when matched by its reflection in the pond. It was meant to give an impression of paradise—in this case a paradise arrived at by setting out from China (balance and tiles) and going by way of Fujiwara Japan (wood and refinement).

Far away from Kyōto, a branch of the Fujiwara established themselves as lords of northern Honshū in the twelfth century. Their administrative capital was at Hiraizumi. For a long time now Hiraizumi has been little more than a name on the map, but in its heyday it was a city with some one hundred thousand inhabitants. The northern Fujiwara took care to dignify their capital with buildings which were evidence of both their political power and their aesthetic taste. Of all its former splendour there is now only one remnant: the Golden Hall of the temple called the Chūsonji. The hall was built to house the mortal remains of three Fujiwara lords and is small, but the wooden structure is superbly decorated inside and out with gold and lacquer, jewels and mother-of-pearl. In their devotion to Buddhism and love of display, the northern Fujiwara rivalled their Kyōto relations, and their career at Hiraizumi is a striking illustration of the spread of Buddhism and the general development of the provinces in the second half of the Heian period. There is also evidence of international trade, in that some of the timbers in the Golden Hall are of wood which must have come from China and the southern Pacific area.

Another famous religious centre in the provinces, this time to the west of Kyōto, is the Itsukushima Shrine on an island in the Inland Sea. A simple Shinto structure must have stood in this area from remote antiquity to serve the religious needs of fishermen and other seafarers, but for many centuries now the shrine has been large and splendid, built over the sea at the head of a small bay with the peak of the island rising steeply behind it. When the tide is out there is nothing but wet sand beneath the buildings, but when it is in, they appear to float on the water. Although the date of the present buildings is not known, their lay-out and architectural style go back to the twelfth century. During this period the shrine came under the patronage of the powerful Taira family, whose leaders lived at Kyōto but had extensive estates in the western provinces. It is recorded that Taira Kiyomori, who liked to relax at Itsukushima, had the shrine completely rebuilt in 1168. A little earlier he had arranged for the presentation of a magnificently illustrated set of Buddhist Sutras. Taira patronage, which climaxed several centuries of court interest in the shrine, shows the degree to which Shinto was receptive to Buddhism in the Heian period. It also shows the way in which a remote country place assumed national significance as the court gradually extended its politics, religion and crafts into the provinces, and was in turn affected by them.

The shrine's architecture exemplifies all this. It is a harmonious and intricate blend of Shinto and Buddhist styles. The bark roofs recall native tradition, the buildings follow the *shinden-zukuri* pattern, and the prototype for the red pillars in the galleries is to be found in Chinese architecture. Nor can the genius with which the shrine is related to landscape and seascape be overlooked. In their graceful ease of construction, open to the sun and air and waves, the Itsukushima buildings even now seem to impart something of the Heian mood of refined simplicity, cheerfulness, and creative use of nature.

Sculpture

Only a few of the Shinto shrines, but all the Buddhist temples contained sculptures, and many of these have escaped the periodic destructions of the buildings which have housed them. This was luckily true even though the Heian sculptor preferred wood to the earlier techniques of working with metal, clay and lacquer. Sculpture after 800 remained religious, continuing to portray Buddhas and their attendants. However, whereas in Nara times these figures had often been naturalistic, sculptors in the ninth and tenth centuries stressed the inherently divine or non-human aspect of the deities, for example by giving the statue more than the usual number of heads and arms, and equipping it with the recognized emblems of such virtues as wisdom, power and purity.

The Shingon sect was most active in commissioning works and training artists, not for art's sake, but for a definite religious purpose. Informing all Shingon sculpture was the idea of the cosmic Buddha, and a desire to show his manifold powers. The sculptures were thought of as physical extensions of the Buddha into this world of space and time, by means of which the believer could literally come into physical contact with him. Great care was given to the posture of the statue, which had to be correct according to Shingon ritual. This concern with ritual and religious power often seems to mar the statues as works of art, but the best of them are impressive in a sombre, arresting way.

Severity gave way after 900 to more colourful and fanciful treatment. Statues were often brilliantly painted, and attention was paid to detail or amusing facial expressions. In many cases this led to elegance and a certain sumptuous 'sweetness' superseding reverence. However, the interior of the Golden Hall at the Chūsonji, with its array of small carvings, shows the Fujiwara love of luxurious refinement without detracting from its devotional effect. The same may be said of the Byōdōin's small angels and heavenly musicians, fixed to the walls around a large seated figure of the Amida *bodhisattva*. Although the Amida in particular anticipates religious trends of the period after 1185, both angels and main figure are Heian pieces, and are major triumphs of the sculptor's art.

Painting

The temples provided workshops for artists as well as sculptors. Shingon also dominated the field of religious painting, which conformed to Chinese styles, usually being done on silk in rich, glowing colours. Shingon's idea that Truth (i.e. the cosmic Buddha) included the unpleasant as well as the agreeable sides of life give its pictures a dramatic energy lacking in the works of the other sects. The intricate designs and beautiful colouring of the Shingon *mandalas* make them works of art, even though they were not intended to be pictures, but diagrams of cosmic unity: painting was a far better medium than sculpture for expressing this idea.

A very important development in the last century of the Heian period was the rise of *Yamato-e*, or Japanese-style painting. In contrast to the curved lines and soft colours of the religious style associated with China, *Yamato-e* artists favoured angular lines and more brilliant decoration. Traditional paintings were designed for display on the walls of temples, but the *Yamato-e* took the form of long scrolls which were to be looked at and put away. Often the scrolls had written stories or explanations to supplement the pictures. The viewer-reader held the unopened portion of the scroll in his right hand, using his left to unroll it and then re-roll as he went along. Thus the pictures were not static representations to be taken in at a glance, but dynamic revelations of their subjects. The idea of scroll-paintings had come from China, where they were chiefly used for panoramic views of landscapes and cities. In Japan they depicted popular legends, scenes from novels, notable political events, and aspects of Buddhist teaching.

One of the three scrolls on 'Legends of Mt Shigi Temple', for instance, tells how a hermit sent his begging-bowl flying down from his hut on the mountain to a rich man's house. When the rich man refused to fill the bowl, it flew back to the hermit followed by all the miser's sheaves of rice. Another Heian scroll is of scenes from the *Tale of Genji* and is imbued with a mood of elegant wistfulness. Painted in the twelfth century, the Genji scroll is thought to be a nostalgic tribute by the decaying courtier class to the days of its glory. Equally famous are the scrolls of frolicking animals. Done in ink, the most amusing sections are satirical, with animals behaving like people. These scrolls were all painted in the twelfth century, before the end of the Heian period. Many others date from subsequent centuries.

In general, the scrolls led painting from the exclusively devotional concerns of the older styles of art to a growing awareness of the pictorial possibilities and challenges of the everyday world and life as it was actually lived, even by commoners. In them, art was free to develop as art, rather than remaining a technique for religious edification. They also had obvious links with the semi-popular literature of the late Heian period. This literature was far from being just another reflection of the court and its concerns, although it was collected and appreciated by courtiers. The *Konjaku Monogatari* (*Tales of Long Ago*), for instance, consists of folk-lore drawn not only from Japan but also from China and India. The book's general inspiration lay in the Buddhism that still joined the three countries' cultures, and it has an appropriately evangelical edge. However, as finally assembled and polished in Heian Japan, its contents owe at least as much to the sparkle of lay and at times plebeian wit as they do to the glow of monkish piety.

Music

As in so many other spheres of activity, the Heian era saw new native developments in music as well as the perpetuation of imported and traditional musical styles. The court orchestra continued to play the *gagaku* music of its Korean and Chinese counterparts, which had been introduced in the Nara period. However, specifically Buddhist methods of composition grew in importance, while Shinto preserved its musical tradition. Individual courtiers lost face if they were not reasonably skilled on such instruments as the flute or lute (a prototype guitar). A distinctively Japanese instrument also came into fashion among the upper classes, the *koto*, a kind of flat harp. Meanwhile, outside the capital, wandering minstrels equipped with lutes began to entertain the people with long, ballad-like recitations of heroes' exploits.

PART III

Medieval Japan

CHAPTER NINE

Rule by the Military Houses

At the end of the twelfth century the government of the country changed in a way that determined Japan's character for the next seven hundred years. Five centuries earlier, the structure of government was transformed by the adoption of Chinese ideas and practices; seven centuries later, confronted by the Western Powers, Japan's leaders deliberately set about remodelling the country into a modern nation-state. The change in the 1180s, which ushered in rule by the military houses, was brought about neither by fear of foreign aggression nor by a desire to benefit from foreign example, but by a shift in the balance of power within Japan.

Japan had now entered a new age, which historians usually call feudal. Like its Western counterpart, Japanese feudalism was to be distinguished by fiefs, vassalage, and a marked military ethos in culture as well as politics. However, fiefs, in the sense of areas of land held under the authority of a military overlord, were not a feature of its early development. It was the institution of vassalage and, above all, the loyalty of individual vassals that enabled the heads of military houses to rule Japan, displacing the civil aristocracy.

Who were these vassals? At first, in the Heian period, they were not a distinct group within society. They were men of the provinces and not of the capital, men of substance, some of distinguished ancestry, who answered a need for order and security as the military forces of the central government became ineffective. They were not a specialist class of fighting men, but rather local administrators and managers of *shoen*, which often needed armed protection. In time leaders with a wide following of dedicated warriors emerged, whose services were called on by the central government itself. It was the bond between military leaders and followers, kept strong by loyal service on the part of the warrior and rewards bestowed bv the leader, that turned fighting men into vassals.

95

The feudal institution of vassalage evolved slowly. In the eleventh century the Minamoto, a family of future military overlords, were campaigning on the court's behalf in the northernmost part of the country. This was a hundred years before they established themselves as effective rulers of the country. Their enemy was the Abe family, who had taken over the province of Mutsu and were openly contemptuous of the court's authority. The exploits of Minamoto Yoriyoshi (988–1075) have been set down in writing, together with those of the warriors from eastern Japan who loyally served him through a long campaign. One incident in the tale reads:

> . . . there was a warrior in Yoriyoshi's army called . . . Tsunenori —a man from Sagami Province whom Yoriyoshi had always treated generously. Though Tsunenori had broken through the victorious enemies around him, he had barely managed to escape, and knew nothing about what had happened to Yoriyoshi. He questioned a soldier, who said, 'The general is surrounded by rebels. Only five or six men are with him; it's hard to see how he can get away.' 'For thirty years now I have been in Yoriyoshi's service', said Tsunenori. 'I am sixty and he is almost seventy. If he must die, I intend to share his fate and go with him to the underworld.' He wheeled and entered the enemy cordon.
>
> Two or three of Tsunenori's retainers were present. 'Now that our lord is about to die honourably by sharing Yoriyoshi's fate, how can we stay alive? Although we are merely sub-vassals, we are men of principle too', they said. They penetrated the enemy ranks together and fought savagely. They killed a dozen rebels . . . and all fell in front of the enemy.[1]

Loyalty was the first duty of a vassal, and in this case it is clear that the warriors with Yoriyoshi were loyal to him and not to the distant court. Of course, loyalty alone would not sustain an enduring relationship. Warriors were loyal to military leaders because they could expect tangible rewards for their services. Men of the emerging vassal class already held positions connected with *shōen* and drew their income from rights to shares in the produce of estates. Great military leaders like Yoriyoshi had it in their power to confirm or enlarge these *shiki* incomes of the local administrators and *shōen* managers, thus creating vassals. It was through loyal service directly rewarded by a

[1] McCullough, 'A Tale of Mutsu' in *Harvard Journal of Asiatic Studies*, Vol. 25, 1964–5, pp. 191–2.

military leader that the provincial *shōen* manager class could hope to better themselves individually.

Yoriyoshi's son, the illustrious warrior Yoshiie (1039–1106) strengthened the bonds binding the Minamoto family and its vassals by leading them to further victories in campaigns in the north of Japan and rewarding them afterwards. Enduring relationships were created not only between individuals but between families. Men who served a Minamoto leader in one generation would expect their sons to serve that leader's son.

Thus by the mid twelfth century military leaders, and not the civilian proprietors of *shōen*, were becoming the real leaders of the *shōen* administrative class. These leaders bound their followers to themselves as vassals by using *shiki* rights which, in the early phase of Japanese feudalism, took the place of fiefs.

In 1156, a small number of warriors settled a dispute over succession to the throne within a few days. This incident (the Hōgen Disturbance) marks the point at which warriors ceased to be subordinates of the civilian families at the court. The leadership of the warrior class was still a matter for dispute between Minamoto and Taira clans. In the winter of 1159–60, the house of Taira crushed the Minamoto (the Heiji Disturbance). Twenty years later the Minamoto fortunes began to revive and before long they swept the Taira into oblivion. This change in military leadership made little difference to the court nobles. They had been the real losers in 1160 and never regained their lost authority.

The Rise and Fall of the House of Taira

The Taira, first of the military leaders on a national scale, prospered in the service of the cloistered Emperors Shirakawa and Toba. But it was the Hōgen and Heiji Disturbances (1156 and 1160) in Kyōto which brought them to the peak of their power. Both outbreaks were celebrated in military romances, written probably fifty years afterward, when men living under a military regime chose to listen to such tales. The events of 1160 also inspired artists one hundred years later to make a set of scroll paintings in the *Yamato-e* style, the *Heiji Monogatari Emaki*. The first scroll describes in word and picture the seizure by conspirators of the retired Emperor Nijō, and the burning of his palace.

The picture, which consists of one unbroken sweep of motion from right to left, commences with a scene showing a mixed mass of ox-carriages of the nobility, armed horsemen, and soldiers and commoners afoot dashing pell-mell toward the Sanjō Palace, where they are brought up short by the surrounding walls, inside which we see a crowd of mounted warriors milling about, while some of their number afoot push the Imperial carriage up to one of the buildings. A military figure is standing on the porch, apparently giving orders. In an adjoining courtyard of the palace is a group of forlorn ladies, while a courtier is fleeing from a murderous-looking soldier. Beyond them the palace buildings are blazing furiously. In the surrounding courtyards, mounted warriors are dashing wildly about, while the miserable residents of the palace are being hacked to pieces or are attempting to leap into a well already overflowing with humanity. Beyond the well on the far side of the palace grounds, we see warriors mounted and afoot passing out one of the palace gates, with heads of two of the defenders stuck on spears carried by two foot-soldiers. Beyond this group, we find the main mass of the attackers surrounding the Imperial carriage and withdrawing in triumph.[2]

The confusion and bloodshed were real enough. But out of this violence emerged reasonable order under a national government in the hands of Taira Kiyomori (1118–81).

Kiyomori, who had backed the right side in the 1156 succession dispute, was just over forty years of age when he routed his Minamoto rivals in 1160. Neither event had been of his direct making. Although he was certainly born to a measure of greatness, history seems to have laid more greatness on him than he either wished to have, or was suited by temperament to bear. In keeping with the military tradition of his house, Kiyomori went about armed with an escort of retainers in the manner of a general, which he was not in fact; and, as a highly privileged subject, he visited the court in state, in ox-wagon and palanquin. But the cultured, civilian aristocrats considered him uncouth. He was certainly forceful when roused, and when he felt that he had nothing to lose by a policy of force. But at times of crisis he was surprisingly timid and he was probably never very clever. In short, the picture of Kiyomori that has come down to us is of a very human person, and in an age when suspicion and cruelty were coming into fashion in politics he was better natured than might have been expected. His most notable act of forbearance occurred in 1160 when, more responsive to feminine appeal than to his advisers' pleas, he spared the lives of the young sons of his defeated foe, Minamoto Yoshitomo (1123–60).

[2] Reischauer and Yamagiwa, *Translations from Early Japanese Literature*, pp. 452–3.

The supremacy of the Taira took a familiar form. Kiyomori deferred to the imperial house, while ruling through the emperor or retired emperor. The Fujiwara kept their high titles and remained powerless. Kiyomori outdid his social superiors in ways now quite familiar, by making the best possible matches for his daughters. As a result, and much to his joy, he became the grandfather of both a future emperor and the head of the Fujiwara house. Other, and usually older, members of the Taira family were given a high proportion of posts in the provincial administration, and they accumulated more than five hundred *shōen*. In addition, the Taira had built up a profitable trade with China, conducted through their territories in the west of Japan. Kiyomori himself did much to improve ports and navigation in the Inland Sea, and this connection with China was a source of strength. But he and his family were kept in power by the loyalty of their warrior adherents, which they retained through grants of *shiki* rights and appointments to local government offices.

The Taira, however, did not hold power for long. They had their enemies among those displaced at court, and by far the most dangerous of these was the senior cloistered emperor, Go-Shirakawa (1127–92), who was an extremely skilful politician. Kiyomori was aware of court intrigues, however, and managed to keep both courtiers and the armed monks of the great monasteries in check. As it turned out, the Taira had most to fear from the Minamoto, who had been left leaderless in 1160, but were still capable of action. A plot in 1180 led to armed conflict which turned into a full-scale war between the Minamoto and the Taira.[3] When Kiyomori died in 1181 he had seen supreme power begin to slip from his family's grasp. Four years later the Taira were utterly defeated by Minamoto forces.

The Heike Monogatari

The rise and fall of the House of Taira is commemorated in the *Heike Monogatari (Tale of the House of Taira)*. This greatest of Japan's war tales has much in common with the European epic *The Song of Roland*: both were recited to generations of listeners; both stirred men time and again even though they were familiar with the heroic tales of battle; and both are, in a sense, religious. One is a work fired with Christian enthusiasm for the crusade against the followers of Mahomet; the other is suffused with Buddhist attitudes towards an

[3] This war between the Minamoto (or Genji) and the Taira (or Heike) is known as the Gempei War.

'unhallowed and degenerate age' and the 'impermanence of all things'.

The *Heike Monogatari* opens with a bell sounding in an Indian temple where the Buddha preached many of his sermons. It goes on:

> The hue of the flowers of the teak tree declares that they who flourish must be brought low. Yea, the proud ones are but for a moment, like an evening dream in springtime. The mighty are destroyed at the last, they are but as dust before the wind.[4]

Taira Kiyomori, pictured as having grown arrogant with power, is one of the two great figures in the story. His pride and success in this life are matched by his terrible death. In his final illness water was poured on him to cool him, but ' . . . it flew off again hissing in clouds of steam and spray, as though it had struck red-hot iron or stone, and the water that did strike him burst into flames so that the whole chamber was filled with whirling fires and thick black smoke'.[5] His death was credited not to old age but to the evil karma that he had accumulated. It was a fate from which neither the recitation of Sutras, nor the power of the gods and Buddhas nor tens of thousands of loyal warriors could save him. The story does not end here, however, for it is concerned with the destruction of the whole house of Taira.

The most attractive figure in the *Heike Monogatari* is Yoshitsune of the Minamoto, the bane of the Taira and the greatest of Japan's popular heroes. He is the 'Roland' of this war tale. Roland has been called ' . . . brave to the point of rashness, provocative, arrogant with the naive egotism of the epic hero, loyal, self-confident, and open as the day . . . '[6] So it is with Yoshitsune:

> Elated with victory, the Genji rode into the sea in pursuit till they were up to their saddles in water and fought among the ships, while the Heike with rakes and billhooks tried to seize Yoshitsune by the neckpiece of his helmet. Two or three times their weapons rattled about his head, but his companions with sword and halberd warded off the attacks from their master as they fought. In the course of this fighting the Hōgwan (Yoshitsune) somehow or other dropped his bow into the sea, and leant out of the saddle trying to pick it up again with his whip. His companions

---

[4] Sadler (translator), 'The Heike Monogatari', in *Transactions of the Asiatic Society of Japan*, Vol. XLVI, Part II, 1918, p. 1.

[5] Adapted from Sadler, Op. Cit., p. 276.

[6] Sayers (translator), *The Song of Roland*, p. 11.

cried out to him to let it go, but he would not, and at last managed to recover it, and rode back laughing to the beach. The older warriors reproached him for this saying: 'However valuable a bow it might be, what is that in comparison with our lord's life?' 'It was not that I grudged the bow', replied Yoshitsune, 'and if my bow were one that required two or three men to bend it, like that of my uncle Tametomo, they would be quite welcome to it, but I should not like a weak one like mine to fall into the hands of the enemy for them to laugh at it and say, "This is the bow of Kuro Yoshitsune, the Commander-in-Chief of the Genji"; and so it was that I risked my life to get it back.' And this explanation drew expressions of approval from all.[7]

Yoshitsune capped a succession of brilliant victories on land with a final triumph at sea. Most of the members of the house of Taira, including Kiyomori's widow and her grandson, the eight year old Emperor Antoku, were lost in this action, which took place in 1185. The *Heike Monogatari* ends with the death of Kiyomori's daughter, the mother of Antoku, who had been spared and had become a nun. The final chapter opens, like the first, with the tolling of a temple bell.

The Success of the Minamoto under Yoritomo

Ironically, the very brilliance of the sea victory (at Dannoura) helped to destroy the victor Yoshitsune (1159–89), who became involved in a fatal quarrel with his elder brother Yoritomo.

Yoritomo (1147–99) was the head of the Minamoto. He, together with Yoshitsune and another brother, were the children who had been spared by Kiyomori in 1160. At that time Kiyomori had sent the thirteen-year-old Yoritomo to live out the rest of his life in the remote eastern province of Izu under the custody of a local Taira vassal. In time, he married the daughter of his guardian and acquired a reputation for leadership among the provincial warrior class of the district, irrespective of traditional allegiance to Taira or Minamoto.

After the final defeat of the Taira in 1185 it seemed to Yoritomo that Yoshitsune threatened Minamoto solidarity. This was mainly because Yoshitsune understandably dallied in Kyōto after Dannoura, enjoying the sweets of victory which included the guileful attentions of the cloistered Go-Shirakawa, and refused to return at once to his brother's headquarters in the east. Yoritomo revenged himself by

[7] Sadler, 'The Heike Monogatari', in *Transactions of the Asiatic Society of Japan*, Vol. XLIX, Part I, p. 238.

rejecting repeated declarations of loyalty from Yoshitsune, hounding him and his immediate family to death four years later.

It is difficult to imagine a greater contrast than existed between Yoshitsune and Yoritomo. The picture given in records of the period makes it plain that Yoritomo was no epic hero. He was a man of achievement, prudent, where his brother was rash, a close man, humourless and determined; the destroyer of many of his own blood-relations but the wise builder of institutions of government that worked well. The manner of his death is somehow symbolic. He was thrown from his horse, not in battle, but while returning from the ceremonial opening of a bridge. According to the romancers of the *Heike Monogatari*, the brilliant success of the Minamoto was due to Yoshitsune. Historians, on the other hand, look to his elder brother Yoritomo as the architect of Minamoto success and the creator of the Kamakura *bakufu*.

The *bakufu* was a system of military government which Yoritomo and his associates devised over a period of years. There is abundant evidence that shortly after the opening of hostilities against the Taira in 1180 Yoritomo was well established in the east of Japan. In particular he controlled the fertile and strategically important Kantō area, the large plain where modern Tōkyō stands. Yoritomo had set up his base of operations, less a fort than an administrative centre, at Kamakura in the southern part of the Kantō plain. He had once managed with a single secretary, but as his responsibilities increased he needed an office, called the *samurai-dokoro*, to help him control his vassals. (It was the grim duty of the chief officers of the *samurai-dokoro* to inspect the head of that over-mighty vassal Yoshitsune when it was sent to Kamakura preserved in sweet *sake*.) As the war against the Taira spread to the west and problems of control multiplied, two more offices were set up in Kamakura. One, the *kumon-jo*, handled documents relating to the imperial court, far to the west in Kyōto; the other, the *monchū-jo*, heard disputes over land rights.

The next stage of administrative development occurred in 1185. At that time Yoritomo was in an awkward situation, with an insecure grasp on the west of Japan, where the Taira had lately held sway, and with the court going so far as to back Yoshitsune against him. He then made a decision of far-reaching importance. He accepted the advice of one of his vassals to 'ask' the court to permit him to appoint *shugo* (constables) in every province and *jitō* (stewards) in all the *shōen*, answerable to Kamakura. Yoritomo was not upsetting the structure of imperial government nor its outgrowth, the *shōen;* and both *shugo* and *jitō* were recognized offices. Moreover, the court had used military men from time to time in the Heian period to restore order in one part of the country or another in an emergency. Now Yoritomo was given the right to maintain order permanently throughout the land through the posting of *shugo* and *jitō*.

The final development of the *bakufu* structure came in 1192. The court, literally over Go-Shirakawa's dead body, awarded Yoritomo its highest military rank. The man who was already by birth the head of the house of Minamoto became *sei-i-tai-shōgun*, and this old title acquired a completely new meaning. Whoever had held it in the past had been empowered to wage war on the Ainu frontier, but Yoritomo was commissioned to govern a country that he had restored to peace. Whoever had held the title in the past had surrendered his sword of office once a particular frontier campaign was over. But Yoritomo intended to remain *shogun* for life, and, what is more, it was widely understood that he would pass his rank on to his heirs.

Originating in the day to day administrative and disciplinary needs of the Minamoto army ostensibly fighting for the court, the Kamakura *bakufu* grew into a machinery of government for the entire country after peace was re-established. Yoritomo's success was partly due to this ability to convert men and institutions from a wartime function to a peacetime one. In a similar way, he developed a centre of government out of his military headquarters at Kamakura, where he stayed even after the fighting was over when it might have seemed appropriate for him to rule the country from its traditional capital at Kyōto. He was an innovator both in regard to major institutions of government and to the seat of government.

Yoritomo thus built his authority not by destroying the existing order but by finding a secure place for himself and his vassals within it. His supremacy depended on the exercise of powers granted by the court and on control over his vassals following their victories, as much as on the victories themselves.

The role of the provincial vassal class in these events should not be minimized. Its acknowledged leader claimed to act for the emperor in all matters of real administrative importance, but the transition to military rule would not have gone so smoothly if Yoritomo had not been able to show a frightened and demoralized court that he had sufficient control over the warriors to stamp out depredations and preserve a general peace. Under the circumstances, the court was willing to legitimize his government with imperial mandates and eventually with the office of *shōgun;* and in so doing it relinquished administrative power. In return, the court received a firm guarantee that the aristocrats and metropolitan clergy would continue to enjoy their *shiki* incomes and their traditional status as social and cultural leaders.

Yoritomo had been born in Kyōto and spent his boyhood there, and he retained a measure of appreciation for the capital and its way of life. It was his destiny to reconcile the aspirations of the rising provincial vassal class and the fears of the established court aristocracy. In doing so he showed himself to be better attuned to the trends of the times than ever Kiyomori had been.

The Hōjō Regency

It is characteristic of Japanese government through most of its history that institutions have been controlled not by nominal leaders, but by a succession of men from great families who 'served' them. So it was with the Kamakura *bakufu*. After the death of Yoritomo in 1199, two of his sons successively held the title of *shōgun*, but did not live long enough to influence events. Thereafter the office was not filled by Yoritomo's blood-relations, but by persons adopted into the Minamoto family. Though these later *shōguns* were of distinguished birth, their title was an empty one. Real power was exercised by successive heads of the Hōjō family who acted as regents for the *shōgun*.

The claims of the Hōjō to power were tested in a series of violent events, culminating in an armed attack launched by the imperial court in 1221 (the Shōkyū War). After years of frustration the retired Emperor Go-Toba (1180–1239) had resolved to recover real authority. The traditional account alleges the cause of the trouble to have been a dancing girl. Go-Toba ordered certain estates to be assigned to her. It so happened that Yoritomo himself had granted these estates to Yoshitoki (1162–1224), the head of the Hōjō family. A most important point was at issue. The authority of the *bakufu* over its vassals rested on just such land rights granted to the vassal by his overlord, with loyal service rewarded by confirmation of these rights. Go-Toba therefore was striking at a foundation of what was beginning to be recognizable as a feudal regime. The retired emperor was rebuked but persisted, and finally declared war on Yoshitoki as an outlaw. Go-Toba had made a terrible mistake. His initiatives revealed not the weakness of the *bakufu* under the Hōjō, but its strength. The great majority of the warrior families in the east remained loyal to Kamakura; and with their support the regime had no difficulty in crushing the forces raised against it by the court.

The man who led the Hōjō to this high point of influence was the regent, Yoshitoki, but nobody at Kamakura had proved to be more resolute in moments of crisis than his sister Masako (1156–1225). This lady had been Yoritomo's wife, and mother of the two sons who succeeded him as *shōgun*. Like many women of the warrior class, she possessed formidable strength of character. When the disconcerting news of Go-Toba's actions first reached Kamakura, it was Masako who had taken the lead in demanding the loyalty of senior Minamoto vassals and advocating an offensive strategy. Her actions only added to prestige already won as a stalwart upholder of her late husband's work. By the time of her death in 1225, she had been a person of consequence on the stage of national politics for nearly thirty years.

The career of Masako, originally the daughter of an obscure country warrior, contrasts strongly with the fate of Go-Toba. The man who was the descendant of emperors and had been an emperor himself ended his days in desolate exile on the Oki Islands. His feelings there were expressed, according to one account, in the following poem:

Even winds blowing from the capital fail to reach these · lonely isles,

But the surging waves from the sea visit me constantly.[8]

But if winds failed to reach the Oki Islands, books did not. The late twelfth century was one of the golden ages of traditional court poetry (*waka*), and poets at this time compiled the thirteenth, and perhaps the greatest, of the imperial anthologies. Known as the *Shinkokinshū*, or the *New Collection of Poems Ancient and Modern*, this anthology contains representative works of a brilliant group of courtier-poets of the time. Go-Toba himself contributed the respectable total of thirty-three poems. He had always taken a keen interest in the work of compilation and devoted his ample leisure on Oki to the final editing and arranging of the 1,981 poems that constitute the completed text of the *Shinkokinshū*. He must have known by the time he died that in poetry, at least, he had striven to good purpose.

The Hōjō continued to do well by ruling wisely. After 1221, imperial princes obedient to Kamakura were placed on the throne in Kyōto. As an additional precaution, a branch of the *bakufu* was set up· in Kyōto to keep a check on politics at court. Custom decreed that the estates of families on the losing side in the Shōkyū War be confiscated.

[8] McCullough, '*Shōkyūki*—An Account of the Shōkyū War of 1221' in *Monumenta Nipponica*, Vol. XIX, p. 209.

Some three thousand estates, many of them in the west, were not kept by the victorious Hōjō but distributed to temples and shrines or assigned to vassals of the *shōgun*. This extensive re-allocation of land in the western provinces enabled the *bakufu* to control the areas where, for administrative as well as geographic reasons, its authority had been rather weak.

After Yoshitoki, the family provided a succession of regents who have been praised for their high character, fair administration of justice and willingness to share responsibility. With these virtues the Kamakura *bakufu* kept the peace, with little resort to force, for decades after the Shōkyū incident. Its most notable administrative achievement in these years lay in the field of law. The Jōei Code, issued in 1232, was intended to be no more than a clear statement of rules for the Minamoto vassals. In practice, however, the rules proved so sensible and the Hōjō so conscientious in maintaining Kamakura's reputation for fair and speedy justice, that the Jōei Code became part of the general legal system and remained one of the chief sources of law until the collapse of the feudal order in 1868.

The Mongol Invasions

Despite the outstanding administrative record of the Hōjō, Japanese historians have felt obliged to criticize them harshly for the way they treated the imperial family in 1221, when not only Go-Toba but also two of his sons were banished and an infant emperor deposed. Yet even their strongest critics have acknowledged that they led their country well in withstanding the Mongol invasions of the second half of the thirteenth century.

For three and a half centuries, contact between Japan and the continent had not only been fairly peaceful (pirates aside) but unofficial. When the T'ang dynasty decayed in the ninth century, the sending of official embassies from Japan became pointless, and the practice ended. It was not renewed during the next three hundred years when the Sung dynasty governed China. However, in the thirteenth century a new and vigorous regime of Mongol origin replaced the Sung, and took the initiative in renewing relations.

In 1264, the Mongol chieftain, Kublai Khan (1215–94), made Peking his capital, a significant event in the establishment of the vast Mongol empire that stretched westward from Korea as far as Europe. Then in 1268, in an effort to extend his sway, the 'Emperor' of Great Mongolia addressed a letter to the 'King' of Japan threatening war if that small State did not acknowledge its inferior status and establish friendly relations with his dominions. The court in Kyōto wavered, but the *bakufu* did not forward any reply to the Mongols.

The first invasion came in 1274, after five more Mongolian missions had failed. Warriors in Kyūshū bore the brunt of the attack at Hakata on the island's north-west coast. This was the very area the Japanese had prepared defensively five hundred years before, when they feared an invasion from Korea that never materialized. The Japanese warriors faced veteran Mongol forces who were better armed. They were saved by their fortitude—and by the weather. The Mongols landed on 19 November 1274, and that evening their experienced Korean seamen urged them to re-embark. A storm that night scattered the fleet and left possibly as many men drowned as had lost their lives in the fighting.

The storm concealed from Kublai the fact that the Mongol army had not broken through Japanese land defences, and, on hearing the news, he simply sent a further mission requiring the King of Japan to come to his capital to do homage. The Hōjō leaders ordered that members of the mission be beheaded on the beach at Kamakura, and laid more elaborate plans to strengthen defences in the west. Control over warriors in Kyūshū was tightened. A stone rampart was constructed along the shores of Hakata Bay in anticipation of new attacks in the same area.

The rampart took five years to complete, but this did not matter since the Mongols were heavily committed in campaigns in south China. In 1281, however, even though they had heard of the preparations, the Mongols did land forces on a broad front on the north-west coast of Kyūshū. The defensive line held for nearly two months, but the winning blows were struck by a typhoon on 15 August 1281. This typhoon has come to be known as the divine wind or *kamikaze*, a name revived during the closing stages of the war in the Pacific (1941–45) for suicide pilots who used their planes to ram enemy shipping. The original *kamikaze* effectively thwarted the Mongols, who lost a great part of their fleet and their army (tens of thousands of men) in attempting to withdraw. The Mongols attacked no more, but fear that they would return lived on.

The Decline of the Kamakura Bakufu

Strangely enough no great epic celebrates the heroism and final victory of the Japanese over the Mongols; only a pictorial record survives. Battle scenes, showing what combatants wore and what arms they carried, are vividly portrayed on a painted scroll with written commentary commissioned by one Takezaki, a participant in the fighting. The record was meant to support his claim for reward, and one scene shows Takezaki cutting a Mongol throat.

Takezaki's claim was one of many. The court, the temples and the shrines which had offered prayers for victory, the *bakufu's* vassals and other warriors who had actually achieved the victory, all felt that they had saved their country. The Kamakura authorities were in a difficult position, for the vanquished foe had left his dead, but no property to be divided among the victors. Therefore the *bakufu* could not meet even legitimate demands for compensation, and its prestige was lowered.

Other factors told against the Hōjō. In the 1290s they decreed a general cancellation of debts. This was seen as a means of helping retainers who were living beyond their income, but inevitably the measure sapped the confidence of creditors in the regime. Furthermore, other powerful families resented the way the Hōjō favoured members of their own family when making *bakufu* appointments. Against this background of discontent, there occurred a change in the quality of leadership as between Kyōto and Kamakura. The last Hōjō regent was named Takatoki (1303–33).

> By day and by night, with wanton acts he dishonoured his glorious ancestors under the ground; in the morning and in the evening, with vain merriment he invited ruin in his lifetime. . . . Those who saw knit their eyebrows, and those who heard uttered condemnations.[9]

Even allowing for exaggeration in the traditional accounts, he must have been a disaster.

While Takatoki was disporting himself, the *bakufu* had acquired a furtive but persistent opponent in the person of the reigning emperor, Go-Daigo (1288-1339). This ruler, like Go-Toba before him, planned to regain full authority; but not for him the impulsive actions of his predecessor. He had ascended the throne in 1318 and rightly saw that his first task was to concentrate in his own hands whatever shreds of power remained to the imperial house. This he achieved in 1321 when he persuaded his father to step down from the position of cloistered emperor, and so terminated the cloister as a separate centre of power.

[9] McCullough (translator), *The Taiheiki—A Chronicle of Medieval Japan*, p. xxxvi.

The next stage in Go-Daigo's plan—the overthrow of the *bakufu* itself—was more difficult to accomplish. In 1331, after much plotting and planning, Go-Daigo and his supporters were successfully attacked by the Hōjō. For the second time in little more than a century the leading member of the imperial house found himself in exile on the Oki Islands.

This cycle of fate was not overlooked by lovers of historical romance. A fourteenth century work, the *Masukagami*, describes Go-Daigo's arrival on Oki in the following way:

> Nothing remained in the way of relics of that former exile. There was a handful of houses and, in the distance, only a shed where the fishermen burnt salt. When he cast his eyes on this most miserable view, all thoughts of himself left his mind, and he recalled instead the events of the past. With sorrow and humility he tried to imagine what it must have been like for that other Emperor to have ended his days in such a place, and he realized that his present exile stemmed from his desire to fulfill the aspirations of his ancestor.[10]

In fact, Go-Daigo did not die on Oki but returned to the mainland and recovered the throne. His son, Prince Morinaga, rallied anti-*bakufu* forces and so weakened Hōjō authority that important warrior families, the Nitta and Ashikaga in particular, ceased to support the *bakufu*. This switching of sides by great eastern warrior families was crucial, and in 1333 in Kamakura Nitta Yoshisada (1301–38) destroyed the last Hōjō regent and all his important kinsmen.

The battle of Kamakura is one of the events commemorated in the *Taiheiki* (*Chronicle of Grand Pacification*), the last of the major war tales. It describes with gusto romanticized and picturesque scenes of death and destruction. This was a battle, so the *Taiheiki* says, 'to decide great things'. No doubt it was, and not only for the individual contestants who took part, man pitted against man, in the style of warfare of those days. The events of 1333 mark the start of a long process of administrative and social disintegration. Yet, so far as the outward form of government was concerned, the battle did nothing to alter the established fact of rule by military houses.

The House of Ashikaga

The Hōjō had been destroyed ostensibly to allow for a restoration of power to the court under Go-Daigo. However, in 1336 another

[10] Keene, *Anthology of Japanese Literature*, p. 250.

military family, the Ashikaga, became the strongest single element in the government of the country.

Go-Daigo had regained power in 1333, but his government was so inept that he soon antagonized his warrior supporters. One of his generals, Ashikaga Takauji (1304–58) took advantage of this to occupy the capital and imprison the ruler. Go-Daigo, who seems to have been at his best in adversity, refused to come to terms with Takauji, and fled into the mountains of Yoshino, south of the capital. There he set up a government in exile which became known as the Southern Court, although members of the imperial family remained behind and collaborated with Takauji. In 1338 the reigning emperor of the Northern Court in Kyōto appointed Ashikaga Takauji as *shogun*. Although the Ashikaga line of *shoguns* lasted until 1573, neither Takauji nor his immediate successors established unquestioned authority.

The principal reason for this lack of control was that the Southern Court under Go-Daigo, his son and his grandson, continued to challenge in open warfare the legitimacy of the Northern Court and its Ashikaga sponsors. Since the Southern Court could raise armies on its own behalf and enjoyed the loyal support of some of Japan's most brilliant generals, the outcome of this war of the Northern and Southern Courts was uncertain for several decades; and it went on disturbing the country until 1392.

The middle decades of the fourteenth century proved to be one of the great divides of Japanese history. Go-Daigo had attempted to revert not to the situation that had existed immediately before the rise of the Taira in 1160, but to the much earlier Nara and early Heian periods when emperors governed in fact as well as name. Now this fragile hope of a complete restoration was shown to be utterly illusory, and with its collapse went what remained of the structure of imperial government at all levels—local, provincial and national. This structure had first taken shape in the Taika Reform. The Fujiwara and cloistered emperors had changed it but on the whole preserved it, and it had survived as a subordinate partner to the Kamakura *bakufu*. After 1336 it became part of the past: a tradition of continuous national administration which had existed for seven centuries, with the imperial court as its focal point for all but the last of them.

Although the old government organized around the throne had diverged considerably from its original Chinese model, the divergence was not due to stupidity or political ineptitude on the part of the

Japanese. Rather, it was the result of a process of creatively adapting the Chinese original to a different, Japanese, situation. The overall success of these modifications—the last significant one was the Kamakura *bakufu* itself—is evidence of something of a flair for politics among the Japanese, and an ability to act constructively in matters of practical administration. The most recent manifestation of these qualities had been the repulse of the Mongols. The defence effort as a whole had been splendidly organized and directed by the Hōjō leaders, and even when the Mongols arrived in Kyūshū these leaders never needed to leave their headquarters at Kamakura.

The early Ashikaga *shōguns* and their advisers inherited their predecessors' political skills and had the sense to attempt to adopt, with some changes, the well-tried structure of the Kamakura *bakufu*. However, owing to the incessant campaigning against the Southern Court, the Ashikaga commanded neither the men nor the wealth to rule the country directly from one centre of government, but had to delegate authority to a number of 'deputies'. They appointed heads of powerful families to the office of *shugo* (constable) with responsibility for wide areas of the country. In time the constables extended their power beyond their original military functions, taking an ever greater share of taxes from estates and acting as civil rulers as well. Historians have come to call them *shugo-daimyō*, in recognition of the fact they were more than officials appointed by the *shōgun* and were becoming territorial lords (*daimyō*). While these men were diverting to their own uses the traditional taxes and *shōen* dues paid in the rural districts, the Ashikaga were finding themselves dependent—in a way no other national rulers had been—on such slim bases of financial support as the *sake* brewer-pawnbrokers of Kyōto.

The Muromachi Bakufu at its Height

Ashikaga Takauji had set up his headquarters in Kyōto, not at Kamakura in the east, in order to meet the military challenge of his opponents. His successors remained in Kyōto, and forty years after the founding of the regime built suitably grand buildings in the suburb of Muromachi. One name given to the Ashikaga regime, therefore, is the Muromachi *bakufu*.

The buildings in Muromachi date from the time of Ashikaga Yoshimitsu (1358–1408). In his lifetime the house of Ashikaga reached its peak. He became *shōgun* at the age of nine in 1368, and during his minority Ashikaga fortunes depended greatly on the highly capable Hosokawa Yoriyuki (1329–92). The older man did not attempt to turn his office (*kanrei* or deputy) into a hereditary one by keeping puppets in the office of *shōgun*, in the manner of the Hōjō. Even so, other constables thought that Hosokawa Yoriyuki was playing an unduly large part in the affairs of the regime and, feeling threatened, forced him to give up his high post after twelve years. Only Yoshimitsu in his prime was able to overawe the constables by a combination of armed force, a strong personality and sense of the dramatic. By balancing the constables, each with his own following of retainers, he managed to produce a stable situation in the country as a whole. There is no question that Yoshimitsu was the most important figure in the years just before and after 1400.

Indeed, the Ming dynasty, which had succeeded the Mongols as rulers of China, recognized Yoshimitsu as 'king' of Japan. In those turbulent times men from Kyūshū and the Inland Sea took shelter from the authorities in defensible inlets from which they sallied as far as Korea, China and even south-east Asia, sometimes to trade and sometimes to attack and pillage coastal settlements. The Chinese called them *wakō*, 'Japanese robbers', and found them very difficult to control. Yoshimitsu managed to restrain the *wakō*. The Chinese then agreed to receive official Japanese missions, which led to a re-opening of trade between the political centres of the two countries, and Yoshimitsu derived considerable income from the proceeds.

It is not surprising that the Chinese took Yoshimitsu to be a king, for he behaved as if he were. The imperial family in Kyōto owed him a great deal, for it was Yoshimitsu who brought the conflict between the two courts to an end in 1392. This involved the return of the southern line's sovereign to Kyōto where he voluntarily surrendered his claims to the throne. In the last years before his death in 1408, the Ashikaga leader behaved very much as if he were on the same level as the emperor in Kyōto. There is even a suggestion that he expected his favourite son to occupy the throne.

Even if in political life the emperor was not important, the court was still able to attract those to whom social standing mattered. Yoshimitsu did his best to link his family with the court and to out-shine it, probably because he enjoyed lavish spending, but partly with the idea of drawing the powerful constables away from the countryside to live in mansions in the capital. They were encouraged to look to Kyōto by the very scale of Yoshimitsu's spending. He built palaces and temples and a retreat called *Kinkakuji* (Golden Pavilion), set among pine trees beside a large pond. The

Kinkakuji exists today as a reminder that although the military houses had deprived the imperial house and the court aristocracy of effective control of the country, the greatest military house now followed the court aristocracy in matters of taste.

CHAPTER TEN

The Failure of Ashikaga Rule: the Vigour of Economic and Cultural Life

The Ashikaga family, so powerful under Yoshimitsu around 1400, failed to keep control of the country in the fifteenth century. Disputes between powerful military houses were so continuous that for the hundred years from the 1470s no central government existed. This century is called the *sengoku jidai*, best translated as the 'period of the country at war'. It is easy to over-estimate the destruction suffered in the *sengoku jidai*. True, Kyōto, once 'the capital of flowers' was reduced to a burnt field, and the appalling loss in metropolitan temples, shrines, palaces and their treasures fully matched the decline in metropolitan political authority and prestige. Nevertheless, in the country as a whole, new social forces were being released which in time produced a better life for more people.

The Collapse of Central Government

The eclipse of the Ashikaga regime can be dated from the violent death of the *shōgun* Yoshinori in 1441. Invited by a leading military man to an outdoor dramatic entertainment at his Kyōto mansion, the *shōgun* was killed by armed men who burst in on the proceedings. The host had feared that his guest might have been planning to reduce his family's power and position. Yoshinori had indeed shown himself to be a forceful ruler. He was succeeded first by one child and then by another, neither of whom had strong regents to help him. The second child, Ashikaga Yoshimasa (1436–90) became a brilliant patron of the arts, but was certainly no soldier. Cultivating the

114

civilized life in the capital, Yoshimasa left war to be waged by men whose ambitions and training fitted them for it. He retained sufficient prestige to prevent the Ashikaga house from being destroyed, but not enough power to keep peace in the land.

The weakness of the Ashikaga was revealed fully during the Ōnin War (1467–77), fought through eleven years within the city of Kyōto and in the neighbouring districts. This terrible conflict between the Hosokawa family and the Yamana family arose from a dispute over who should control the affairs of the *bakufu* at its centre in the capital. Yoshimasa, living on the very edge of the fighting, pursued his own private interests, and was no more effective in governing the country than the emperor himself. Both *shōgun* and emperor remained simply symbols of a political unity that was to be the chief casualty of the fighting.

As the war dragged on, the great military families realized that fighting in the capital was of less importance than what was happening in the provinces. The troops went home to put down risings, leaving Kyōto burnt and looted. However, when those military leaders who had been appointed *shugo* (constable) by the Ashikaga returned to the provinces they found that the *bakufu* no longer had the power to support them. When armed conflicts broke out in the decades after 1477, the *shugo* had to fend for themselves. Very few succeeded in holding their positions against attack by new families (often their own vassals or relations). The Hosokawa, though reduced in power, remained influential, but other families disappeared altogether.

The new local rulers were the territorial lords, or *daimyō*. They were to play a major role in the next four hundred years of Japanese history. Generally speaking, the domains of the *daimyō* were not as large as the areas that had been assigned to the ousted constables. But these domains, though relatively small, were naturally compact units, lending themselves to easy defence and close control within their area. Self-reliant, the early *daimyo* had virtually no contact with the capital. They made their own rules for governing the lands that they controlled and protected. Long-standing links with the capital were broken, as neither the name of the emperor nor the command of the *shōgun* any longer carried weight in the provinces. Most important of all, *shiki* rights to income from the *shoen*, the estates that had sustained court life for so long, were swept away.

With no income being sent to the capital the court was reduced to poverty. 'Common people made tea, and sold it in the garden of the Palace, under the very shadow of the Cherry of the Right and the

Orange of the Left. Children made it their playground. By the sides of the main approach to the Imperial pavilion they modelled mud toys; sometimes they peeped behind the blind that screened the Imperial apartments.'[1] So say traditional accounts, which also allege that emperors had to sell their calligraphy in order to maintain themselves. What is certain is that important court ceremonies—including the funeral rites of Emperor Go-Tsuchimikado in 1500—had to be postponed because the imperial treasury was empty. Moreover, many aristocratic families who had served the court for nearly a thousand years, found that they had to flee to the provinces and ' . . . began to live directly off their lands in a final desperate attempt to salvage a living from their inheritances.'[2] They soon lost their identity as courtiers.

The *daimyō* were not the only men to emerge with greater authority as Ashikaga and *shugo* rule collapsed and *shōen* were obliterated. In this age of warfare, peasant farmers struggled to secure and improve their position. Led by local men they united to defend themselves against conflicting armies, and authorities who levied heavy taxes. Their united protests were sometimes violent. The point is not that peasants protested, but that during the years of no effective central rule they organized themselves efficiently. They managed to present a united front against powerful military men and to govern themselves for years at a time. The most successful group of self-governing peasants held together for nearly a century under the leadership of members of a radical religious sect. In less spectacular fashion, agricultural villages in many parts of the country became self-governing, with their own village headmen and their own rules. *Daimyō* left such villages to manage their own affairs, provided that they paid taxes. On the other hand, *daimyo* tried to keep direct control of their warrior vassals, who were potential rivals, by getting them to live near the main castle of the domain and not in the countryside.

The Vigour of Economic Life

The growth of many new centres of political power was matched by economic developments in the countryside. Smaller centres of activity overshadowed Kyōto, formerly the one great centre of economic life. Each *daimyō* needed wealth as well as armed strength to sustain himself as an independent ruler. The *daimyō* able to exploit the mineral wealth

[1] Murdoch, *A History of Japan*, Vol. I, p. 633.
[2] Hall, *Government and Local Power in Japan 500–1700*, p. 204.

of their territories (gold, silver, copper) were particularly powerful; and miners proved useful as sappers in attacks on enemy fortifications. But, in general, the wealth of the domains was drawn from the hard work and enterprise of farmers, merchants and artisans.

For many years, from Kamakura times, agricultural production had been rising with improved technology (use of the water-wheel) and more intensive use of the land (double-cropping). The wholesale trade in agricultural products, particularly rice, grew larger; and trade between regions increased. In the troubled years after the Ōnin War, *daimyō* offered protection to merchants and encouraged enterprises such as the holding of regular markets and the manufacture of special products such as swords and armour, textiles and salt. Merchants were given official approval to trade within *daimyō* territories. The growth of *jōkamachi*, or towns-below-the-castle, where the warrior vassals, merchants and artisans gathered, fostered the growth of markets and commercial organizations that were taxable. However, the basis of *daimyō* power was still control over their retainers and over land. Since the bulk of the population remained rice-farmers, the *daimyō* needed to control rice-producing river valleys and coastal plains. They built protective forts on higher ground where the natural defences of steep mountains dominated the flat, productive valleys that no *daimyō* could afford to lose.

With the decline of Ashikaga rule, two *daimyō* families, the Hosokawa and the Ōuchi took over the official China trade from the *bakufu*. These families were geographically well placed to undertake such a commercial venture. Their territorial base was in the area of the Inland Sea, which had been the scene of considerable maritime trade, foreign as well as domestic, from ancient times. The Hosokawa, who dominated the eastern end of the Inland Sea, were supported by the merchants of Sakai; the Ōuchi, from territories further west, operated through the northern Kyūshū port of Hakata. Both Sakai and Hakata were old-established trading ports and during the Muromachi period their citizens enjoyed a high degree of political independence. Rivalry between men from these two 'free cities' led to fighting in the Chinese port of Ningpo in 1523, but it was the Ōuchi who controlled the official China trade in the ten years before it ceased in 1549.

These voyages to China (there were eleven between 1433 and 1549) stimulated economic activity in Japan, especially in the towns of Sakai and Hakata, but they were by no means so vital to Japan as foreign trade is today. Swords, copper ore, sulphur and fine woods (the last re-exported from south-east Asia) were the most important Japanese exports.[3] Copper coins were a major import from China, with silks, porcelain and books. In the days before the Japanese minted their own coins satisfactorily, Chinese coins were commonly used. The payment of salaries and taxes, the sale of produce and land were transacted either in coin or in terms of coin. Availability of currency greatly facilitated the use of credit, which, in turn, stimulated economic activity.

Cultural Life in the Period of the Country at War

The new castle-towns, more secure and sometimes wealthier than the capital itself, attracted working artists of various kinds during the *sengoku jidai*. Kyōto ceased to dominate the nation's culture as it had done under Yoshimitsu at the beginning of the fifteenth century, and even under Yoshimasa sixty years later. Yet a common cultural life, disseminated by travellers, proved stronger than political divisions. Indeed, cultural continuity has been one of the most remarkable characteristics of Japanese civilization; the traditional arts of present-day Japan assumed their classic form in the century of war that ended four hundred years ago.

The priest Sesshū (1420–1506) raised to new heights the *suiboku* style of painting, in which black ink and water are used to produce varying shades on white absorbent paper. After working with Japanese masters in Kyōto, Sesshū left for China just before the Ōnin War to improve his mastery of a style that was Chinese in origin. As it turned out, he probably learned more from finer Chinese paintings that had already been brought over to Japan than he did through visiting China. Returning home, Sesshū found Kyōto ravaged by war, and settled in the far west of the country, where he enjoyed the patronage of the wealthy and powerful Ōuchi family. Here he produced notable landscapes: single paintings designed for hanging, as well as scrolls. One splendid scroll, fifty feet long, shows rural scenes from early spring through summer to autumn and then winter. One senses that Sesshū intended to portray not only a journey through the seasons but a pilgrimage through life. The scroll is more than a dazz-

---

[3] On one expedition 37,000 swords were shipped to China. These were obviously not the great works of art forged by master craftsmen of Kamakura which surpassed the fine Spanish swords. As warfare changed from individual combat to the deployment of large formations of foot-soldiers, artisans turned to the mass-production of shorter, utilitarian swords.

ling display of *suiboku* techniques; it seems to depict a man's spiritual experience.

Sesshū's genius is individual, and yet, like the temple-artists of the Nara and Heian periods, he was an active participant in the Buddhist culture of east Asia. However, while earlier religious painters, especially in Heian times, had looked principally to Shingon, Sesshū and the other members of the *suiboku* school drew their inspiration from the Zen sect of Buddhism, which had been developing in China since the seventh century. Both Shingon and Zen held to the idea of a cosmic Buddha who was fully and perfectly embodied in the material world and the experience it offers, rejecting the older Buddhist tradition that this world and life were nothing but illusion. Shingon had surrounded the doctrine of the divine permanently pervading the universe with an atmosphere of extreme awe, mystery and incantation. Shingon art, therefore, was appropriately elaborate and symbolic. Zen, on the other hand, despised ritual and icons, and sought to present the basic teaching of immanence as directly as possible. Consequently, its art, though concerned with the same 'truth' as Shingon art, differed strikingly from the latter in approach and mood. The *suiboku* painters chose for their subjects seemingly ordinary scenes which they nevertheless managed to infuse with a strong sense of the ideal or divine. In doing this they developed a style that was a kind of austere impressionism, abandoning the rich colours of earlier painting for the noble simplicity of black ink on white paper.

Sesshū thoroughly understood Zen and practised it. There was nothing specially remarkable about this, since Zen ideas saturated Muromachi culture. What was remarkable was that in him a deep appreciation of Zen philosophy was married to an unsurpassed mastery of the techniques of ink painting, which require faultless control since a stroke once made cannot be changed. Sesshū always painted with meticulous skill, displaying command of line and angle, but he grew bolder as he grew older. Perhaps it was simply a matter of greater confidence with his brush. More probably, it was due to a deepening of his Zen convictions, together with the impressions gained from the travels he loved to make in his own country in spring and early summer, when the harsher outlines of the Japanese landscape are softened by haze. Whatever the reason, Sesshū in his prime went further than any other *suiboku* artist in China or Japan in developing the impressionistic style, and by the time he died he had painted some of the world's greatest pictures. These paintings have a dominant quality of idealized simplicity that appeals to people of all ages and cultures, because there is no need to have the kind of fore-knowledge which the Shingon *mandalas* and other icons demand in order to appreciate them fully.

It had long been customary to offer flowers in front of Buddhist statues. In the fifteenth and sixteenth centuries there developed rules for the arrangement of flowers in the houses of the great as well as in temples. In these early days of flower arrangement as a distinct art, the original form was the *tatebana* (standing flower) arrangement. Impressive to look at, it was intended not only to please his senses or display the skill of the arranger, but to make a spiritual impact on the beholder by recreating a scene that was true to nature. *Tatebana* were constructed to suggest the sacred hill of Sumeru, famous in Buddhist literature, with mountain peak, waterfall, hills, the foot of the mountain and a town suggested by the green foliage of certain trees and plants used in fixed combinations and positions. Fewer flowers were used than might be expected. Balance was essential, but unnatural symmetry was to be avoided. At this time, and until the nineteenth century, flower arranging was a masculine art—practised by priests, nobles and warriors—and flowers were arranged for a hero's departure to battle as readily as for his wedding.

The tea ceremony also owes much to patronage by members of the warrior aristocracy during the *sengoku jidai*. It is much more than a meeting of friends to quench their thirst. At its best it is a formal social gathering of connoisseurs, free for a time from the cares of the world to give themselves to appreciation of what is modestly beautiful. The prescribed setting is removed from the everyday world, but reminiscent of it in essentials: a tea house, just nine feet square, set in a garden, with a stone water-basin, lantern and toilet. Entering the room, one becomes not a spectator but a participant. The smell of incense, the sight of a scroll hung in an alcove with a simple flower arrangement below, subtly stimulate the senses. The simmering of the iron kettle over a charcoal fire is likened to the sound of the wind in the pine-trees. Tea—thick, green and bitter—is made with the utmost economy of movement. After each participant has sipped a bowl of tea, the conversation turns to the quality of the tea bowl itself and associated subjects.

Participants in the tea ceremony today are heirs to an ancient tradition. Monks brought the plant from China because they found drinking tea helped to keep them awake during long hours of meditation, and popularized it as the secret of long life. Then these monks came to realize the social and aesthetic potential of their habit of drinking tea together; they created the tea ceremony, and in doing so discovered one of the most perfect expressions of Zen simplicity and reliance on the power of suggestion. One of Yoshimasa's many cultural advisers, the Zen priest Nōami (1397–1471), recommended the ceremony to the pleasure-loving but sensitive *shōgun*. This had remarkable consequences, for Yoshimasa took up the tea ceremony and patronized the arts associated with it. In his tea house, regarded as a model by later generations, and in a larger building nearby, the *Ginkakuji* or Silver Pavilion, the barbarian-quelling general and his circle met together. The standards of taste they set then are still respected. Just as the tea ceremony should retain a sober, modest beauty, so should the porcelain tea bowls and the buildings in which it is practised.

One of the classic forms of theatre in Japan, the *nō* drama, was another product of Muromachi high society. It was created between 1350 and 1450 by two men, Kanami Kiyotsugu (1333–84) and his son Zeami Motokiyo (1363–1443), who were supported by the *shōgun* Yoshimitsu at a critical juncture in their lives. In his younger days Kanami earned his living as a working actor and learned the skills of acting, writing and making music while giving a kind of vaudeville performance at temples and shrines, which charged entrance money to a public that included uneducated country people out for some jollity as well as cultivated aristocrats. The discernment and patronage of Yoshimitsu relieved Kanami and his son of financial worries, and enabled them to concentrate on a smaller circle of discriminating patrons. As a result, they eliminated the realistic stories and sets, the farce, and the acrobatics from their programmes, and in their place used the more elevated language and themes of aristocratic literature, together with stately dances derived from Buddhist rituals and official court celebrations. These and kindred changes transformed the old plebeian theatricals into a highly refined art form, in much the same way as monks and men like Yoshimasa constructed a unique ceremony out of the drinking of tea.

Aesthetic refinement characterizes all the two hundred and forty plays which now form the repertoire of classical *nō*. *Nō* reflects the Muromachi preoccupation with Zen, as does the style of acting favoured by Zeami. In fact, Zeami did more than anybody else to create the *nō* theatre. He not only composed most of the major plays, but also wrote treatises to explain the underlying principles of his art. In these essays, he points out that 'no action' is more important than action. The most meaningful moments in a performance are those when an actor has just finished a gesture or a dance or a speech and then, in complete silence and stillness, manages to do more than merely hold the attention of spectators. He actually intensifies it. Thus, *nō* has been built on Zen techniques of suggestion and stylized implication.

But unlike the tea ceremony, *nō* did not grow out of Zen alone. It embodied in one grand summation achievements and attitudes that had gone into the making of Japanese culture since archaic times. The masks worn by the actors when playing female and certain male roles are evidence of the continuing vitality of a craft that goes back to the Nara period. Similarly, the splendid *nō* costumes, which show up all the better on a stage customarily bereft of scenery, are superb examples of the silk-weaving and silk-dyeing industry, centred on Kyōto and already a thousand years old. On the literary side, Kanami and Zeami culled sections of text and ideas for the stories of their plays from a wide variety of existing sources. 'Courtly' literature, Buddhist Sutras and hymns, local legends, tales of Heian celebrities, exploits of latter-day military heroes—all were grist to their mill. Yet the *no* plays were original; the authors had the genius to fuse a variety of materials into literary masterpieces which genuinely reflect the outlook and concerns of Muromachi times.

In addition to their aestheticism, the *nō* plays are profoundly religious; and this aspect, too, reveals a subtle blending of diverse elements. Imbued through and through as they are with the spirit of Buddhism, originally a foreign and court-sponsored religion, they nevertheless have connections with Shinto and native folk tradition. Sometimes the relationship is direct—a legend used is a specifically Shinto legend, or a deity portrayed or mentioned is a specifically Shinto deity. But indirectly all *nō* performances have a relationship with Shinto, since the construction of the stage—with its floor of sacred cypress wood, its replica of a shrine roof, and its decor of pine trees and white sand—deliberately recalls the plays' origins in the shrines and their round of public festivals. Although the mood and style of acting owe much to Zen, most of the plays have a definite doctrinal message, stressing the need for qualities like faith, reverence and compassion, despite the fact that these virtues were the concern of the older Buddhist sects, rather than Zen.

In sum, the *nō* plays are striking testimony to the ability of Japanese culture to assimilate not only foreign ideas and discoveries but also elements from its own past into a new and exciting synthesis.

It is a culture which relies heavily on established traditions; yet in its great moments, and in response to new developments and influences, it can reshape traditions in a satisfying way.

Today *nō* appeals only to small groups of devotees, but when it developed in the fifteenth century, it was widely popular. Players from the capital were invited to entertain gatherings in provincial castle-towns, and this practice was so widespread that one military ruler advised his successors in the 1480s not to spend money on bringing actors from Kyōto but to train local talent. Musicians were also in demand, for the mood of a play was evoked by the rhythm and melody of drums and flute as much as by voices and dancing.

Several plays would be presented in one programme, and in order to arrange such programmes the repertoire was divided into five categories: deity plays, hero plays, heroine plays, mad person plays and devil plays. One play would be chosen from each category to form a varied bill of fare. Since *nō* treats all its themes seriously, short farces (*kyōgen*) were also staged to provide light relief for the audience, and rest for the actors. These *kyōgen* preserve the light-hearted and unreflecting spirit of the holiday crowd and are of some value as sources for social history.

What follows is a summary of the play *Funa Benkei*. It was written as a 'concluding piece' to end a programme. *Funa Benkei*, like all *nō* drama, is lyrical in intent: it sets out not to tell a story but to create a mood.

The spectators sit some distance from the polished wooden stage, nineteen feet five inches square, with its own roof supported by pillars. There is no scenery except a permanent painting of a pine tree on the wall at the back. A gallery leads off to the left, where a striped curtain hangs, ready to be drawn back and up as the actors enter. To the rhythmic accompaniment of drums and a flute, Yoshitsune, three retainers and the faithful monk Benkei make their entrance. The actors, a boy playing Yoshitsune and an older man the part of Benkei, stand in splendid costumes of heavy silk and brocade. A song by Benkei and the retainers, sung to musical accompaniment, is repeated by a chorus of eight to ten men in plain dress, and then followed by a travel song by Benkei who explains that they are leaving for Kyūshū. With Yoshitsune's misfortunes in mind the travellers sing the words:

> Unlike when years ago he started hence
> Against the rebel Heike troops,

> Now with heavy heart he mounts the boat
> With a small band of trusty followers.
> Uncertain is the lot of man,
> As floating clouds and running water!

While the boat is being made ready, the lady Shizuka, Yoshitsune's mistress, indicates that she wants to go with them. Benkei protests.

Benkei: May it please my lord, though I hesitate to mention it, I now see that Lady Shizuka is coming with us. Under the circumstances it seems unsuitable; it would be well if she were firmly ordered to return home.
Yoshitsune: Let Benkei deal with this matter as he thinks best.
Benkei: Very well, my lord. I will go to Lady Shizuka's lodgings and convey to her your lordship's decision.

(Plainly Yoshitsune is not the man he was in the *Heike Monogatari;* legend has changed him from a fighting gallant into a pitiable fugitive.)
Lady Shizuka enters. The actor is a man wearing a 'young woman' mask that covers his face. The mask seems expressionless, but a good actor can suggest many moods. Distressed and disbelieving, Shizuka seeks Yoshitsune out, but he tells her to return. In high-pitched song the chorus bemoans the situation.

> How can my lord leave Shizuka behind,
> How can my lord leave Shizuka behind,
> Since 'shizuka' means calm weather?
> The enduring troth we plighted
> Calling the gods to witness
> Has been of no avail.

Shizuka weeps in stylized manner, bringing up the hand and forearm before the eyes, with head lowered.
With his fan, Benkei gestures as if to fill a cup with wine for Shizuka. She sings; she puts on a tall gold hat and then to the accompaniment of chanting (the words are full of allusions to Chinese literature) she dances slowly and gracefully one dance and then another. The dances over, her golden hat fallen to the floor, she leaves the stage in tears. The first act has been brought to a close.
The second act is the final part of the play and also the climax of a programme. The action is more stirring, the rhythm of the music and

the dancing faster and more dramatic. The boat (a framework to suggest reality) sets out at Benkei's insistence, despite signs of a storm and the fears of Yoshitsune's other retainers. Benkei promises the boatman that he will be made 'controller of shipping for the western seas' when his master's fortunes are restored. They press on, the boatman's actions with a bamboo pole suggesting the helmsman's struggle to control the boat in rough water. Then Benkei, looking towards the curtain, sees rising from the waves the spirits of dead Taira warriors who have come to wreak their vengeance on Yoshitsune and his band for their defeat and drowning at the battle of Dannoura.

The curtain is pulled back. A single, ghostly figure advances. It is wearing a mask of crescent shape, the eyes ringed with gold to indicate the supernatural. A wig of black hair falls down its back. Its costume is of gold brocade and heavy silk.

> Behold me!
> I am the ghost of Taira-no-Tomomori,
> Scion of the Emperor Kammu,
> In the ninth generation.
> Hail, Yoshitsune!
> I have come
> Guided by your oarmen's voices. . . .
> I, Tomomori,
> Will drag down Yoshitsune
> Under the waves beneath which I sank.

The ghost of Tomomori dances, leaping violently, and mimes the words of the chorus as they describe his sword fight with Yoshitsune. They tell how Benkei intervenes, saying 'Swords are of no avail', and how Benkei rubs his beads, and prays to the Buddhist guardian kings. His prayers are answered.

> The still-pursuing spirits are put to flight
> By Benkei's prayers;
> Then on the tide they drift away
> Leaving no trace upon the foaming waves.[4]

The actor who plays the ghost returns to the gallery. The play is over.

[4] The words are quoted from Nippon Gakujutsu Shinkōkai, *The Noh Drama—Ten Plays from the Japanese*, Vol. I, pp. 167–82.

CHAPTER ELEVEN

Buddhism in the Kamakura and Muromachi Periods

In 1180 the Tōdaiji in Nara was burnt by the Taira because its monks had meddled in politics. Eager to consolidate the authority of his regime in Kamakura after his victory, Minamoto Yoritomo contributed handsomely to the rebuilding of the temple and attended the service of dedication in 1195, as did the emperor and the court. The new buildings were not as grand as the original ones, but statues made for them reflect vividly the late twelfth century revival of Nara styles. Guardian deities in the new south gate, great muscular giants with violent facial expressions, are shown in vigorous movement. Such sculpture is evidence of the genius of a group of Kyōto artisan-artists, the chief of whom was Unkei. He and his workshop associates constructed wooden statues for temples both in Kyōto and in Kamakura. Their striking return to Nara vitality and realism was short-lived; even the Unkei school soon turned out statues more in keeping with the gentler, more idealistic Heian style, which remained popular down to recent times.

Buddhism might be outwardly rehabilitated by the rebuilding of its temples, complete with great sculptures. But buildings can survive long after the decline of the spiritual life lived within them; and each generation had to learn anew what Buddhism was about.

When I turned eight years old I asked my father, 'What sort of a thing is a Buddha?' My father said, 'A Buddha is what a man becomes'. I asked then, 'How does a man become a Buddha?' My father replied, 'By following the teachings of Buddha'. 'Then, who taught Buddha to teach?' He again replied, 'He followed the teachings of the Buddha before him'. I asked again, 'What kind of Buddha was the first Buddha who began to teach?' At this my father laughed and answered, 'I suppose he fell from the sky or else he sprang up out of the earth'.

126

My father told other people, 'He drove me into a corner, and I was stuck for an answer'. But he was amused.[1]

The boy was Yoshida Kenkō (1283–1350), the son of a Shinto priest, who was to distinguish himself as a poet and obtain a post at court. He eventually retired to become a Buddhist monk, but his writings show him to have been a worldly-wise gentleman, with a keen sense of what was beautiful in this changing world and a nostalgia for the golden days of life at court in the Heian period. His reminiscences are well worth reading as a statement of what is regarded even now in Japan as good taste, but his religious views are not startling because he did not press for answers to the problems of existence.

Some Buddhists carried their personal quest for truth beyond the normal limits of established religion. Some became hermits, like Kamo no Chōmei (1154–1216). His career resembles that of Kenkō in that he had a close family connection with the Shinto priesthood but as an individual achieved prominence in the literary circles of the court. Suddenly, however, at the age of fifty-three, he too became a Buddhist monk, and in his case severance with the world seems to have been complete. He retired first to one mountain hermitage and then to another, and shortly before he died, evocatively described the physical and spiritual life he had led in these retreats. The very title of Chōmei's memoir—*Account of a Hut Ten Feet Square (Hōjōki)*—indicates that he had forsaken the world not for the rich and gregarious monasteries of Hieizan, but for the privations of a hermit's solitude. He declares that he does not regret his choice and links it with a series of disasters that had befallen Kyōto in the early 1180s: fire, whirlwind, earthquake and famine.

> Strange to relate, among the sticks of firewood were some to which bits of vermilion or gold and silver leaf still adhered. This, I discovered, came about because people with no other means of living were robbing the old temples of their holy images or breaking up the furnishings of the sacred halls for firewood. It was because I was born in a world of foulness and evil that I was forced to witness such heartbreaking sights.[2]
>
> * * *
>
> Sometimes I pick flowering reeds or the wild pear, or fill my basket with berries and cress. Sometimes I go to the rice fields at the foot of the mountain and weave wreaths of the fallen ears.

[1] Keene (translator), *Essays in Idleness—The Tsurezuregusa of Kenkō*, p. 201.

[2] Keene, *Anthology of Japanese Literature*, p. 202.

Or, when the weather is fine, I climb the peak and look out toward Kyoto, my old home, far, far away. The view has no owner and nothing can interfere with my enjoyment.[3]

*   *   *

I do not prescibe my way of life to men enjoying happiness and wealth, but have related my experiences merely to show the differences between my former and present life. Ever since I fled the world and became a priest, I have known neither hatred nor fear. I leave my span of days for Heaven to determine, neither clinging to life nor begrudging its end. My body is like a drifting cloud—I ask for nothing, I want nothing. My greatest joy is a quiet nap; my only desire for this life is to see the beauties of the seasons.[4]

Although Chōmei did not set himself up as a teacher restating the truths of the Buddhist religion for the benefit of others, a spirit of evangelism was abroad and in the Kamakura period it revolutionized Japanese Buddhism. Tendai and Shingon had already carried the religion, its arts, and its opportunities for education far and wide through all the provinces. But though their Mahayana doctrines were comprehensive and distinguished by compassionate concern for all beings, in practice they remained monastic and their spiritual riches were restricted to the few who could become monks. Now, owing to the efforts of a handful of notable evangelists, Buddhism became genuinely popular, stripped of many of its esoteric trappings and brought down to the level of the common people.

Hōnen (1133–1212), Shinran (1173–1262) and the spread of Amidism

Born the son of a country official, Hōnen showed such intelligence that he was sent to the capital to study at the Tendai headquarters on Hieizan. He fulfilled his early promise, outstripping his teachers in understanding the many works of Buddhist learning used for training monks in the Tendai sect. One of his teachers, frustrated after hours of argument with Hōnen, became so angry that he struck him with a wooden pillow—only to confess, after he had thought about it, that Hōnen was right. To have reached this point in one's studies would be enough for some people, but Hōnen went on discussing the varied teachings of Buddhism and questioning one expert after another. For nearly thirty years he remained on Hieizan, dissatisfied, until one day

[3] Keene, Op. Cit., p. 208.
[4] Ibid., p. 211.

in the year 1175 he came across the writings of a Chinese priest named Shan-tao who had lived five hundred years before. The following passage, in particular, impressed him. It concerns the Amida *bodhisattva* who is supposed to have made a great vow, declaring that he would not enter nirvana until all other beings could do so.

> Only repeat the name of Amida with all your heart. Whether walking or standing, sitting or lying, never cease the practice of it even for a moment. This is the very work which unfailingly issues in salvation, for it is in accordance with the Original Vow of that Buddha.[5]

At last Hōnen was satisfied. He was sure that he had the key to one of the most difficult problems posed by the Buddhist religion: how to break the cycle of existence, to be reborn not in this world but in paradise. Briefly, the key lay in a transfer of merit from Amida to those who believed in him. Hōnen decided to repeat the words *Namu Amida Butsu* (Homage to Amida Buddha) as a token of his complete trust in Amida, who would come down to welcome him when he died and take him back to his Pure Land. Years of scriptural study preceded his choice of the words *Namu Amida Butsu* as the one sure means of piling up sufficient merit for salvation.

Hōnen did not insist that his fellow men follow him through the same process of study and self-cultivation. On the contrary, he taught a practice so simple that it could be undertaken not only by monks who could devote their full time to it, but by busy officials, wives of aristocrats, farmers, or anyone else. He wrote letters to people who could not come to see him in person, and for a leading aristocrat of the day, Fujiwara Kanezane, a book, the *Senchakushū*, setting out the main points of his teaching. To make it abundantly clear that the practice of repeating the name of Amida, the *nembutsu* as it was called, was superior to all other practices (elaborate ceremonies in temples for example) he taught it separately from all other aspects of Buddhism.

People responded to his call because of its simplicity and because of the efforts he made to reach out to them. Another reason can be seen in the following story about a pious and learned monk who, after reading the *Senchakushū*, went to bed thinking how biased it was. He had a dream.

[5] Coates and Ishizuka (translators and editors), *Hōnen the Buddhist Saint*, Vol. II, p. 184.

He thought he saw an immense number of invalids in the western gate of the Tennōji Temple, all in great distress, when a holy man came with a bowl of rice gruel, which he was putting into the mouths of the sick people with a spoon. When he asked who this was, he was told 'Hōnen Shōnin', whereupon he awoke and thought to himself, 'Here I was thinking the *Senchakushū* a one-sided performance, and this dream must be a rebuke to such a thought. This Hōnen is surely a holy man who knows the faculties of men and the peculiarities of the time. Now, sick people in the first stages of their disease, are able to eat all such fruits as the orange, citron, pear and persimmon, but later they cannot eat even the like of these, being able only to wet their throats with a little bit of thin rice gruel just to keep them alive. And so this exclusive preaching of nothing but the *Nembutsu* is really the same thing. The world is now submerged under the flood of the five corruptions, and the beneficent influence of Buddhism is constantly on the wane. Society is degenerating, and we are now like people afflicted with a sore disease. We can no longer eat the orange and citron of the Sanron and Hossō,[6] nor the pear and persimmon of the Shingon and Tendai. There is nothing for it but to take the thin rice gruel of the *Nembutsu*, if we would escape the round of birth and death.'[7]

Behind this story lay the general idea that at a certain time after Buddha's death the world would enter an age of complete degeneration, and Buddha's teaching cease to be effective. In Japan, in 1175, when Hōnen started his mission, political and social life were indeed in turmoil, and it was known that the great Buddhist monasteries were inward-looking and overly concerned with ritual and scholarship. In a period of catastrophe which appeared to confirm traditional prophecies, people in all walks of life were particularly ready to listen to Hōnen's message.

Although Hōnen's evangelical activity marks the beginnings of Amidism as a separate sect, there had been earlier practitioners of the *nembutsu*. Among the most notable of these were Kūya (903–72), who took his message to the people with singing and dancing, and Genshin (942–1017), who made more of an impression on the aristocracy than on the people with his book *Ōjōyōshū* (*Essentials of Salvation*). This was a best-seller describing in graphic terms the horrors of hell and the joys of Amida's Pure Land. The great Fujiwara Michinaga himself died in 1027 with the name of Amida on

[6] Sects founded in the Nara period.

[7] Coates and Ishizuka, Op. Cit., Vol. II, p. 317.

Itsukushima Shrine on an island in the Inland Sea. Shrine dances are performed on the raised stage

Nō drama: built over the water just out of sight to the right of the top picture is one of the oldest *nō* stages in the country—Shizuka's dance from the play *Benkei in the Boat*—a *nō* musician playing a hand-drum called the *tsuzumi*.

Sesshū's Landscapes of the Four Seasons—Winter (monochrome)

his lips, and holding in his hand five coloured strings attached to a statue of the *bodhisattva*. His family later gave Amidist teachings their classic architectural and sculptural form by building the Byōdōin at Uji to represent Amida's paradise. The superb gilded statue of Amida in the central pavilion, surrounded on the high white walls by fifty-two carved figures of angels and *bodhisattvas* on clouds, must have prefigured for many a believer the scene of Amida and his attendants come to welcome him into the Pure Land at his death.

In contrast to the Byōdōin's Phoenix Hall, which set a pattern for other aristocrats to follow, Hōnen asked for nothing more as a memorial temple to himself than the thatched cottage in which a family practised the *nembutsu*. His disciples carried on his work, not only in the capital but in distant provinces, preaching a message of salvation for people of all classes and both sexes.

Shinran (1173–1262), who taught in eastern Japan for some twenty years after 1207, was the most important and most radical of Hōnen's disciples. Shinran broke his vows as a monk, marrying and having a family, but nevertheless he continued his vocation as a preacher of Amidism. Acutely aware of his own weakness, he relied more than any Pure Land teacher before him on the super-abundant power of Amida. Man was so weak that he could not save himself; complete faith in Amida alone would save him. Even faith, so Shinran said, was the gift of Amida, the source of all spiritual strength, and for him the words *Namu Amida Butsu* became a way of expressing gratitude for the gift of faith that leads to salvation.

Both Hōnen and Shinran insisted that the *nembutsu* must be said with a believing heart. However, there was a difference in their fundamental attitudes towards the practice. Hōnen had thought that the greater the number of repetitions the greater the believer's chances of rebirth in the Pure Land. Therefore he advocated continuous calling on the name of Amida. This implied that religion was a matter of performance, demanding both will-power and physical effort. Shinran, on the other hand, regarded the desire to save oneself as selfish. Selfishness could lead only to rebirth in this world and not the Pure Land. His complete reliance on Amida's saving power made him feel that even one heartfelt invocation would serve as well as Hōnen's tens of thousands a day.[8]

[8] 'From the time Hōnen began to repeat the name seventy thousand times a day, he did nothing else day or night. And if anyone came to ask questions about religion, while he seemed to be listening to the questions, he lowered his voice, but really did not cease repeating the *Nembutsu* for a moment.' Ibid., Vol. II, p. 188.

This doctrinal divergence had practical implications. Clearly, if repetition mattered, then faith was still tied to the monastic way of life and its opportunities for undistracted practice of the *nembutsu*. But if the really important thing was underlying faith in Amida and not constant verbal affirmations of such faith, then Shinran was right in encouraging his followers, through the example of his own marriage, to go on living in society, doing their work and raising their families, yet confident all the while of ultimate redemption by Amida. His gospel of pure grace switched the emphasis of Japanese Buddhism from monks to the laity.

The sects that regard Hōnen and Shinran as their founders, the Jōdo and the Shinshū, have long been the two largest Buddhist sects, and as early as the thirteenth century, enthusiastic followers of Amidist tenets were able to raise the funds to build the well known statue of Amida in Kamakura, apparently without official support. Nor were Hōnen and Shinran the only successful evangelists. The founder of the Ji sect, Ippen (1239–89), using the same methods as Kūya three centuries before him, persuaded the common folk to follow him in singing and dancing in praise of Amida. His travels around the country, preaching the *nembutsu*, have been commemorated in a biographical scroll, unsurpassed in its depiction of landscape and an interesting record of the ordinary life of the times, with which the Amidists were so closely connected.

Nichiren (1222–82)

Nichiren had none of the advantages of high birth, as he was born to fisherfolk of Tainoura. Nevertheless, his studies at a local temple earned him a chance to go to Hieizan, where he stayed for ten years. He returned to his home by the eastern seacoast, and in the quietness of the countryside prepared himself for a life of fervent evangelism.

Like Hōnen and Shinran before him, Nichiren rejected the prevailing belief in lavish ritual and emphasis on study as the means of salvation. He, too, preached a simple message easily understood by ordinary people. He took the Lotus Sutra as the one and only key to salvation, regarding it as a return to the original teaching of Saichō. He taught his followers to repeat the formula *Namu Myōhō Renge Kyō* (Glory to the Sutra of the Lotus of the Supreme Law) as a declaration of their faith.

Nichiren was concerned with society as a whole, as well as individuals. His sense of duty to the world took him to Kamakura early in his ministry. He prophesied woe to the nation in a manner that marks him off both as a nationalist and as a remarkably intolerant Buddhist. Japan would be punished with calamities and invasion by the Mongols, he insisted, unless officials suppressed all Buddhist teachings but his own. Many years later, when his prophecies seemed to be coming true, Nichiren reacted to the news that the Hōjō had executed Mongol ambassadors with characteristic spleen: 'It is a great pity that they should have cut off the heads of the innocent Mongols and left unharmed the priests of Nembutsu, Shingon, Zen and Ritsu, who are the enemies of Japan'.[9] He was forced to leave Kamakura because of opposition and when he returned unrepentant, he was banished. Taking this as proof that he was right, Nichiren resumed his denunciations of government officials and other Buddhist leaders as soon as he was free to do so. In 1271 he was taken before a court, found guilty of treason and exiled to the island of Sado.

It is believed by his followers that Nichiren was actually condemned to death on this occasion but miraculously spared. On the way to the execution ground he dismounted and challenged the god Hachiman and the sun goddess to honour an oath they once made to protect those who proclaimed the truth; and at the place of execution, he prepared himself by uttering the words *Namu Myōhō Renge Kyō* as he awaited the final stroke of the sword. It never came. He was saved by a lightning strike or a fire-ball which threw the proceedings into total confusion: the executioner could not execute and a badly shaken government substituted exile for death.

Whatever actually happened, exile convinced Nichiren more than ever that he was destined to save Japan. In 1274 with the Mongols at the gate, the Hōjō pardoned him, presumably for the sake of national solidarity. He was well received when he returned to Kamakura, but the government still declined to take his ideas seriously and he withdrew to the solitude of Fuji's foothills. This time he had left Kamakura of his own free will. Even if he was secretly disappointed by his failure to convert the nation, he did not lose heart and spent his time writing letters and thinking about the future. His mind was fixed on a mystic vision which now included other nations besides Japan. He believed that once its government and people followed him in single-minded devotion to the Lotus Sutra, his country would stand at the centre of a reinvigorated Buddhism spreading through the known world.

[9] Quoted in Sansom, *Japan—A Short Cultural History*, p. 336.

Then the golden age . . . will be realized in these days of degeneration and corruption, in the time of the Latter Law. Then the
establishment of the Holy See will be completed, by imperial
grant and the edict of the Dictator, at a spot comparable in its
excellence with the Paradise of Vulture Peak. We have only to
wait for the coming of the time. Then the moral law will be
achieved in the actual life of mankind. The Holy See will then
be the seat where all men of the three countries [India, China,
and Japan] and the whole world will be initiated into the mysteries
of confession and expiation. . . .[10]

Nichiren's gospel did not die with him. His followers organized
themselves into a separate sect that bears his name. This Nichiren
sect has always been smaller than the rival Pure Land schools. Nevertheless its numbers are substantial, and there has been a significant
revival in recent times of its founder's idea of a national religion playing a leading part in the political life of the country.

Dōgen (1200–53) and other Zen monks

Dōgen, born into a noble family and with every prospect of doing well
at court, turned his back on public life. After studying in the
monasteries on Hieizan, he turned away from orthodox Tendai
teachings. He became interested in the practices of Zen, newly
established in Japan by the monk Eisai (1141–1215), who had
brought back ideas still flourishing in China. Dōgen, too, made the
journey to China in search of a monk who could teach him the way to
self-realization. At length a monk of the Ch'an (in Japanese Zen)
sect recognized that Dōgen had become enlightened through seeing
into his own being. He returned to Japan in 1227 after four years
overseas. So successful was he in transmitting Zen practices of
meditation that they have flourished to this day, especially among
better educated people.

Dōgen's way of meditating, the most distinctive part of his teaching,
was popular only in the sense that everyone was free to practise it. In
fact, relatively few were prepared to take his slow way to enlightenment which encouraged a growing awareness of one's Buddha nature
through the practice of sitting cross-legged in silent meditation with
body upright, 'like a dead tree'. Dōgen added to this practice the tasks
of daily life as a form of religious exercise, in the spirit of George
Herbert's verse:

[10] Tsunoda, *Sources of the Japanese Tradition*, p. 230, slightly altered.

> A servant with this clause
> Makes drudgery divine,
> Who sweeps a room as for Thy laws
> Makes that and the action fine.

The people who came to Dōgen's temple were thus thrown back on themselves in their search for enlightenment, being forced to use and develop their own resources of character and to go without such aids as prayer or ritual.

The *Eiheiji*, Dōgen's Temple of Perpetual Peace, a centre of religious training, is built well away from the cities in the foothills of mountains that face the Japan Sea. Its situation is symbolic of Dōgen's attitude to temporal power. He rejected worldly honours in the form of a temple built for him by the Kamakura regime, and reluctantly accepted but never wore a purple robe sent to him from Kyōto by the emperor. He claimed that he was heir to a tradition far older than the government in Kamakura, transmitted directly from one Buddhist master to another in a chain beginning with the historical Buddha himself. He never tried to secure official recognition, but the Sōtō sect of Zen, recognized after his death as having been founded by him, is today the largest single Zen sect.

Not all Zen monks were as unbending towards the government as Dōgen; and Eisai, already an old man when Dōgen visited him, had needed *bakufu* protection against the jealous schemings of Tendai and Shingon monks favoured by the Kyōto court. In fact official support has been one of the mainstays of Zen, which has always been highly regarded by the country's leaders. The great Zen temples were built with official encouragement, first in Kamakura and then in Kyōto. These buildings had architectural features which were new to Japan, and whenever they have been destroyed by earthquake or fire, the government of the day has helped rebuild them in the original style. Military men, in particular, liked the idea of religious exercises that cultivated a strong, self-reliant character, and kept the body and mind under control.

One Zen monk in the fourteenth century had a spectacularly successful career as an adviser to rulers as different as Emperor Go-Daigo and Ashikaga Takauji, both of whom turned to Musō Sōseki (1275–1351) for spiritual and temporal counsel. Sōseki persuaded Takauji to follow Emperor Shōmu's example in building a temple in each province as a way of spreading Buddhism. But the success of Zen monks lay not in converting the masses but in raising the level of civilized life: painting, the tea ceremony, literature and learning. Serving as advisers on foreign affairs, Zen monks acted as a bridge between Japan and China.

Garden design also came under Zen influence. Musō Sōseki was an accomplished landscape artist, making use of trees and water in relatively large spaces. Though most gardens associated with Zen temples are plentifully planted with trees and shrubs, the Zen monks also introduced a distinctively different form of Chinese garden to Japan: a garden without water, of rocks and raked sand, with few plants of any kind. Such gardens were intended for meditation, not for physical exercise. The small sixteenth century garden of the Daisenin in Kyōto, for example, can be interpreted as representing the course of human life from youth to maturity in a river of white sand. Tall stones set at the end of the confined space symbolize sacred mountains and a waterfall. At the foot of the waterfall the stream of sand is constricted with rocks and seems to flow turbulently through a narrow channel representing the impulsiveness and complexities of youth. The stream passes through a barrier of rock, typifying the barrier of doubt. Then the sand broadens out and bears a rock shaped like ·a 'treasure ship'. The broadening reflects the peace attained through enlightenment. The rock may be interpreted as carrying the treasures of experience, or as carrying the viewer into the oneness of nature.

Zen masters claimed to perceive an underlying unity and purpose (that is, a full revelation of the Buddha) in the apparently meaningless jumble of the material world. While they shared with Shingon teachers the goal of enlightenment in this life (*satori*), they took their own path. Eisai, Dōgen and the others insisted that enlightenment was an intensely personal and private experience, and the essence of the discipline given in a Zen monastery lies in quiet meditation. Two things, however, are impressed on novices: that all experiences are of equal spiritual significance (drudgery is divine); and that reasoning is futile. Zen holds that nobody can actually think himself into a state of enlightenment, still less depend on the logical arguments of others. Rationality must eventually give way to intuitive insight, which alone frees a person to live naturally and spontaneously 'as birds in the forest, and fish in the water'.

Attachment to the commonplace and reliance on understanding things for oneself are two important principles of Zen's still-living philosophy. They also underlie Zen aesthetics, which frown on anything gaudy or elaborate, and emphasize, on the one hand, naturalness and, on the other, a kind of reflective restraint that deliberately leaves room for the imagination. The 'no action' of Zeami's dramatic theory, like blank spaces in *suiboku* painting or rock-and-sand gardens, is a contrivance to jolt the respondent into the self-realization of enlightenment.

The words *wabi* (lonesomeness), *sabi* (oldness, ordinariness) and *yūgen* (mysteriousness) are often used to describe Zen taste. Yoshida Kenkō remarked, 'There is something forlorn about the waning winter moon, shining cold and clear in the sky, unwatched because it is said to be depressing'.[11] This is prose; but in literature Zen belongs especially to poetry, and in many of its aspects may be summed up as a poetic attitude to life. Snatches of non-Japanese verse, like William Blake's aspiration 'to see a World in a grain of sand' or Hopkins's praise of 'all things counter, original, spare, strange', illustrate the same approach and show the universality of the Zen outlook. Yet fragments are only fragments, and can be misleading if quoted out of context. Better still as a guide to Zen is the *Shinkokinshū* poem:

Miwataseba	When I look out
Hana mo momiji mo	There are neither blossoms nor maple leaves—
Nakarikeri	Only a few thatched huts
Ura no tomaya no	down by a bay,
Aki no yūgure.	And an evening in autumn.

---

[11] Keene, *Essays in Idleness*, p. 20.

PART IV

Early Modern Japan

CHAPTER TWELVE

Sixteenth Century Japan

The arrival of the Portuguese in Japan in the early 1540s, followed a generation later by the Spaniards, came towards the close of the Iberian peoples' great age of exploration, and revealed to the Japanese the existence of a civilization other than that of east Asia. Since the fifteenth century, the westernmost Europeans had been crossing uncharted seas and visiting strange continents for reasons of trade and conquest, and with a burning desire to spread the Catholic faith. Yet, hardy adventurers and dedicated missionaries though they were, they more than met their match in the outstanding Japanese political and military leaders of the time.

After a century of widespread turbulence, Oda Nobunaga (1534–82) and Toyotomi Hideyoshi (1536–98), working to much the same purpose, gradually compelled their fellow *daimyō* to submit to their political control, taking care to link their fortunes with the name of the emperor. This development marked the end of the era of the country at war (*sengoku jidai*). A third *daimyō*, Tokugawa Ieyasu (1546–1616), profited most by the reunification. Shortly after 1600, he established the Tokugawa *bakufu* which was to govern the country in deep and lasting peace for two and a half centuries.

Not even the eventual downfall of the Tokugawa regime could undo the national reunification that had given rise to it. Equally irreversible was a growing indifference to traditional religion among the ruling classes, the first signs of which may be dated to about 1550. First contacts with the West; increasingly effective national unity; growing secularization: the beginnings of modern Japan are to be found in the events of the sixteenth century.

Nobunaga and Hideyoshi

Warfare was in Oda Nobunaga's blood, as was the case with so many other men of the samurai local-official class. At the age of twenty-five he gained control of his native province, Owari, after eight years of conflict with various relatives. Already he was thinking of extending his influence westwards into the Kyōto region; and the following year, 1560, he won the crucial battle of his career. In what is known as the battle of Okehazama, he made a surprise attack on the camp of Imagawa Yoshimoto with a relatively small body of troops. Imagawa, who was *daimyō* of Tōtōmi and Suruga, also had designs on Kyōto and had invaded Owari on his way to the capital. Nobunaga protected himself from further attacks from the east while he was away in Kyōto by making alliances with Tokugawa Ieyasu (Mikawa province), Takeda Shingen (Kai province), and the powerful Hōjō family in Sagami. Having taken these precautions he at last entered Kyōto in 1568 together with a member of the Ashikaga family, Yoshiaki, whom he duly had appointed *shōgun*. The Kinai

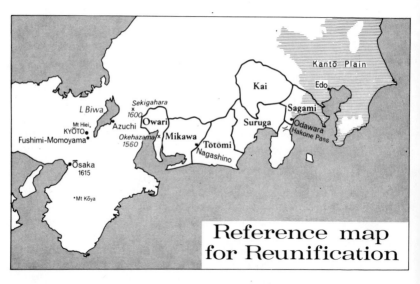

Reference map for Reunification

(Kyōto-Ōsaka) district was of great value to Nobunaga. If he could keep military control of the capital, then the emperor and *shōgun* would be obliged to formally sanction his schemes for further aggrandizement. Nobunaga soon found, however, that his mere presence in this key area was not enough to reduce it to political obedience, and almost to the end of his life he was occupied with strengthening his hold over it.

Ashikaga Yoshiaki resented having no power, and started intriguing against his upstart patron from Owari. Nobunaga, aware of what was going on, had no difficulty in chasing Yoshiaki out of Kyōto when matters came to a head in 1573. The glory of the Ashikaga family, which had long flickered fitfully, was finally extinguished.

The Buddhists proved far more troublesome, but Nobunaga's solution to the age-old problem of priests meddling in politics was devastating in its completeness. The Tendai monks had always made full use of the strategic advantages that came from their possession of Hieizan. The mountain overlooked Kyōto, making it easy for its occupants to launch sudden attacks on the city. It had served just as well as a sanctuary in times of trouble, because civil rulers and warlords alike were reluctant to attack so sacred a place. Nobunaga had no such scruples. In 1571, he had his troops surround Hieizan. The thickets on the lower slopes were set alight, and the soldiers killed everyone trying to escape. Tens of thousands of monks, women and children died in the slaughter, and one of the great treasure-houses of east Asian art and culture was reduced to ashes.

Nobunaga realized that the political independence of the Buddhist sects stood between him and national domination. The man whose motto was 'Rule the Empire by Force' began his momentous siege of the Shinshū fortress-temple of Ishiyama Honganji in 1570. Situated on an island in Ōsaka, it was virtually impregnable so long as the monks could bring in supplies and reinforcements by sea from provinces outside Nobunaga's control. In 1580, after ten weary years of effort, he was at last in a position to arrange the surrender of the Ishiyama Honganji through the good offices of the emperor. Its exhausted defenders were allowed to leave peaceably. Twelve months later the emperor intervened again; this time to save the historic Shingon monasteries on Kōyasan from a punitive expedition despatched by Nobunaga.

Once he had quelled his religious opponents in the central provinces, Nobunaga was free to extend his dominion. In the east, in alliance with Ieyasu and the Sagami Hōjō, he destroyed the powerful Takeda family domain in Kai in 1581. In a previous campaign against Takeda, at the battle of Nagashino in 1575, Nobunaga used firearms, first introduced by the Portuguese thirty or so years earlier, in a new and deadly fashion. Sustained volleys from the disciplined troops decimated the Takeda cavalry.

In 1581, Nobunaga also sent armies westwards, to do battle with the Mōri family, who ruled all the provinces between Kinai and the western tip of Honshū. These armies were led by two of his best generals, Akechi Mitsuhide and Toyotomi Hideyoshi. The campaigning was inconclusive, and in the summer of 1582, Akechi returned with troops to Kyōto, surrounded the monastery where the unsuspecting Nobunaga was staying, and killed him. Akechi's success was short-lived. Hearing the news of Nobunaga's death, Hideyoshi immediately made peace on favourable terms with the Mōri *daimyō*, marched his soldiers in the direction of Kyōto at top speed, and destroyed Akechi and his army.

Nobunaga's great energy and military talent took him far towards his goal of gaining control of the entire country by stages. The mixture of innovation and soundness of judgment with which he pursued his ambition marked him off from other *daimyō*. His success was largely achieved by brute force, but he never lost sight of the need to consolidate his military gains by attending to matters of civil administration. He built castles of great strength at strategic points, principally Nijō in Kyōto, and Azuchiyama on the shore of Lake Biwa overlooking the main road to the capital from the east. These castles provided him with administrative centres as well as security. Within the provinces that fell to him he standardized the currency, kept highways in a proper state of repair, abolished customs barriers, and in general did all he could to promote trade and industry.

Nobunaga was dead; but Hideyoshi went on to complete his former overlord's plans for unification, and at the same time to leave his own indelible stamp on his country's history. Hideyoshi's was a truly remarkable career. A peasant's son, he became *de facto* ruler of Japan, corresponding by letter with the emperor of China and the king of Spain on equal terms. Not until the nineteenth century did individuals have another opportunity to rise so far.

Though a seasoned warrior, Hideyoshi seldom missed a chance to talk peace in the interests of avoiding futile loss of life. He preferred to conquer not by using force but by making a convincing show of it. A characteristic victory was that won in 1582 over the huge Mōri domain. Unable to take the major border stronghold of Takamatsu (modern Okayama prefecture)[1] by direct assault, the attacking troops were ordered to raise the level of water in its protective moats until the castle was gradually flooded into submission. Campaigns in 1585 brought the northern provinces and Shikoku under Hideyoshi's sway. Two years later he achieved his most brilliant feat of arms, in Kyūshū. The Kyūshū *daimyō* had long been independent of any

[1] See map on page xi

central control, and one of them—the Shimazu family of Satsuma province (Kagoshima prefecture)—had recently subjugated most of the island. In 1587, Hideyoshi advanced into Kyūshū with some two hundred and thirty thousand soldiers. After fierce fighting the Shimazu armies retreated to their base in the domain capital at Kagoshima, and anxiously awaited the battle that would decide the fate of the empire. Hideyoshi encamped with his host in the hills above the town, and waited. He won his war of nerves. Peace was arranged on terms that allowed the Shimazu to keep all their original domain but deprived them of their conquests in the northern half of the island.

In 1590, Hideyoshi fought his last battle on Japanese soil, against the Hōjō family's castle at Odawara in Sagami. He employed the familiar tactic of surrounding the castle with an overwhelming force and waiting for the inevitable surrender. This time, however, when it was all over, he departed from his usual practice of confirming his opponents in a substantial part of their holdings. The Hōjō had been given ample opportunity to make a peaceful submission in the years before 1590, but had insultingly refused to do so. Hideyoshi now ordered their leaders to commit suicide, and handed over their entire domain on the rich Kantō plain to Tokugawa Ieyasu who had been his most prominent ally in the Odawara campaign. At the same time, Ieyasu agreed to surrender his ancestral lands in Mikawa and Tōtōmi for redistribution among some of Hideyoshi's retainers. By this manoeuvre Hideyoshi moved the power base of the second most important warlord in Japan one hundred and fifty or so miles further east, across the Hakone pass and well away from the strategic heartland of the empire in the Kinai district.

Ieyasu's transfer is typical of the way in which Hideyoshi sought to stabilize the existing power structure in what he saw as his own and the national interest. His unification was based neither on outright despotism nor on visionary ideas, but on precedent and a prudent assessment of actualities. The *daimyō* were not eliminated as a class, although many *daimyō* families lost territory to Hideyoshi's most capable and trustworthy followers. All *daimyō*—old and new—were required to swear a solemn oath of allegiance to the emperor, promising at the same time to obey the commands of his regent (i.e. Hideyoshi) 'down to the smallest particular'.

For better administrative control, the whole country was surveyed in detail. So thoroughly was this enormous task carried out in the years between 1582 and 1598 that Hideyoshi and his advisers came to know the exact extent of every *daimyō's* domain, the mountains and rivers it contained, and the locations of its towns, villages and roads. They also learned the kinds and quantities of crops and manufactures. This was military intelligence of the first order, but information derived from the survey was even more valuable as an indication of taxable resources. *Daimyō* revenues could now be levied by the central government with a high degree of accuracy and fairness.

Hideyoshi also realized that the problem of *daimyō* allegiance was part of the wider problem of general pacification. Since the end of the Heian period a vast quantity of arms—mainly swords—had been produced in Japan, and these were widely distributed among the population. (The situation may be compared to the present-day prevalence of firearms in the United States.) Internal peace depended on a sweeping domestic disarmament. Hideyoshi enforced this in 1588 with his 'sword-hunt' decree in which he instructed peasants everywhere to hand over swords and armour to their official superiors. The metal collected would, he announced, be used for the manufacture of a huge statue of Buddha in Kyōto, and so those who obeyed promptly would make things easier for themselves both in this and the next world. Defaulters were severely treated by inspectors sent out to supervise the sword-hunt, which proved successful in its primary aim of disarming the population. It also marked an important stage in differentiating between the samurai, or warrior vassals, and the peasant masses. Hitherto there had been no sharp distinction, but from then on the large class of samurai-farmers (from whose ranks Hideyoshi himself had come) was forced to choose between soldiering and farming; no longer could its members do a bit of both.

Military success, therefore, was capped by political domination, and Hideyoshi trod the well-worn path of consolidating gains in the field with a mixture of imperial mandates and high court titles. He was appointed regent (i.e. *kampaku*, the position long held by the Fujiwara) in 1585 and chief minister (*dajō-daijin*) in 1586, and in 1592 he passed on the post of regent to his nephew and started calling himself *taikō*. This title literally means 'great small side-gate', and had been conferred on retired regents in the past. He never held the office of *shōgun* due to his humble birth and the fact that Ashikaga Yoshiaki was still alive. It is probably best to think of Hideyoshi as chancellor. Like Taira Kiyomori in the twelfth century, his supremacy was complete but died with him.

Hideyoshi made up his mind that his authority should continue in his own family, but he was dogged by misfortune. He had made his

A detail from the scroll Matsuzaki Tenman Engi (Kamakura period)

Teahouse (Kōtōin) at the Daitokuji temple Kyōto (Muromachi period)

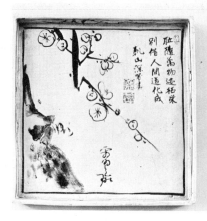

Three minor paintings from early modern times: a cormorant by the renowned swordsman and artist Miyamoto Niten (1584–1645): a dish by Ogata Kenzan painted by his elder brother Kōrin with plum blossom and characters: a movable screen dated 1575, with hawks, symbolic of samurai, prominent in art as in national life

nephew, Hidetsugu, his heir in 1592 because his only son had died in infancy two years earlier and he despaired of having more children. Then, the following year, his favourite concubine had another son, who was called Hideyori. Delighted with this turn of events, Hideyoshi resolved to make the new baby his appointed successor. To do this, he had to disinherit Hidetsugu. The task was not difficult, as his nephew had earned a reputation for dissipation and cruelty. But Hideyoshi went to extremes against his former heir. In 1595 he ordered him to commit suicide and then had all his wives and children killed in a public and brutal way. It has been suggested that Hideyoshi's mind was somewhat affected during these last years of his life. Certainly, his treatment of Hidetsugu's household differs markedly from the generosity he had customarily shown his political foes. Yet the succession problem was a unique one, and the way he handled it cannot really be compared with his attitude towards other weighty matters. Moreover, the problem was virtually insoluble in the conditions of the time, because the *daimyō* were still free to contest national leadership for themselves after Hideyoshi's death, and because the principle that national leadership should be determined in terms of national, not family, interest was by no means established.

Hideyoshi's attempted solution was therefore understandable, but was sadly mistaken. Too much was at stake to leave to an infant— Hidetsugu at any rate had had the merit of being a man in his twenties. Again and again in his dying moments Hideyoshi called on the greatest *daimyō* to swear support to Hideyori. They swore readily enough, but his own attitude towards Nobunaga's grown-up sons in 1582 must have made him realize the uselessness of such promises.

Other troubles which clouded the hero's old age were an abortive war against China and increasing anxiety about Christianity. The war with China actually took place in Korea, and dragged on for most of the 1590s. Hideyoshi travelled to Kyūshū to take charge of the arrangements for the initial attack by an army of well over one hundred thousand men in 1592, but never crossed to the mainland to command his troops in person. The Japanese invaders overran most of Korea in the early stages of the fighting, and on several occasions defeated Chinese armies sent to intercept them. Nevertheless, the combination of Chinese intervention and Korean naval successes was too much for the Japanese, who eventually could do no more than occupy the southernmost districts of the peninsula around Pusan.

Troops were withdrawn on both sides and campaigning petered out between 1593 and 1596, while the Chinese government and

Hideyoshi tried to negotiate a way out of the impasse. Neither party would accept the other's terms, however, and Hideyoshi, in a fury, dispatched another hundred thousand men to conquer China in 1597. This second attack fared no better than the first, and one of Hideyoshi's deathbed pleas the following year is supposed to have been: 'Let not the spirits of the hundred thousand troops I have sent to Korea become disembodied in a foreign land!' True or not, those who directed affairs after him lost no time in withdrawing all Japanese soldiers from the mainland.

Korea was devastated and the Ming dynasty of China seriously weakened, but Japan herself had gained absolutely nothing from her aggression. Indeed, however one looks at them, these military expeditions were a gigantic failure. Why did Hideyoshi undertake them? One theory is that he ordered the western *daimyō* and their troops to Korea in order to keep them out of mischief at home; in other words, as part of his domestic pacification. Yet there is no evidence that the *daimyō* involved were particularly restless, and as for the allegedly footloose common soldiers, administrators responsible for the land survey and sword-hunt could surely have found a way of restraining them short of foreign involvement on this scale. If new territory had to be conquered as a kind of safety valve, why not sparsely inhabited and poorly defended Hokkaidō? It is also wrong to ascribe the invasions to incipient madness on Hideyoshi's part. The 1592 expedition was a masterpiece of logistics, conceived and supervised by him personally when he was at the height of his powers, immediately after the triumph at Odawara. The bare fact is that all his life Hideyoshi had talked from time to time of making war on the mainland, and the fall of Odawara in 1590 provided the first opportunity to put his dream into practice.

> A Caesar, he ere long to Gaul,
> To Italy a Hannibal!

If the continental ventures had succeeded, they would have given Hideyoshi an international reputation comparable to that he already enjoyed within Japan, and would have presumably opened the way to full-scale trade relations with Korea and China at a time when all legitimate trade had been suspended by the two neighbouring States. The plans miscarried because Hideyoshi did not perceive the essential difference between war at home and war overseas. When he and his fellow *daimyō* fought each other, no matter how bitter the strife, they were all Japanese nationals and heirs to a common political tradition. This meant that an amicable and durable settlement of disputes could eventually be arrived at under the aegis of the throne. In Korea and China, however, the Japanese, quite apart from the size of their task, were opposed to whole peoples who had a national will to resist them. Thus, when Hideyoshi, following his usual policy, made a show of force and then waited for useful negotiations, these were not forthcoming. He then had to choose between ignominious withdrawal or conquest of China, something which the Japanese at the time could not have achieved.

Hideyoshi's reactions to Christianity illuminate the character and motives of an extraordinary man, the key figure in the reunification of his country; but some Western commentators have fallen into the error of grossly exaggerating the role played by their own civilization in early modern Japanese history. At first, Hideyoshi was content to follow Nobunaga in tolerating the new religion. Although there were always some around him who detested Christianity, a few of his vassals and the people connected with his private life were converts. His attitude, when he visited the Jesuits in their stronghold in north Kyūshū in the summer of 1587 on his way back to Kyōto after the conquest of Satsuma, was very friendly. In return for various favours the missionaries entertained him on board a small Portuguese warship. No sooner had Hideyoshi resumed his triumphant journey homewards, however, than he issued an edict denouncing the Jesuits for encouraging the persecution of believers in Buddhism and Shinto, and for allowing Portuguese merchants to sell Japanese overseas as slaves. He further ordered that all foreign priests should leave the country within twenty days.

This expulsion edict, for all its rigour, was not properly enforced. The Jesuits—who were unable to give a convincing reply to the charges Hideyoshi had levelled against them—made an elaborate pretence of going away to Macao. However, most of them went into hiding in the districts round Nagasaki where they had already gained much support, and where as semi-fugitives they carried on quietly with their work of converting the heathen. Hideyoshi, for his part, seemed willing to let the matter rest, for no Japanese converts were punished at this time even though he must have known that the Kyūshū Jesuits had not obeyed him. There were even a number of foreign priests virtually on his doorstep in Kyōto, including the aged Father Organtino whom Hideyoshi liked and protected. Relations between the missionaries and the Japanese authorities were never quite so happy after 1587 as they had been before, but there was a period of watchful calm until the next storm broke in 1597. Early in that year Hideyoshi had twenty-six Kyōto Christians mutilated and executed. The leaders of this group were seven Spanish Franciscans who had entered the country illegally and had proceeded to preach their faith openly in Kyōto and Ōsaka in defiance of Hideyoshi's instructions, an action which greatly angered the more prudent Jesuits. This second persecution of 1597 was more severe than that of ten years earlier in that it led to actual martyrdoms, yet compared with religious persecutions in Europe and later in Japan, it was a small affair. Once again, after his initial outburst, Hideyoshi followed a policy of leniency toward both the missionaries and the three hundred thousand or so Japanese converts.

What explanation can be given for Hideyoshi's sudden changes of attitude towards Christianity? As national ruler his attention was almost entirely taken up with internal pacification, external conquest, and the succession question. It is in terms of these issues that scholars should seek to understand him, remembering at the same time that he was an autocrat who continually needed to assert his authority. The 1587 expulsion edict may well have been intended from the first to be no more than a strong warning. Having just overcome the Shimazu warlords of southern Kyūshū he was perhaps unpleasantly surprised to discover how powerful Christianity had become in the island's northern provinces. With converts numbered in hundreds of thousands and including local *daimyō*, and with the major port of Nagasaki virtually governed by the Jesuits, the new religion was much more influential there than in the capital. In fact, the general situation would have been all too reminiscent of the Shinshū settlements against which Nobunaga had struggled. The obvious way to prevent matters getting out of hand was to sharply curtail any offensively zealous missionary activities. This the 1587 edict achieved, and in 1590 Hideyoshi took over the administration of Nagasaki. However, if anti-Christian policies had been pressed too far, there would have been a definite risk of disrupting the valuable trade with Macao.

A similar chain of circumstances no doubt lay behind the martyrdoms of 1597. Spaniards and a few Japanese had been anxious for some time to break the Portuguese monopoly over foreign trade by introducing regular commerce between Japan and the Philippines. The Japanese, though, were aware that Spain could threaten them militarily in a way that Portugal could not, and Hideyoshi adopted a typically half-warlike, half-conciliatory policy towards the authorities in Manila. Matters were brought suddenly to a head by an encounter between Hideyoshi and the Spanish captain of a galleon that had run aground off the coast of Shikoku. The ship, the *San Felipe*, carried a very valuable cargo of gold which Hideyoshi contrived to have confiscated. The Spanish captain bravely objected, and it is said that one of his companions foolishly boasted that the armed might of Spain was made all the more irresistible by its links with the spiritual power of Catholicism. Hideyoshi then may have decided to show the governor in Manila and the king in Madrid that his word alone was law in Japan. The unfortunate Franciscans, and the even more unfortunate Japanese converts who died with them, were obvious instruments to this end, since the friars had entered the country by a subterfuge, not as priests but as members of an official embassy from Manila. Certainly, Hideyoshi was infuriated by the *San Felipe* affair. Some of the words he allegedly used on the occasion are:

> My States are filled with traitors, and their numbers increase every day. I have proscribed the foreign doctors; but out of compassion for the age and infirmity of some among them I have allowed them to remain in Japan; I shut my eyes to the presence of several others, because I fancied them to be quiet and incapable of any bad design, and they are serpents I have been cherishing in my bosom. . . . I am not anxious for myself; so long as the breath of life remains, I defy all the powers of the earth to attack me; but I am perhaps to leave the empire to a child, and how can he maintain himself against so many foes, domestic and foreign, if I do not provide for everything incessantly?[2]

Castles, Palaces and Decorative Arts in the Momoyama Period

Architecture and art in the Momoyama period (1586–1615) were the forerunners of a secularized society. Nobunaga's and Hideyoshi's policy of reunification seriously damaged the Buddhist sects, many of which had already been weakened by the disappearance of the *shōen* system. No longer could the monks compete with other leadership groups as equals in terms of property rights and military strength. Moreover, Buddhists' loss of political independence was matched by a weakening of their cultural influence; the nation's unifiers chose to demonstrate their power, openly and lavishly, in the erection of castles and palaces, not temples.

[2] Murdoch, *A History of Japan*, Vol. II, p. 289.

He [Nobunaga] decided to build the castle completely of stone—
something, as I have said, quite unknown in Japan. As there was
no stone available for the work, he ordered many stone idols to
be pulled down, and the men tied ropes around the necks of these
and dragged them to the site. All this struck terror and amazement
in the hearts of the Miyako [Kyōto] citizens for they deeply
venerated their idols. . . . He constructed a moat around the
outside, spanned it with drawbridges, and placed different kinds
of birds and fowls in the water. . . . He decreed that while the
work was in progress none of the monasteries either inside or
outside the city should toll its bells. He set up a bell in the castle
to summon and dismiss the men, and as soon as it was rung all
the chief nobles and their retainers would begin working with
spades and hoes in their hands. He always strode around girded
about with a tiger skin on which to sit and wearing rough and
coarse clothing; following his example everyone wore skins and
no-one dared to appear before him in court dress while the
building was still in progress. Everybody, both men and women,
who wanted to go and view the work passed in front of him;
while on the site one day, he happened to see a soldier lifting
up a woman's cloak slightly in order to get a glimpse of her
face, and there and then the king struck off his head with his own
hand.

The most marvellous thing about the whole operation was the
incredible speed with which the work was carried out. It looked
as if four or five years would be needed to complete the masonry
work, yet he had it finished within 70 days.[3]

Previously castles had been little more than temporary fortifications of hilltops, but Father Frois' description of Nobunaga at work on
his Nijō castle in 1575 makes it clear that by the Momoyama period,
they were built to last and to resist attacks by firearms. The defences
consisted of moats, normally sixty-five feet wide and twenty feet deep,
with impressively solid stone ramparts fifty feet thick at the base and
sloping at an angle of more than forty-five degrees. The area thus
enclosed was divided up into a system of courts, intricately designed
and planned for defence. The main court contained the central
tower or keep, a structure of three to seven storeys known as the
tenshukaku ('guardian of the sky'). The keep served as an observation
tower, a command post and an armoury, sometimes as the living

[3] Cooper (editor), *They Came to Japan, An Anthology of European Reports on Japan,
1543–1640*, pp. 94–5.

quarters of the lord of the castle and always as a symbol of his power widely visible from the surrounding plain. Stone was used for the foundations of the keep and the subsidiary towers and buildings, but their superstructures were of wood and white plaster. It is this mixture of stone and wood that gives the Japanese castle its air of great strength combined with a soaring lightness.

What Nobunaga had done at Nijō, Hideyoshi was to surpass with his castle in Ōsaka. This was the greatest fortress of them all, with a seven-storey keep, and Frois was to live long enough to be shown over it by an exultant owner:

> He acted as a guide just as if he were a private individual, opening doors and windows with his own hands. And so in this way he led us up to the seventh story, describing on the way all the riches that were stored away on each floor. Thus he would say, 'This room which you see here is full of gold, this one of silver; this other compartment is full of bales of silk and damask, that one with robes, while these rooms contain costly *katana* [swords] and weapons'.[4]

In addition, Hideyoshi built two notable palaces in or near Kyōto. One of these was his *Jurakudai* (Ten Thousand Pleasures) mansion, completed in 1588; the other was at Fushimi-Momoyama, and it is from this building that the art period gets its name.

Grandeur and elaboration also marked the Momoyama style in furnishing and equipping the castles. Sculpture, in the old sense of creating Buddhist images which were works of faith as well as art, was not revived. In its place developed carving of a mundane but dexterous style: birds, emblems, flowers and animals to adorn the interior and exterior walls, and, especially, the gateways of the new homes of the great. Painting also turned away from the austere idealism of the *suiboku* masterpieces to something more grandiose and colourful. Even in its fifteenth century Muromachi heyday, Buddhist culture under the influence of Zen had shown signs of incipient secularization. Zen thinkers and artists had insisted that religious enlightenment was to be found in nature and everyday life. From this it was no great step to accepting things just as they are, without giving them spiritual significance. Moreover, from orthodox points of view, Zen had made the fundamental mistake of substituting art for religion.

[4] Cooper, Op. Cit., p. 136.

The Momoyama period produced two artists of truly outstanding talent, Hasegawa Tōhaku (1539–1610), and his rival Kanō Eitoku (1543–90). The latter assured the fame of the Kanō school with its blending of the *suiboku* style with *Yamato-e*. The school's founders, Kanō Masanobu (1434–1530) and his son Motonobu (1476–1559), had both received the patronage of the Ashikaga family, and despite political changes their successors remained official artists down to the nineteenth century. Kanō painters worked on a large scale, usually using gold and several other bright colours on the plaster walls, the sliding doors, and the portable screens which served as room-dividers of the castle-palaces. Well versed in the artistic traditions of both China and Japan, they had the technical skills to depict European subjects in addition to traditional ones. In general this art was decorative, and those who executed it were supremely competent decorators rather than individual geniuses of Sesshū's or Tōhaku's stamp. Nevertheless, the sheer virtuosity with which the Kanō artists worked must be admired. Their flamboyant style reflected the outlook of patrons who had mastered their world and were eminently at home in it.

Contact with the Outside World

The Iberian peoples transformed neither the economy nor the religious life of the country to which they came. Missionaries did have some impact, but it was largely confined to north Kyūshū, and Christianity did not displace Buddhism. Direct trade between Europe and Japan was not important in the sixteenth century. The Portuguese found that what the Japanese really wanted from abroad were Chinese silk fabrics; as a result of Chinese reactions to *wako* depredations, Japanese were not permitted to go to China themselves to buy them. For their part, the Chinese were eager to import silver, of which Japan then seemed to have an inexhaustible supply. Thus, the Portuguese, established in Macao in about 1556, conducted an extremely profitable carrying trade. Their ships took Chinese silk to various ports in Kyūshū, and in return brought back loads of silver which they then sold at a great profit on the Chinese market. Some gold was also brought to Japan, and Japanese exports in addition to silver were swords, lacquer-ware and copper.

The Portuguese poet Camoes, in his epic poem *Lusiadas* celebrating the greatness of Portugal, wrote:

He Iapao, onde nace a prata fina
Que illustrada será coa ley divina

O Japan, land of fine silver,
In future you will shine with
the Divine Law.[5]

But neither Christianity nor foreign trade emerged as central issues of
Japanese history in the sixteenth century. Contact with Portuguese
and Spaniards left social traces as in the words for bread (*pan*) and a
type of sponge cake (*kasutera*, i.e. Castile). *Tempura*, a dish of fried
seafood, is usually thought of as typically Japanese, but is almost
certainly of Portuguese origin. Tobacco had its first planting about
1600, with the result that Japanese authorities legislated against
it while James I of England was composing his famous *Counterblast To
Tobacco*, and with as little effect. Cotton, re-introduced by the Portuguese, became a major agricultural and industrial crop in the course
of the next two centuries.[6] Potatoes and sweet potatoes were
seventeenth century importations; the former are still called *jaga-imo*,
or Jakarta potatoes. With the exception of cotton, all these crops,
together with pumpkins and sweet-corn, originated in America as
fruits of the American Indians' independent development of agriculture. The Europeans had, in pursuit of their own ambitions,
introduced Japan to the new world in addition to their own small
corner of the old.

---

[5] Quoted also in Boxer, *The Great Ship From Amacon—Annals of Macao and the Old
Japan Trade, 1555–1640*, p. 1.
[6] Cotton seems to have been originally introduced much earlier in the Heian
period, but in the meantime cultivation had ceased.

CHAPTER THIRTEEN

Administration Under the Tokugawa

While Hideyoshi lay dying in the summer of 1598 he arranged for five of the greatest *daimyō* to govern the country as a council of regents on behalf of his five-year-old son, Hideyori. The regents naturally had to give most of their time to the administration of their own large domains, and Hideyoshi intended them to do no more than keep watch over relations between the military leaders and the imperial court, the loyalty of the *daimyō* to the house of Toyotomi, religious affairs and Japan's foreign relations. In practice, supervision meant keeping a close check on the activities of a group of five commissioners, who were personally less powerful than the regents but had earned Hideyoshi's trust as competent administrators.

Mixed government by regents and commissioners managed to organize the recall of Japanese troops from Korea towards the end of 1598, but began to fall apart soon after that. The most powerful regent was Tokugawa Ieyasu; it turned out that he had an able and implacable foe in one of the commissioners, Ishida Mitsunari. This man never tired in his attempts to stir up trouble for Ieyasu by inciting the other *daimyō* against him. In the delicate situation following Hideyoshi's death the preponderance of Tokugawa power was too great to be left alone. Ieyasu had either to take the final steps which would ensure the supremacy of himself and his sons, or face the prospect that jealous rivals would wait for a chance to humble them forever.

Ishida's schemings forced the issue. On 21 October 1600 an army eighty thousand strong, led by him but provided by a coalition of 'western' *daimyō*, attacked the same number of 'eastern' troops under the command of Ieyasu. Ishida's forces were defeated. This decisive encounter took place at Sekigahara, some sixty miles north-east of Kyōto. Fifteen years later, Ieyasu completed the chain of events begun at Sekigahara by besieging and eventually destroying the

156

headquarters of the Toyotomi party in Ōsaka castle. The luckless Hideyori died in the flames of the final attack.

The Sekigahara and Ōsaka campaigns gave Ieyasu and his heirs military control of the entire country. Authority won by arms had been the basis of every system of political control since the surrender of the court aristocracy to the Taira and Minamoto warrior families in the twelfth century. Therefore Tokugawa rulers certainly did not break any new ground in the way they achieved power. Nor were they unusual in the steps they took to shift the source of power from the battlefield to the palace, the castle, and the council chamber, and in general to convert a position of mere might into one more decently clothed in ideas of right. But while there may have been plenty of precedents for these policies of stabilization and legitimization, what was extraordinary was the resounding success with which the Tokugawa pursued them. The Tokugawa *bakufu* or government set up its headquarters in Edo on the Kantō plain, in time creating a metropolis out of what had been a fishing village surrounded by marshland. It lasted for over two hundred and fifty years, until 1868. For most of this long period, Japan lived at peace both with the outside world and within her own frontiers.

The New Shogunate

After Sekigahara, Ieyasu immediately attended to the important matter of titles. Fortunately for him, Yoshiaki, the titular Ashikaga *shōgun*, had recently died; and although the authentic genealogy of the Tokugawa house did not stretch back beyond the fifteenth century, Ieyasu had little difficulty claiming appropriate Minamoto lineage to take the title of *sei-i-tai-shōgun* for himself and his descendants. The court meekly issued the formal letter of appointment towards the end of 1603.

Ieyasu was *shōgun* for only two years, since in 1605 he arranged for the title to be passed on to his son, Hidetada. He lived on for another eleven years, and in his ostensible retirement was as busy as ever, but he preferred to watch over the affairs of the nation and his house, rather than be concerned with details of routine administration. Hidetada, in turn, transferred the office of *shōgun* to his son, Iemitsu, in his own lifetime. After his father's death in 1632, Iemitsu ruled in his own right until he died in 1651, leaving the ten-year-old Ietsuna as his successor.

The Early Tokugawa Shōguns

Name	Born	Shōgun	Died
Ieyasu	1542	1603	1616
Hidetada	1578	1605	1632
Iemitsu	1604	1623	1651
Ietsuna	1641	1651	1680

The device of having the court appoint their successor while they themselves were still hale and hearty allowed the first two *shōguns* to make sure that there would be continuity of policy, and generally strengthened their administrative system during the critical years of its foundation. Indeed, so well in this and other ways did Ieyasu, his son, and grandson perform their basic task of consolidation, that in 1651 the regime not only surmounted the immediate problem of having a child *shōgun* but remained fully effective even when Ietsuna grew up too sick to govern.

How did these three men contrive in fifty years to settle the affairs of twenty to thirty million others for generations to come? Basically, the answer is that although Ieyasu, Hidetada and Iemitsu accepted the existence of other centres of power and privilege besides the Tokugawa house, they managed to build a governmental machine which would control all of these rival *élites* indefinitely. Like Hideyoshi, the Tokugawa leaders contented themselves with ruling as 'first subjects', and deferred to the court by acknowledging the titular sovereignty of the emperor. Also, like Hideyoshi, they tolerated, within fairly broad limits, the independence of both *daimyō* and religious sects. Unlike Hideyoshi, however, they used their sweeping authority as *shōguns* to regulate the activities and relationships of court, *daimyō* and clerics so as to keep these groups in a state of perpetual subordination.

The great and abiding importance of the office of *shōgun* lay in the amount of effective control it conferred on its holders. Whoever held it possessed a right to command which could extend, if need be, to each man, woman or child in the country, and to every acre of land in the country. An important point is that the successive Tokugawa *shōguns* were all formally nominated to their position by the emperor. In other words, in form and in constitutional theory they ruled Japan not in their own sovereign right, but because the emperor had called on them to do so; from the outset they were supposed to be guardians of the nation as well as Tokugawa family chiefs. By the seventeenth century, of course, the office of *shōgun*, together with its general prerogatives, was of respectable antiquity. Ieyasu, Hidetada and Iemitsu never neglected to learn from the past, in particular from the career of Minamoto Yoritomo and the history of the Kamakura shogunate in the thirteenth century after Yoritomo's death.

In addition to questions of institutional authority and historical precedent, the personal qualities of the first three Tokugawa *shōguns* did much to confirm their family's power. All of them were cautious and hard-working men who, although they surrounded themselves with capable advisers, nevertheless reserved the right to make final decisions. Hidetada appears somewhat prim and colourless in comparison with the other two, but there is no doubt of his administrative ability. Iemitsu is alleged to have been imperious and capricious. He certainly behaved like a strong ruler and it was in his time that the *bakufu's* control system was 'perfected'; but whether he was really moody or not—or whether even if he were, this in any way affected the issues at stake—is hard to say.

Ieyasu's career is the most controversial. His was a seemingly ordinary nature which rose to a series of great occasions. Alone of the three he had to distinguish himself in warfare as well as statecraft, and he alone can be called a self-made man. His early life was spent in fighting and otherwise working his way back from the adversities of a youth spent as a political hostage to the Imagawa family. At this time not only was Ieyasu himself a captive, but the Tokugawa group of hereditary warrior-retainers teetered on the brink of complete dispersal.

The traditional picture of Ieyasu is one of a crafty and grasping old man, and Japanese children are probably still told that 'Ieyasu ate the pie Nobunaga made and Hideyoshi baked'. Ambition never led him astray, however. On the contrary, self-control and a truly marvellous patience stamped his character from childhood. He was also lucky, in surviving so many battles in the first half of his life, and in that his health, of which he took scrupulous care, allowed him to outlive his great contemporaries by a useful margin of twenty or thirty years. Above all, he was lucky in having capable sons to take over the family fortunes when he died. Even though he was hardly a family man, and his wives and children meant little to him, the question of succession determined many of his attitudes. Certainly, in a period of thrusting and showy egotists who wanted as much as possible for themselves, the Tokugawa *daimyō* laboured quietly for the good of his household, retainers as well as children, and refused to compete for purely personal glory.

Ieyasu was always simple and frugal in his own habits, his only entertainment being hawking. He was notoriously careful with money, and there is a story that when he accidentally discovered that his ladies-in-waiting did not eat many vegetables if they were well salted, he promptly instructed his cook to make their dishes as salty as possible. Yet, as the years drew on, the retired *shōgun* wished to establish a reputation for benevolence, although this attitude did not extend to Hideyori. If benevolence means a good-natured regard for people in general, despite a lack of strong ties with particular individuals, a willingness to see other points of view, and a desire to work with others and not against them, then Ieyasu was benevolent. During his last few weeks on earth the old man completed long-standing arrangements to have himself deified, perhaps hoping to continue even after death the 'watching brief' he had come to exercise during life. If he does indeed live on as some sort of kindly, protective spirit among the cool huge cedars and clear mountain streams of his shrine at Nikkō he will have had the reward of seeing his descendants preside for centuries over a peaceful and generally prosperous society, and the further satisfaction of knowing that the end of Tokugawa greatness was not altogether unworthy of its beginnings.

Regulation of Elites: Buddhist Sects and the Imperial Court

Detailed regulations for important groups or classes underpinned the Tokugawa administrative system. Such regulations took the form of basic codes which were reaffirmed and sometimes revised at the accession of each new *shōgun*. One set, issued between 1601 and 1616 and known collectively as the regulations for Buddhist monasteries (*jiin hatto*), left doctrine and internal sect organization largely in the hands of the clergy, but made aggressive propaganda an offence and put the management and taxation of temple estates under *bakufu* supervision. These and later rules for religious houses were enforced by an important group of *bakufu* officials, the temple magistrates (*jisha bugyō*). Such legislation made Buddhism, and Shinto, completely dependent on Tokugawa protection.

The court received similar treatment. Laws for noble families (*kuge sho hatto*), dating from 1615, imposed stringent restrictions on the personal freedom of movement of the emperor and his courtiers. Not only were they confined to Kyōto, but even within their ancestral city they were not supposed to move outside the palace and its grounds. One regulation told the nobles that they were 'strictly forbidden, whether by day or by night, to go sauntering through the streets or lanes in places where they have no business to be'. Even more obvious was the determination to prevent the emperor from taking any active part in the political life of the country. To this end, the *bakufu* insisted on regulating senior court and ecclesiastical appointments; the monarch was left with nothing but the style of sovereignty, the 'right' to appoint the *shōgun*, and his traditional religious functions as chief mediator—between heaven and earth according to Confucian notions, or between his divine ancestors and his subjects in the Shinto rituals. Yet although the Kyōto Court lived as a sort of prisoner of the Edo *bakufu*, the Tokugawa authorities took care to make it a gilded captivity. Following the precedent set by Yoritomo and the Hōjō regents, they always spoke to and of the court in an extremely respectful fashion. Whenever the Kyōto palaces and nobles' residences fell into a state of disrepair or were damaged by fire or tempest, the Edo government hastened to rebuild them. Most important of all, the imperial and other court families regularly received an adequate, if hardly princely, income from certain shogunal estates set aside for their material support.

Central Government and Local Autonomy: the Baku-Han System

Hideyoshi, it will be remembered, had appreciated the need to reduce the *daimyō* to a state of permanent submission to the central authority, but had not done very much in practice to bring this about. The Tokugawa, with characteristic efficiency, made good this short-coming at the first opportunity, aware that, unlike Buddhists or court, the domain lords were in a position to resist them with force. Consequently, the law for the military houses (*buke sho hatto*), promulgated in 1615 on the morrow of Ieyasu's culminating victory at Ōsaka castle, ranks as the most important single enactment of the regime. Its provisions applied to all *daimyō* equally. The military lords were forbidden to: move troops outside their own frontiers; form political alliances among themselves; maintain more than one castle in their domain; marry without shogunal approval. Later prohibitions made it illegal for *daimyō* to do such things as coin money, enter into direct relations with the court or foreigners, or build large ships except for trade. The military house legislation succeeded in its primary object of protecting the Tokugawa against *daimyō* attack, and ushered in the long period of Tokugawa peace. Civil war, like religious war, became a thing of the past.

The obedience of the *daimyō* was exacted under the guise of vassal loyalty. Those among them who had not already done so, had to tender written oaths of obedience to Ieyasu after 1600 acknowledging him as their feudal overlord. These pledges were renewed by each successive *daimyō* of a *han*, and by all the *daimyō* whenever a new *shōgun* took office. Lords who disregarded Tokugawa wishes could be punished as disobedient vassals; the shogunate would reprimand them, retire them, or—in extreme cases—confiscate their fiefs.

The traditional feudal code of conduct between members of the military *élite* also justified the imposition of the alternate residence system (*sankin kōtai*). Taking up the old custom of homage, by which a vassal had been expected to go every so often in person to pay his respects to his overlord, the Tokugawa both regularized and bureaucratized it. By the time of the third *shōgun*, Iemitsu, all *daimyō* virtually without exception and throughout their reigns had to spend alternate years living at Edo, supposedly in attendance on the *shōgun*. Actually, they only met the *shōgun* once or twice a month at highly formal audiences. The rest of the time the *daimyō* spent in their Edo mansions or *yashiki*, attending to their own domain affairs and private pleasures. Something which before 1600 had been occasional and personal now became periodic, unavoidable and completely impersonal.

The alternate residence system effectively shackled the power of the *daimyō*, especially as they had to leave their wives and eldest sons behind in Edo when they returned to their domains. Only a very persistent and ingenious lord could plot rebellion if he had to spend half his time in the shogunal capital away from his territory in the country. Moreover, the costs of the regular journey to and from Edo, to say nothing of the expense of maintaining a permanent establishment there, taxed the financial resources of even the largest *han*.

Central control was only one facet of Tokugawa government; local autonomy was also an integral part. Throughout their history as national rulers, the *shōguns* retained direct control over no more than about a quarter of the territory and people of Japan. This area had as its two focal points the Kantō plain and the Kinai district, and was known as the *tenryō* or 'heavenly domain'. The remaining three-quarters of the country was parcelled out among the *daimyō* to rule as their own domains (*han*). In addition to functioning as local entities *han* were combined with the *bakufu* to form a unique, viable, and interdependent national political order.

The two hundred and sixty domains varied greatly in size. The largest was that of the Maeda family in Kaga (Ishikawa prefecture) and Etchū (Toyama prefecture) provinces, with an official productive capacity of over five million bushels of rice (1,000,000 *koku*). At the other end of the scale lay numerous holdings rated either at or not very much above the 10,000 *koku* mark, which was the minimum needed for *daimyō* status. All domains were technically self-governing units, subject only to the broad requirements of Tokugawa hegemony and national policy. This meant that the laws in force in a domain issued from its own administrative capital or castle-town, not Edo; and that the supervisory officials were its own *han* samurai who were appointed by and responsible to the local *daimyō*, not the *shōgun*. In the field of taxation, the *han* governments collected and spent revenues as they pleased, and the shogunate had no customary right to impose regular taxes outside the *tenryō*.

There were, however, restraints on the exercise by the *han* of both administrative and fiscal independence. In the first place, no *han* government could flout the general regulations of the *bakufu* on such matters as religion, monetary policy, civil war or relations with the Kyōto court. In the second place, many of the smaller *han* were instructed to follow shogunal practice in day-to-day administration. Thirdly, even though a direct levy on *han* revenues was adopted only once or twice by the *bakufu* as a last resort in times of grave financial crisis, individual *han* frequently found themselves compelled to contribute to costly public works schemes (road building, castle repairing, land reclamation) in Edo and elsewhere in the shogunal territory. As already pointed out, failure to comply with the *bakufu's* injunctions or requests could speedily land a *daimyō* in trouble as a disloyal vassal. Finally, the *shōgun's* prerogatives as feudal overlord allowed him to intervene at will in the domestic affairs of a *han*. Although cases of intervention were quite common, the *bakufu* cannot be said to have abused this right. It was usually driven to act either by a dispute within the *han* over succession to the position of *daimyō*, or by outbreaks of serious peasant unrest which the local authorities could neither settle nor control.

Restraints and qualifications notwithstanding, a *daimyō* was generally speaking lord of all he could survey—and often a good deal more —from the top of his castle's keep. It would be more accurate, if less colourful, to say that the *han* bureaucracy was lord of all it could survey. For, in domain affairs as much as in their relations with the *shōgun*, the *daimyō* were 'victims' of bureaucratization; most of the authority they had wielded at the beginning of the seventeenth century as personal rulers quickly passed to councils of hereditary 'clan elders' (*karō*). Such councils were the local equivalents of the *shōgun's* senior and junior councils, and under their general control the routine administration of the domains was carried on by a small number of high ranking officials (*bugyō*) and deputies (*daikan* or *gundai*) in charge of groups of villages. In all but a few *han* the samurai had become permanent residents in the castle-town by 1650. Other factors were also at work to bring about a steady accumulation of power at the centre. The most notable of these was the policy whereby *han* administrations as well as the *bakufu* paid a fixed stipend to increasing numbers of samurai, and so resumed administrative control over lands originally granted to middle-rank retainers as petty fiefs. Bureaucratization and centralization, on an admittedly piecemeal and local scale, were the order of the day.

The development of hereditary ruling councils owed much to the *daimyō's* periodic absences in Edo fulfilling the obligations of the alternate residence system. The device of a 'travelling Cabinet', i.e. the *daimyō* taking one or more of his elders with him to Edo, enabled him to keep in touch with *han* affairs. Nevertheless, of necessity much of his governing authority had to be entrusted to those ministers he left behind in the castle-town, and even when the *daimyō* was physically in his domain, the prospect of having shortly to leave it again doubtless deterred him from interfering in the elders' decisions. There was never a time in the Tokugawa period when a strong-willed *daimyō* could not make his influence felt, but all would-be potentates had to take full account of both national policy and established local practice.

The political fragmentation involved in the *baku-han* system naturally made for an irrational duplication of administrative functions, and inevitably produced an over-abundance of officials. However, it also gave the entire country the elementary political disciplines of effective law and order and tax collection, not only at the local-regional but also at the local-village levels. Moreover, despite the regionalist and pluralist assumptions of the system, resemblances between one governing authority and another (i.e. *han* and *han*, *han* and *bakufu*) were sufficiently close to create a common political culture, an experience of government which was shared across the nation and which affected all classes. Willingness to obey the commands of official superiors, even in the matter of taxes, and the existence of a common political culture, enabled the country's leaders after 1868 to proceed rapidly with their self-appointed task of building a unified and progressive nation state.

Local autonomy also provided for useful initiatives. In finance, for example, nearly all the *han* governments were confronted by the same shortage of revenue that plagued the *bakufu;* but after 1800 a few of them hit on remedial policies which were remarkably successful, more so than those attempted by the shogunate. In intellectual matters also, the system allowed for considerable diversity, with some *han* developing distinctive traditions of scholarship and education which were to stand the entire nation in good stead in the troubled years after 1840, and were the ideological mainsprings of its march toward modernity.

It is true that local autonomy was an integral part of the Tokugawa system, in the sense that the *han* had existed from the first as semi-independent and functioning entities. It is also true in the sense that they became even more closely integrated in the overall administrative structure as time went on, and were able to consolidate their position relative to the *bakufu*. To talk of the 'Tokugawa system' or the 'shogunate' is useful when discussing the administrative structure and developments of the seventeenth and early eighteenth centuries, but after that these terms reflect progressively less of the actual state of affairs and, in particular, the distribution of power. For the later period, *'baku-han* system' is a more accurate description. This development was facilitated by the seventeenth century switch from force to moral persuasion as a political means. Just as important, however, was the gradual association of all the *daimyō*, not just a section of them, with the prevailing power structure, which caused a blurring of divisions and a general softening of traditional attitudes.

From Ieyasu's time, the great majority of *daimyō* had been divided into two classes: *fudai* and *tozama*. The former were literally the 'hereditary vassal lords', the successive heads of families which were already Tokugawa vassals before the fateful battle of Sekigahara. The *tozama*, by contrast, were the 'outside lords', whose ancestors had been Ieyasu's peers in 1600 and had only sworn allegiance to him after his victory. *Fudai han* were usually small, but they were strategically placed around the Kantō plain, along an axis to the Kinai district, in Kinai itself, and on the borders of large *tozama han*. The *fudai daimyō* (about one hundred and thirty families) provided the shogunate with its councillors and senior officials, and those who received such appointments naturally wielded far more power, and enjoyed greater prestige, than they would have had as minor territorial lords. It was the *fudai han* which most faithfully followed Tokugawa precedent and exhortation in internal domain organization and legislation. It is not surprising, therefore, that the *fudai* houses should have been very closely identified with the *bakufu*. Its fortunes were their fortunes.

Traditionally, the *tozama* were objects of Tokugawa mistrust, and though territorially strong, these lords could never hope to occupy the positions in the shogunal administration open to their *fudai* colleagues. Nevertheless, even the *tozama* benefited from long-term changes. By 1700, it was no longer feasible for any group of *daimyō* to foment rebellion. Long periods of cohabitation in Edo, a city which was birthplace and childhood home of most of the domainal lords as well as the scene of their later compulsory residences, doubtless created all kinds of informal bonds and similarities of outlook among them, and between them and ranking members of the Tokugawa lineage. Marriage and adoption, the latter being freely used to ensure that no *daimyō* family should die out for lack of heirs, worked to the same end. Before long, many of the military lords were related to each other several times over, and similar links bound them to the Kyōto nobility and the Tokugawa house itself.

By about 1800, Tokugawa administration at its topmost level had evolved into an elaborate coalition of different interests. These interests retained their separate identities, and important ties between them were frequently familial and tacit, rather than formal and institutional. The antagonisms that had once held sway were now little more than inherited memories, and there was a general acceptance of the existing regime for the sake of the rewards it conferred on *daimyō* as well as *shōgun*, on clan elder as well as Tokugawa retainer. Beneath this pattern of government by a coalescence of *élites* lay the pluralistic structure of the *baku-han* system, with its diversification of administrative authority into one semi-national and numerous local and autonomous power centres.

Structural pluralism was not confined to politics. It existed in other spheres, notably education. More important still, even though the system has long since been disposed of, the underlying principle of rule by a diversified establishment, each element of which enjoys its own recognized power base, has survived down to contemporary times.

Foreign Policy and Closure of the Country

The *shōguns* and their ministers determined the course of Japan's relations with the outside world from 1600 to the 1850s. They had a duty not only to protect the court and to keep peace within the country by controlling the *daimyō*, but also to ward off any foreign threat to the emperor's dominions. The Mongol attack in Kamakura times was precedent for this; and at the very end of the Edo period, when Westerners intervened in force in Japanese affairs, the Tokugawa went down to the cry of *'sonnō jōi'*—'revere the emperor, and expel the barbarian!'

The first two Tokugawa rulers followed Hideyoshi in favouring the 'southern barbarian' trade, but did so amidst growing difficulties abroad and mounting apprehension at home. The custom of sending licensed trading vessels (*go-shuinsen* or 'red seal' ships) overseas, which had begun in the 1590s, flourished after the turn of the century. These boats carried special passports, stamped with the vermilion seal of the *shōgun*, authorizing them to engage in foreign trade. Without such a document, Japanese merchants could not lawfully participate in ventures of this kind. The majority of the vermilion seal ships sailed either to Indo-China or the Philippines. They took cargoes of swords, lacquer-ware, precious metals, grain, fish and horses, and returned home with silks, antique china, incense and precious woods.

Ieyasu, who liked to learn about the outside world and was better educated than Hideyoshi, no doubt had various considerations in mind when he encouraged the licensed trade. There is evidence that he wished to build up Japan's maritime commerce so his countrymen would no longer be overwhelmingly dependent on foreign traders. Apart from giving Japanese a far greater share of the trading profits, this policy held out some hope of avoiding the religious problems that had come with the Spaniards and Portuguese. Moreover, the *bakufu* could use the license system to swell its own revenues by collecting fees, allocating permits to members of the *shōgun's* household, or stipulating that it should receive a percentage of a voyage's earnings. Finally, by permitting authorized trading only, the authorities could suppress undesirable practices like piracy and smuggling. The crews of even the licensed ships were not beyond reproach, however, and Ieyasu had to deal with a series of protests about their conduct overseas.

For fifty years Portuguese, Spaniards, Chinese and Japanese had been busy trafficking, competing and quarrelling among themselves. Shortly after 1600, first the Dutch and then the English appeared in the north Pacific. The two Protestant countries were at war with the Iberian nations in Europe and across the world, and no sooner had their nationals begun to trade at the port of Hirado, not far from

Nagasaki, than the Portuguese requested they be crucified as pirates. Ieyasu quite properly replied that they had done no harm to him or his subjects.

Meanwhile, within Japan, the political tide began to run strongly against the Catholic converts and their Jesuit mentors. Bands of Christian samurai had fought for the Toyotomi defenders of Ōsaka castle in 1615, and the year before, Ieyasu had issued an expulsion edict calling for the removal of all foreign priests and friars and announcing the prohibition of Christianity in Japan. This meant that for the first time native Catholics were in danger of being punished for their faith. The European missionaries tried their usual tactic of going through the motions of obedience while waiting for better times. Some immediately went into hiding up and down the country. Others actually travelled to Macao, but returned to Japan surreptitiously together with reinforcements for the mission. The hoped-for improvement in the general political climate never took place. Instead, after 1618 a full-scale persecution of Christians developed. The initiative for this came from the *shōguns* Hidetada and Iemitsu, and all the *daimyō*—none of whom were now Christian—had sooner or later to follow suit in their own domains. The *incognito* missionaries were rounded up one by one over the years and usually tortured to death. A priest could escape this fate by renouncing his faith; and a few did in fact prefer the life of a renegade to the anguish of a martyr.

Since one of the purposes of this terror was to dissuade Jesuits and others from entering the country by stealth, the authorities had to hold out a very real prospect of inevitable arrest and lingering execution. With the Japanese Catholics, on the other hand, the persecutors definitely sought not martyrdom but recantation. Tens of thousands did recant, but several thousand others, including women and children, bravely died for the religion foreigners had taught them. Others, but only a few hundred, had gone to live in the Philippines and Indo-China shortly after Ieyasu published his edict.

The persecution had already achieved its object, with Christianity no longer openly practised anywhere, when in 1637 the final convulsion of the Shimabara rebellion occurred in northern Kyūshū. Some thirty thousand peasants in the formerly Christian *han* of Arima revolted against the tyranny of the local *daimyō*, and set up a defensive stronghold on the Shimabara peninsula east of Nagasaki. The shogunate had great difficulty in suppressing the rising, and had to ask the help of Dutch ships which shelled the rebels from the sea while government troops engaged them on land. To add to the *bakufu's* discomfiture, the rebels openly proclaimed their allegiance to Christianity. After massacring the defenders of Shimabara and deliberating for about eighteen months, Iemitsu and his ministers decided to introduce further stringent controls over relations with foreign countries.

By 1639 a series of measures were enacted which are commonly called the *sakoku* or 'closed country' policy. Although in fact Japan was never entirely closed, external contacts were reduced to the absolute minimum. In substance, it was decreed that in future: no Japanese could leave the country; no Catholic national could enter the country; and all foreign trade and diplomacy had to be conducted at Nagasaki. The first stipulation speaks for itself. The second was directed specifically against the Portuguese. Japanese-Spanish relations had never been happy, and had been brought to an end by the shogunate in the 1620s. The English had withdrawn voluntarily in 1623, because they could not make their trading activities pay. With the Portuguese now excluded, even though they were at last ready to refrain from helping missionaries, only the Dutch were left. In obedience to the *shōgun's* decree, the Hollanders moved from Hirado to Nagasaki where, together with the Chinese, they continued to export and import on a much reduced scale. Nagasaki was directly administered by the shogunate, so all remaining foreign trade was subject to the full rigour of the new laws.

The 'closed country' policy remained in force for over two hundred years. The only slight loopholes were a semi-licit trade between Satsuma *han* (Kagoshima prefecture) and Okinawa and so with China, and at times between Kaga *han* (Ishikawa prefecture) and the Chinese mainland. There are indications that around 1770 the chief minister of the shogunate, Tanuma Okitsugu (1719–88), contemplated a relaxation of the laws in order to improve Tokugawa finances by developing foreign trade. However, Tanuma lost his position before he had time to implement this idea, and his successor, Matsudaira Sadanobu (1758–1829), was determined to maintain the existing arrangements.

It fell to Matsudaira Sadanobu to counter a Russian threat to Hokkaidō in the last decades of the eighteenth century. For the previous one hundred and fifty years the Russians had been steadily pushing eastwards across northern Asia. By 1780, they were established on the Pacific coast and were visiting Hokkaidō to trap fur-seals. This northern island still lay on the edge of the empire so far as the Japanese were concerned, and was largely unsettled except for Ainu.

Parties of Japanese fishermen and traders visited it each summer, but returned south in winter. The danger was that the territory would slip from Japanese control by default. Sadanobu and his colleagues acted energetically. Survey teams were sent to chart the northern seas and make maps of the island, and the Russians were informed that Hokkaidō belonged to Japan. As a further precaution the shogunate itself began to administer the region in 1799. Until then the island had been a sort of administrative appendage of the Matsumae *han* located on its southern tip. Napoleon's invasion of Russia in 1812 put an end to Japanese concern: then and for many years afterwards, the tsars were too preoccupied with European affairs to worry about their remote frontier with Japan.

Thus, the major factors which moved the shogunate to close the country were: trade that, from the Japanese point of view, meant an exchange of precious metals for articles they could well do without; mistrust of a new proselytizing religion that had flourished in an area hundreds of miles from Edo where the Tokugawa had little military strength; and the final shock of the Shimabara rebellion. As time passed, it became more and more difficult to reverse this policy. Like its White Australian counterpart, it became a bulwark for vested interests of all kinds, ethical and cultural as well as political and commercial. For the authorities to have gone back on it after, say, 1750, would have called into question all the other fixed determinants of their regime, such as the relegation of the imperial court to a purely ceremonial function and the subjection of the *daimyō*. Moreover, after the beginning of the eighteenth century, the Tokugawa lacked the clear military pre-eminence they had enjoyed earlier and so were less and less in a position to take this kind of risk.

What were the long term effects of *sakoku*? Japan did not participate in the great scientific discoveries of seventeenth century Europe and the early stages of the industrial revolution. In 1650 the country had been more or less the technological equal of Europe; two hundred years later this was demonstrably not the case. On the other hand, thanks in part to closure, Japan was free during these centuries to make significant national developments in political and social organization, and also in commerce and culture. Above all, she did not suffer the fate of many Asiatic countries, regardless of whether they became colonies or not, of having a ruling class so permeated with Western influences that it eventually became hopelessly alienated from the masses. Japan remained cohesively Japanese, and was able not only to preserve but to gain strength from her national characteristics when hit by the full tide of Westernization after 1850. In short, one might say that Tokugawa foreign policy was one of the things that allowed the country to prepare for modernization in its own way.

Bureaucratization and the Changing Role of the Samurai

Modernization is not just a matter of technology. It also involves rule by bureaucracies; that is, rule which is in principle organized, orderly and rational. The accompanying table shows how the shogunate was organized: it depended for its efficiency on a division of labour between the various branches of government, and its authority reached down to the mass of the people. This hierarchy of authority remained clear and firm, with its parts interacting in a generally orderly fashion, throughout the two hundred and sixty years of effective Tokugawa government. Individual caprice, or even considered personal judgment, carried relatively little weight in routine administration, with men preferring to base their decisions on consensus and precedent and have them enforced through published regulations and statutory codes. As might be expected, documents proliferated under such a system; both within the ruling samurai class, and between them and their subjects, official business (information, petitions, opinions, decisions etc.) was very largely a matter of written records.

Such administrative organization and orderliness of themselves denote a considerable element of rationality, and although a rational instrument of power can be used for irrational and evil ends, Tokugawa Japan escaped this situation. The people who decided policy were high-ranking bureaucrats and stood in the direct tradition of bureaucratic rationality. Furthermore, Tokugawa policies were not based on some dictate of unreason, such as excessive nationalism or blind expansionism. They were Confucian in inspiration, and Confucianism held that actions should spring from reason rather than impulse. This is not to say that the governmental system had no irrational features whatsoever. One obvious irrationality concerned recruitment to the bureaucracy: only men of warrior status could obtain official posts. This was true of both the shogunate and the *han* administrations, and it limited the field for recruitment to about five per cent of the population. But even allowing for this and other objections, the broad truth stands: for its place and time, Tokugawa administration was a rational form of government, the publicly proclaimed aims of which were order and welfare.

TOKUGAWA POWER STRUCTURE

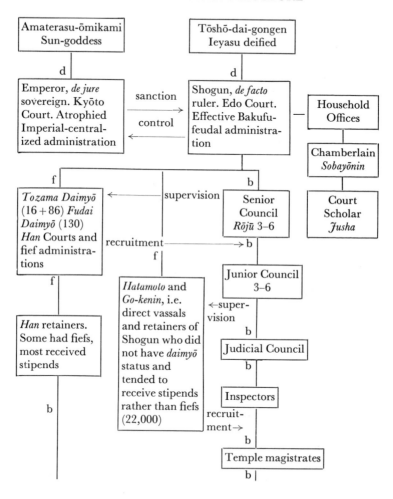

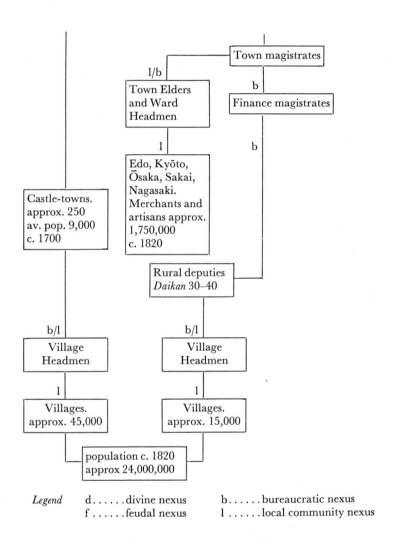

Legend d . . . . . . divine nexus   b . . . . . . bureaucratic nexus
       f . . . . . . feudal nexus   l . . . . . . local community nexus

Bureaucratization was not confined to the administration, but affected Tokugawa society at all levels. Most importantly, it altered the role of the samurai class after 1600. True, the samurai continued to be organized along military lines. This meant that until 1868 its senior members were those families whose ancestors had held high military rank at the time of Sekigahara while the rest were descended from the common foot-soldiers of Nobunaga's and Hideyoshi's day. Moreover, the first article of the laws for the military houses ordered the warriors to pursue military arts as well as learning. Nevertheless, despite these traces of their origin, the samurai as a class became bureaucratized. They stopped being rural, illiterate warriors, and started to be educated bureaucrats who lived in Edo or the numerous castle-towns which were the administrative capitals of the *han*.

This was a tremendously significant development. It is also very well documented. Records of the 1650s and 1670s show that the samurai transition from a military to a civilian function had been virtually completed by then, and that people were aware of its implications. The following quotation is from a play written somewhat later, in 1717. A samurai wife is reprimanding her young son (Torajirō) for playing something like cops and robbers with one of the household's servant boys (Kakusuke).

Narrator : The two boys trade blows accompanied by fierce shouts.
Osai : Fie, fie! A little of that mischief goes a long way. (To Kakusuke) You foolish boy. You're big enough to count as a man, but you're so silly the others won't even take you to Edo. Instead you pick on a small child you might easily hurt. Supposing you damaged the wall of the teahouse, what would you do then? And you, Torajirō, why do you make friends with that simpleton? I'm writing down every naughty thing you do in my note-book, and when Father comes back you can be sure I'm going to tell him.
Torajirō : No, mother, I'm not being naughty. I'm a samurai, and I'm practising how to use a lance.
Osai : For shame. You're ten years old, a big boy, and you still don't understand the simplest things! Of course you're a samurai, but look at your father. He's enjoyed his lordship's favour and his stipend has been increased, not because he's handy with weapons—there's nothing remarkable about *that* in a samurai—but because he performs the tea ceremony so well. That is why his

services are in demand and he is treated with such consideration. Now, while you're still young, you should learn how to hold the tea ladle and how to fold the napkins. I'll get a terrible reputation if people start saying that you children are being brought up badly while your father's away in Edo. I'll be mortified. Yes, I can see why they say that a boy should be trained by a man. Go to your grandfather's and study the *Great Learning*. As for you, idiot, escort him there and bring him back before dark.[1]

From about 1650 onwards polite accomplishments vied with routine administration as the major preoccupation of the country's rulers. There was no longer any real military role for the samurai class. They served as escorts or ceremonial guards, but no more. Hereditary troops who found themselves without enemies, domestic or foreign, could hardly be expected to remain full of martial vigour for generation after generation. Consequently, though samurai did retain an ancestral memory of themselves as warriors, together with a code of soldierly virtues like courage, loyalty, frugality and endurance, the great majority of them lost the taste for war.

The shogunal and domain authorities, bent on peaceful administration of a peaceful country, were probably pleased to see this happen, despite official protestations to the contrary. Certainly, after 1650 they made sustained efforts to educate the former fighters in the ideas and methods of Confucian, non-military government. The authorities also directly contributed to the erosion of their military base by allowing senior retainers to dispense with horses, which had been essential in the armed struggles of bygone times but proved difficult and costly to keep in the towns, and do away with the groups of personal followers whom they were supposed to maintain at their own expense for use in emergency. These 'rear-vassals' formed the basic fighting strength of the various *han* and the shogunate, but maintaining them was a heavy burden on senior retainer incomes and there seemed little justification for them once peace was securely established. Though by no means all the rear-vassals disappeared, this was the tendency, and along with the various other factors mentioned, led to a situation neatly described by Professor Totman: 'In short, the strength of the Edo government lay not in its capacity to fight but in its capacity to prevent a fight from starting.'[2]

[1] Keene (translator), *Major Plays of Chikamatsu*, pp. 278–9.
[2] Totman, *Politics In The Tokugawa Bakufu 1600–1843*, p. 63.

Taxation and Fiscal Problems

If the samurai had to give up thoughts of gaining fame as a warrior, he could at any rate hope to prosper as an accountant. The abacus was one of the things which replaced the sword as a means of achieving wealth and influence. Peaceful, orderly government meant that most political decisions concerned questions of taxation, currency and finance; and after 1700 the ruling class devoted much of its energy to keeping the administration solvent.

One difficulty has already been alluded to: the fact that the *bakufu* normally imposed taxes only on *tenryō* territory. Consequently, it exercised many of the functions of a national government, while for revenue purposes it had access to no more than one quarter of the national wealth. Even within this limitation, the traditional tax structure left much to be desired. Orthodox Confucianism considered land the sole respectable source of personal livelihood and government revenue, and it esteemed peasants next after samurai. Such views were fine in theory, but in practice they resulted in the agrarian class having to shoulder an inequitably heavy tax load. Moreover, in the actual payment of taxes by the peasants there were numerous discrepancies and loopholes. Government procedures for assessment and collection made the village (*mura*), and not the individual farmer, the basic unit, and taxes were levied annually in the form of an agreed percentage of the village rice crop, with villages having the right to appeal for a reduction in years of poor harvest. In the *tenryō* the amount customarily taken worked out at between thirty and forty per cent. Elsewhere, in the *han*, the rate may have been somewhat higher.

The system as a whole rested on the meticulous cadastral surveys which had started under Hideyoshi and continued well into the seventeenth century. Thereafter these surveys diminished rapidly. Bureaucratic inertia and the cutting of direct samurai ties with the villages doubtless played a part in this development, but it has also been suggested that the shogunate and *han* governments were fearful of serious peasant opposition to regular reassessments. Whatever the cause, official laxness in record-keeping led to a situation in which cultivators whose fields were registered had to meet tax obligations in full, while owners of unregistered land usually managed to pay less than their fair share. Moreover, since there was a big increase in agricultural productivity, governments progressively collected less than their stipulated entitlement even from registered land.

Meanwhile, outside the rural sector altogether, the growing and prospering merchant community of the towns and cities had relatively little taxation. It is true that the shogunate and *han* governments, after much hesitation on ideological grounds, moved slowly towards a policy of licensing guilds, whose members paid an annual fee, or 'thank-money', to the authorities. With fewer doctrinaire scruples, forced loans were imposed on exceptionally wealthy merchants and, when the chance arose in the late Tokugawa period, on individuals in the emergent class of peasant-entrepreneurs. These forced loans may be reasonably regarded as a crude form of personal income-tax. In similar manner, domains would order quite savage cuts in samurai stipends for a given year. Despite these shifts and changes, however, taxation in the country as a whole remained primarily a matter of agriculture and agriculturalists.

By 1700 the shogunate had exhausted its reserve funds, and faced a perennial problem of keeping receipts and expenditures in some kind of balance. The eighteenth century therefore saw the steady development of those guild taxes and levies on wealth already mentioned, and even some flickering interest in expanding foreign trade as a source of revenue. Other devices included recoinage and official land reclamation schemes, especially under the *shōgun* Yoshimune (r. 1716–45), whose purpose was to enlarge the tax base.

The *bakufu* availed itself of its prerogatives as the country's sole minting authority to debase the currency, reaping a handsome profit in the process. Its power was on the whole judiciously used; in an era of persistent inflation with money of any kind in insatiable demand, debasement proved one of the most successful means of avoiding serious financial difficulties. A much more respectable, but less fruitful, course of action was retrenchment of government and private (mainly retainer) expenditure. Policies of fiscal austerity, implemented through a series of sumptuary edicts, harmonized with the prevailing Confucian-samurai ethic and so found favour with a number of eminent *bakufu* leaders, if not their subjects.

By one means or another, the shogunate managed to keep on a reasonably even financial keel. Normal expenses were at worst only a little more than normal income; it was the disaster years of famine, fire, castle reconstruction, and extraordinary shogunal ceremony which really upset the financial apple-cart. Yet there existed sufficient resilience, and even a spirit of innovation, to see the system through its blackest periods. For example, in spite of the failure to revise the basic tax registers, there occurred a steady improvement in the financial machinery of government at its upper levels: budgeting, auditing, transport and storage of grain, and so on. Even more striking is the fact that there was a cumulative swing away from the land-tax. It has been calculated that 'In 1841 forty-eight per cent of *bakufu* income came from sources other than agricultural taxes, and half of this was direct merchant levies'.[3]

Perhaps the *bakufu's* greatest asset lay in its sheer size. The smaller domains tended eventually to slide into complete bankruptcy, and conditions in many of the large ones stood hardly better. The shogunate, on the other hand, might incur debts, but its immeasurably greater resources and prestige, to say nothing of its role as the author of national monetary policies, preserved its credit. A kind of enforced transition from 'household' to deficit financing ensued, with rulers seeking to curb the volume of year by year debt rather than eliminate it. Their struggles were rewarded with financial survival—until the final catastrophe of Western intervention in the 1850s totally destroyed the regime's fiscal credibility, along with its military and political standing.

The Shogunate, 1651–1837

The first three Tokugawa *shōguns* had been dominant personalities actively engaged in establishing the basic system of government, and exercising what was virtually a king's power to make and unmake. Their successors were not necessarily cast in a different mould, but they came to office when the system was already in being. They had to rule as part of the established bureaucracy, abiding by existing laws and conventions and depending on the advice of serving ministers. This was obviously the case when the reigning *shōgun* happened to be a child, but even adult *shōguns* after 1651 found their freedom of action restricted in a number of ways. For example, after he moved into his official residence in the grounds of Edo castle, a *shōgun* was not supposed to leave it again except for ceremonial and very costly outings like military reviews and ritual visits to Ieyasu's burial place at Nikkō.

The emperor in his palace at Kyōto, the *shōgun* in his castle at Edo: both were in a sense prisoners of State. The comparison cannot be made too strict because, unlike the emperor, the *shōgun* was virtually irremovable once he had taken office, and his seal was needed on all important laws and government notices. Moreover, several of the later *shōguns* played an active role in political and cultural life. Nevertheless, despite these residual powers and continuing participation,

[3] Totman, Op. Cit., pp. 87–8.

there was a definite trend away from the 'absolute monarchy' of Ieyasu's and Iemitsu's day to a more 'constitutional' type of rule, and whether or not individual *shōguns* were in fact influential appears to have been largely a matter of personal circumstance and choice.

Mid-Tokugawa Period Shōguns

	Name	Born	Shōgun	Died
4	Ietsuna	1641	1651	1680
5	Tsunayoshi	1646	1680	1709
6	Ienobu	1663	1709	1712
7	Ietsugu	1709	1712	1716
8	Yoshimune	1684	1716	1751
9	Ieshige	1711	1745	1761
10	Ieharu	1737	1760	1786
11	Ienari	1773	1786	1841

At first sight, the political history of Japan under these *shōguns* appears to consist mainly of periodic swings between an energetic and self-consciously upright government often bent on reforms conservative in inspiration (early Ietsuna, early Tsunayoshi, Ienobu, Yoshimune and early Ienari), and a more lax administration that allowed for enterprise and freedom as well as wastefulness and corruption (late Ietsuna, late Tsunayoshi, Ieharu). The tensions provoked after 1684 by division of responsibility between the great public office of Councillor and the private shogunal household post of chamberlain, with the issue at length being decided in favour of the former, come into the picture as a secondary and hardly more exciting theme.

However, there were important long term changes taking place in the quality of administration, and these changes had a cumulative and, above all, irreversible effect. One of them was the process of bureaucratization and civilianization. Another was the *bakufu's* capacity to accommodate itself to, and even profit from, the commercialization of the economy. Both trends were part of the established political and social order under Ienari. His period of rule also saw the successful stabilization of a third great area of political activity and development; the relationship between the *bakufu* and the *han*. Ienari's private life complemented this public trend. His domestic arrangements were especially liberal, and many of his more than fifty children raised to adulthood were married or adopted into *daimyō* families, *tozama* as well as *fudai*.

CHAPTER FOURTEEN

Society and Culture in Early Modern Japan

The formal ordering of Tokugawa society depended on considerations of birth and hereditary status, which were reinforced by visible distinctions in dress, speech and etiquette. A four-class system was adopted, based on the one used in China, and the great bulk of the population were officially divided into samurai, peasant, artisan and merchant classes. In addition there were small separate categories of Kyōto courtiers (*kuge*), priests, and outcastes (*eta* or *hinin*). Although such social stratification assumed in principle that every individual would inherit his parents' occupation and status in life, things never worked out quite this way in practice. Nevertheless, even the partial success of the Tokugawa class system contributed enormously to the regime's stability.

In what ways was the hierarchical theory impaired or ignored in practice? In the first place, artisans could never be distinguished properly from merchants. Both groups lived in urban communities, and naturally came to be classed together as *chōnin*, or townsmen. Secondly, although villagers remained at least nominally peasants so long as they lived in the country, all through the Tokugawa period people moved from rural areas into towns, and there was a considerable development of trade and manufacturing in the villages themselves. Thirdly, samurai frequently became *rōnin* ('wave men', i.e. vassals without a lord), drifted about and sank into the ranks of commoners. In the seventeenth century, men often found they were *rōnin* through no fault or wish of their own, as a result of a major political upset such as the enforced transfer of a *daimyō* or confiscation of a domain by the *bakufu*. But an individual samurai was always free to sever relations with his ancestral lord voluntarily, and many took this step both before and after 1700. Especially in the last hundred years of the period, there was some movement the other way—up from the general populace into the privileged *élite*. Either governments chose to reward suitably deserving and affluent subjects by granting them samurai status (in many cases it was a matter of outright sale), or private samurai households sought to better themselves financially by adopting a prosperous merchant's son as heir and marrying him to a daughter if they had one.

In effect, then, for most purposes the four classes were reduced to two—samurai and commoners. The samurais' great badges of rank were the two swords they were always supposed to wear in public, and their distinctive hairstyle. This primary distinction was maintained fairly rigorously down to the end of Tokugawa rule in 1868 and for some years afterwards, but it was never absolute. Indeed, in many ways gradings within the samurai class had a greater rigidity than the division between that class as a whole and the rest of the population, since *daimyō* and other high-ranking military families formed an exclusive group, as did court nobles and outcasts.

The most striking development in the formal social order, however, lay not in coalescence of classes or movement from one class to another. It was a change of relative advantage within the existing system, between the samurai and the merchants. Official dogma had ranked the merchants below other commoners because they did not produce anything. Like the samurai they lived off the work of others, but they did not share the samurai responsibility for administration and general welfare. In the eyes of the more hidebound Confucian theorists, merchants were little better than cunning parasites. Despite such prejudice the Tokugawa period saw a steady enrichment of the officially despised merchants and a growing indebtedness of the ruling samurai class. Samurai owed money to merchants not only as private individuals, but also in a public and administrative capacity as more and more of the *han* governments were obliged to borrow heavily from the great wholesale trade and banking concerns that grew up in Ōsaka.

The 'rise' of the merchants has been persistently seen as somehow subverting Tokugawa 'feudalism' and contributing in an important way to its final overthrow in 1868. This view, which in its cruder form amounts to a total explanation of Tokugawa-period history, smacks more of doctrinaire Marxism than objective study of the facts. The merchants certainly did 'rise', and in a manner that decisively affected the further development of Japanese culture and history. For a variety of reasons, however, it is better to think of relations between merchants and samurai in the Tokugawa period as essentially complementary and symbiotic, not predatory and antagonistic.

Monetization and the Development of a Market Economy

Merchants throve because government as organized by the Tokugawa necessitated a widespread and lasting expansion of domestic trade, together with an increasing use of money and credit. This was the continuation of a trend that had already begun in the *sengoku jidai*. Yet in those early days, *daimyō* preoccupation with military strength meant that they encouraged trade and industry only within certain fixed, i.e. strategic, limits, and while incessant warfare stimulated economic development up to a point, beyond that point it must have had a retarding effect due to insecurity and lack of confidence in the future. Earlier still, in the Nara, Heian and Kamakura periods, commerce and manufacturing had been extremely localized. They really had flourished only in the Kinai and Inland Sea areas, with outlying centres of activity in such places as Hakata, which was the main port for voyages to the mainland. The market economy in those days was restricted socially as well as geographically. Goods produced or brought into the country benefited only a tiny proportion of the population consisting of civilian and military aristocrats, and the senior clergy.

After 1600 all this changed quite rapidly. Money penetrated into all areas of the country, finding ready acceptance by classes which hitherto had not used it. This monetization of the economy made possible nation-wide transactions of a long-term nature, and caused the disappearance of barter and sporadic fairs. It also led to widespread reliance on credit; not long after 1700 the great Confucian scholar Ogyū Sorai (1666–1728) complained that the entire military class was living 'as in an inn', i.e. consuming now and paying later. Sorai noted further that 'of all the ages since the beginning of the world, it is only in the last hundred years that we have had a world in which money is indispensable'.[1]

Trade and its associated credit facilities developed spectacularly during the seventeenth century as a result of achieving political and social stability. The transformation of the samurai into a class of urban consumers, and the need of the *daimyō* for cash and credit to meet the expenses of the alternating residence system, are two examples of how political requirements set the pattern for economic

---

[1] Sorai, *Taiheisaku*, in *Nihon Keizaishi Gaisetsu*, p. 216.

growth. Lower down the social scale, the rulers' semi-contemptuous attitude that merchandizing was fit only for merchants created a fund of occupational skills, indeed, occupational pride and integrity, in that section of the population which engaged in trade. Tokugawa merchants certainly had a sense of independence within the general political and social system, which perhaps explains why they did not attempt to make themselves independent of it.

The deliberate inclusion, again for political reasons, of the great centres of economic activity within the shogunal territory or *tenryō* contributed both to commercial expansion and merchant confidence. Nagasaki, Kyōto, Ōsaka and Edo each possessed a considerable internal market, but their linking in a common administrative nexus fostered the exchange of goods and services on a really large scale. Furthermore, Tokugawa rule, for all its occasional harshness, gave the inhabitants of these cities more security and greater opportunities than they would have enjoyed in the average castle-town. Nagasaki, Kyōto and Ōsaka were predominantly townsmen's cities, administered by no more than a skeleton staff of samurai officials. As for Edo, even though it was the home of almost half a million Tokugawa retainers and their families, merchants could generally rely on the law to protect them, and they were not slow to form *machi-yakko*, or townsmen's fraternities, to defend themselves against bullying and other maltreatment from their social superiors.

Even if there had not been so many administrative factors to force the pace, the Tokugawa peace would have been enough to promote economic development at a somewhat slower rate. The nucleus for expansion was already there, in the age-old commercial experience and requirements of the Kinai district around Kyōto and Ōsaka.

Men from Ōmi—a province that encircles Lake Biwa and is therefore not far from the old centres of national life—were especially famous for their commercial astuteness and enterprise. Pedlars from this area, carrying loads of ribbons, cloth, cosmetics and medicines, had traditionally travelled far and wide in the agriculturally quiet season of summer, visiting villages all over Japan but particularly in the north. In the Tokugawa period Ōmi merchants, still favouring the northern provinces, traded in fish-meal fertilizer, bought up parcels of land here and there, lent money, and engaged in the manufacture of vegetable oil, *sake*, soya bean paste and soy sauce. They exploited to the full the opportunities provided by the first concerted efforts to develop Hokkaidō, which took place early in

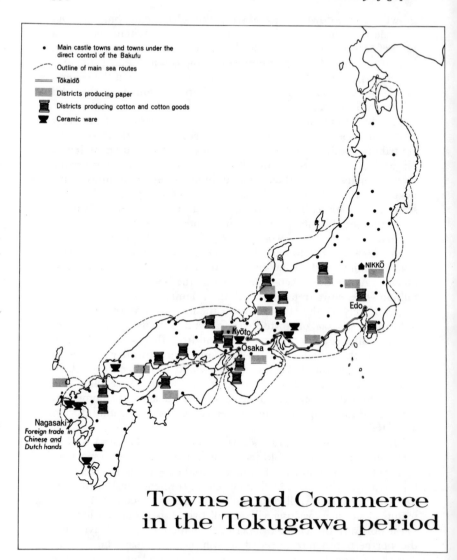

Main castle towns and towns under the direct control of the Bakufu

Outline of main sea routes

Tōkaidō

Districts producing paper

Districts producing cotton and cotton goods

Ceramic ware

NIKKŌ

Edo

Kyōto
Osaka

Nagasaki
Foreign trade in Chinese and Dutch hands

Towns and Commerce in the Tokugawa period

the Tokugawa period. The northernmost island was a plentiful and virtually untapped source of fish, and rich new fisheries, which supplied food as well as fertilizer, came into existence on the basis of an official monopoly granted to men from Ōmi. Such activity led to a number of proverbs, such as 'beggars from Ise, robbers from Ōmi', and 'a carrying pole of the Ōmi men is worth a thousand *ryō* of gold'.

In the country as a whole, commercialization and monetization had two great effects. In the first place, it provided for a rise—slow, but persistent and real—in mass living standards. Countless articles in daily use and humdrum habits of living, today considered traditionally Japanese, had their origin in Tokugawa times so far as the bulk of the population is concerned. The 'typical' Japanese house—made of wood with a tiled roof, raised straw *tatami* floors, and movable lattice and paper (*shōji*) interior walls—is one instance. Others are the everyday use of china and lacquer-ware, the consumption of tea and refined *sake* on a wide scale, the increasing demand for 'luxury' foods like sugar and fruit, and the wearing of cotton clothing by all classes. The second great consequence of commercialization derived from the fact that it involved local and village production for a national market. The rural populations in the various regions tended to specialize in the production of certain goods, in order to 'export' them elsewhere, usually by way of Ōsaka. Thus, despite the continuing administrative fragmentation, Japan became unified as an economic entity for the first time in its history.

Villages Drawn into the National Economy

In each *han* the castle-town played an important part in these developments, since it represented a local centre of consumption and of necessity obtained the bulk of its supplies from villages in the domain. Tax rice was just one element in these supplies and the fiscal policies of *han* governments fostered the production of other food-stuffs and rural goods for sale outside their territories on the national market. The growth of such towns, founded all over the country in the space of a few decades, can only have been a shock to the agrarian economy, drawing it out of a static and self-sufficient past into a bureaucratic and increasingly commercialized future.

Within the villages, which contained about eighty per cent of the total population, commercialization made itself felt in the steady switch from subsistence farming to cash crops, the growth of tenancy, and the emergence of an active gentry-entrepreneur class. It also meant a gradual rise in living standards for most villagers, as can be discerned from the following general description of rural conditions in the closing decades of Tokugawa rule:

> Living standards varied widely with the region, and there was undoubtedly a great gap between richer and poorer. Conditions also varied greatly with the season. A succession of harvest failures could mean appalling distress. This does not, however, seem to have been the normal state of affairs. The living standards of Japanese farmers in all but what we might call the backwoods areas seem to have risen steadily throughout the Tokugawa period, and by the 1860s many farmers enjoyed a level of material comfort which was scarcely available to even quite powerful samurai two and a half centuries before. The existence of shops in the village is a sure indication that peasants bought their wares, which included a good deal beyond the bare necessities. Any village which was not too far off the beaten track could expect to be entertained from time to time by travelling theatrical troupes and many villages maintained a permanent theatre, sometimes with quite elaborate stage machinery. The farmer's life must have been a hard one, as indeed it still is, and his standard of living was considerably lower than that of his counterpart in the cities, as again it still is, but there is no convincing evidence that desperate and inescapable poverty was the common lot of the traditional farmer.[2]

The growth of towns and the opportunities they offered for non-agricultural employment gradually ended the traditional system of indentured and hereditary servants that made possible the operation of large farms. Yet even when they began paying their workers a wage in addition to their keep, it was difficult for the big farmers to obtain satisfactory help for what they were able, or willing, to pay. The only solution was for the big holdings to be broken up into small plots of arable land which were leased to other members of the village. A system of petty estate owner and dependents gave way to one of landlord and tenants. The proprietary families frequently retained a small acreage of land for direct cultivation, but their income as agriculturalists now derived mainly from rents, not from what they produced themselves. Tenants of a particular landlord were frequently people whose ancestors had been either his ancestors' kinsfolk or his ancestors' serfs. Some customary and semi-paternalistic relationships were kept up between the two groups,

[2] Crawcour, 'The Japanese Economy on the Eve of Modernization', in *The Journal of the Oriental Society of Australia*, Vol. 2, No. 1, p. 37.

but it tended to be more and more openly recognized on both sides that the fundamental link between them was the purely economic and contractual tie of rent and cultivation rights.

By no means all the residents in a village divided neatly into the two categories of landlords and tenants. The majority had always been small cultivators who ran family farms, and following the break-up of the larger holdings many people in this group took the opportunity to lease additional land. Below the small-holders a landless element appeared, families who owned little more than their house plots and who eked out a living by working for neigh-bours or in nearby towns. Thus, after about 1800, except in those few remote areas which had not yet been really touched by the market economy, Japanese villages might well contain represent-atives of all the following groupings: landlords, small-holders who owned all the land they cultivated, small-holders who also rented land, tenant cultivators and landless workers.

Despite increasing differentiation along these lines, the village retained a strong sense of itself as a corporate, 'family' entity. Traditions of neighbourliness and mutual cooperation did not die out; indeed, this spirit had to be maintained to cater for such important matters of public welfare as irrigation rights and use of common land. Furthermore, the village continued to be one unit for purposes of taxation and general administration. Nevertheless, in cold economic terms its life no longer revolved around a handful of large holdings, run by an 'extended family' (i.e. owner's family, plus relatives, plus servants), but was almost exclusively sustained by small, 'nuclear family' units (i.e. grandparents if any, parents, eldest son, eldest son's wife if any, dependent juveniles) working farms of two to three acres. Small holdings of this type had tradition-ally prevailed in the Kinai region and had been plentiful enough elsewhere, but they now became the standard Japanese farm. In face of the changes being wrought by commercialization, their great advantage was that they could be worked by the cultivator and his closest kin without having to employ more distant relatives or engage outside help.

With these changes in land tenure and farm household organiza-tion went a marked increase in agricultural production. Not only were more of the staples (rice, millet, soya beans, barley, wheat) grown, but new or exotic crops like cotton, hemp, potatoes, tea, tobacco, ginseng, sugar, dye-plants, and vegetable oils, were culti-vated on a wider scale than ever before. Similarly, sericulture

From earliest times fishing had been important, but offshore fishing prospered with the introduction of nets in Tokugawa times. Many coastal villages, hitherto dependent on agriculture also, switched entirely to fishing. In addition to Hokkaidō, there were particularly rich grounds off Chiba and Kōchi prefectures

underwent a dramatic expansion. The mere fact that most peasant families were now working primarily for themselves must have helped to raise output, and in the case of tenanted land, even though more output meant a bigger slice of rent for the landlord, it also left the cultivator with a larger residue.

It has already been shown how the pattern of land-holding changed as a result of commercialization; and most of the other causes of increased agricultural production can be linked even more directly with the growth of the market. Fish-meal fertilizer, for instance, which gave far better results than the traditional applications of humus and night-soil, came into widespread use in the Tokugawa period, and was something that had to be brought into the villages from outside and sold to the peasants for cash. Another potent source of new production was land reclamation and preparation of new fields for cultivation. Owing to the considerable outlay of capital involved, new-land schemes were only worthwhile if their produce could be sold outside their immediate area. As knowledge and, more specifically, knowledge of opportunities for enrichment grew, so did the use of better strains of seed, and the practice of double cropping which facilitated the spread of new crops. Last but not least was the regional specialization in cash crops, including silk.

Through all these changes the landlord (former large-holder) class remained influential. Its members stayed in the villages, and even though particular landlord families sometimes came to ruin, other families from lower down the social scale prospered sufficiently to join the topmost group. Whatever their ancestry, the wealthiest familes generally bore the burden of local administration, sharing the all-important office of village headman between them. The headman, in essence, was a villager turned official, and it was through him that the rulers communicated with the mass of their subjects. He was responsible to the domain or shogunal officials for the general government and welfare of the village and, in particular, for its payment of taxes. The headman was also supposed to represent his charges in their dealings with authority, to protect them, and to speak up for their common interests if need be. His dealings with the outside world depended on the keeping of records and the exchange of official documents, and his relations with his fellow villagers were governed by the intangible but pervasive force of local custom and consensus.

Only the most wealthy, and consequently most leisured and

literate, families could undertake such responsibilities. In return, they received from the nation's rulers such marks of public esteem as the right to wear one sword and assume a surname. Within the village, everybody deferred to them, and they had ample opportunity for discreet manipulation of affairs in their own interests. It is also apparent that families in the village upper-crust acquired considerable learning and more than a tincture of polite accomplishments. They tended to live quietly and to favour the study of Japanese history and literature, yet many of their members also took up more practical subjects like medicine and agricultural science.

Just as important as the administrative duties and cultural attainments of the Tokugawa landlord class were its entrepreneurial activities. Landlords who did retain a portion of their patrimony under direct cultivation generally pioneered the growing of new and commercial crops in accordance with the most up to date methods; while rents, even if received in kind and so needing conversion into money, provided a basic store of capital for money-lending and the opening up of new lands. New lands had the additional advantage of not being noted on official tax registers until the governing authorities ordered fresh surveys and revised assessments, and this happened less often as time went by. Landlords also actively engaged in rural industry. *Sake* brewing and soy sauce manufacture were the bases of many a gentry fortune. Hardly less common were silk reeling, silk weaving, cotton ginning and spinning, dyeing, vegetable oil manufacture, lumber and transport.

The development of this rural landlord-entrepreneur *élite*, with representatives in just about every village in the land, looms as one of the two or three most significant Tokugawa legacies to modern Japan. It deserves all the attention historians now seem ready to give it, even if this means that interest focuses on only a small section of the peasantry. The perhaps bitter truth is that until very recently history has been the record of the activities and aspirations of *élite* groups, not the masses.

City Life and City Culture

There is scarce a house in this large capital, where there is not something made or sold. Here they refine copper, coin money, print books, weave the richest stuffs with gold and silver flowers. The best and scarcest dies, the most artful carvings, all sorts of musical Instruments, pictures, japan'd cabinets, all sorts of things wrought in gold and other metals, particularly in steel, as the best temper'd blades, and other arms are made here in the utmost perfection, as also the richest dresses, and after the best fashion, all sorts of toys, puppets, moving their heads of themselves, and numberless other things too many to be mention'd. In short, there is nothing can be thought of, but what may be found at Miaco, and nothing, tho' never so neatly wrought, can be imported from abroad, but what some artist or other in this capital will undertake to imitate.[3]

In this fashion did the worthy Engelbert Kaempfer record his impressions of Kyōto in 1691. During the previous hundred years the city had made a striking recovery from the devastation it had suffered in the Ōnin and subsequent wars. In the artistic sphere, this resurgence amounted to a renaissance, in the vanguard of which were artist-craftsmen like Honami Kōetsu (1558—1637) and Tawaraya Sōtatsu (c. 1570–1643). The former came from a family of professional sword-sharpeners, but won renown as an 'amateur' potter, calligrapher, lacquer artist, decorative painter and metal worker. The latter, a far more obscure figure, probably started his career as a fan decorator, but later took up other forms of painting.

During the Tokugawa period, although Kyōto retained its pre-eminence in the manufacture of brocades and other works of fine craftsmanship, it was surpassed by both Ōsaka and Edo in population and general commerce. Between them, the three cities comprised the apex of national economic activity. Ōsaka flourished as a place of exchange serving the whole country, and as the great source of large-scale credit, especially for the *han* governments, and of commodity supplies, especially for Edo. Edo, with its population rising to one million, ranked as the foremost centre of consumption, not only in Japan but in the world. An inkling of the bustle of big city life and the truly astonishing diversification of trade and manufacture can be gained from documents such as the official permission to form a shipping federation, granted in 1784 to twenty-four Ōsaka trade guilds. Goods handled by this group included the following: ashes, baskets, books, carpenters' squares, charcoal boxes, clogs, clothes boxes, copper, cotton, cotton goods, cotton wool, dried fish and other dried foods, drugs, face powder, fertilizers, grindstones, hemp cloth, incense, iron, iron nails, ivory ornaments, lacquer-ware, oar

[3] Kaempfer, *The History of Japan*, Vol. III, p. 21.

wood, oil, paints, paper, parasols, porcelain, rags, sandals, seaweed, socks, straw matting, tobacco, umbrellas, varnishes, wax and wire.

Generally speaking, the firms that qualified for guild membership were sound concerns which had continued over several generations. Their structure represented a skilful blending of the principles of family ownership and corporate management. The founder's descendants usually remained at any rate in formal control, but in practice the crucial decisions were often left to persons of proven competence, like the nominal proprietor's female relatives, or trusted clerks. The latter usually entered the business at an early age as live-in apprentices and, if sufficiently industrious and able, could hope eventually to join the 'inner' family, either by being adopted into it or by being set up in branch houses of their own. On occasion, the corporate spirit was reinforced by a written set of 'house rules' or guides to business practice, which emphasized the conservative virtues of thrift, diligence and caution.

> There are many examples in this world of people eventually going bankrupt by risking not only their own capital but even borrowed money. After all, though it may be a slower process, if you pay for all your personal expenses out of the profits of the trade in which you originally prospered, regard the money which you have as your stock in trade and work single-mindedly at your own business, it is only natural that as a divine reward your house will continue.[4]

So, in the early eighteenth century, wrote one of the founding fathers of the Mitsui Company in a testament for those who would come to occupy his place.

Beneath the crust of respectable and officially protected family businesses, lay the turbulent arena of one-man and one-generation enterprises. Many people in the cities sought to make, and enjoy, a modest fortune for themselves without being too scrupulous about the means they employed, and without worrying unduly about posterity. As a result, there occurred an upsurge of attitudes, part mercenary, part hedonistic, rooted in the aspirations and diversions of the ordinary man and woman. This spirit was traditional Japan's version of bourgeois individualism, and its early flowering was wonderfully captured in the novels and short stories of Ihara Saikaku (1642–93).

[4] Crawcour, 'Some Observations on Merchants', in *The Transactions of the Asiatic Society of Japan*, Third Series, Vol. 8, p. 78.

Saikaku took as his main themes the two great concerns of the impermanent 'floating' world: money and erotic love. He treated them in a witty, anecdotal, and thoroughly realistic manner that still provides good reading. In particular, his stories about how to make (or lose) money are convincing sketches of contemporary city life, short on characterization but full of humorous allusions and local colour. One incident concerns a group of young men sent by their parents to the home of a celebrated miser to pick up advice on how to make good. The new year festivities are not yet over, and while waiting in the front parlour the visitors listen to the noise of somebody grinding an earthenware mortar in the kitchen, and happily speculate on the nature of the refreshments which they are sure they will be served. The host enters and the conversation turns to the meaning of various new year customs, all of which he manages to link with the practice of parsimony. Finally he remarks, 'Well now, you have kindly talked with me from early evening and it is high time that refreshments were served. But not to provide refreshments is one way of becoming a millionaire. The noise of the mortar which you heard when you first arrived was the pounding of starch for the covers of the account-book.'[5]

Saikaku was himself a successful merchant who retired early to take up a life of letters. He wrote for, and principally about, the people he knew best, his fellow townsmen in Ōsaka and Kyōto. The same is true of the great dramatist, Chikamatsu Monzaemon (1653–1725). Anything but narrowly academic in the pursuit of his craft, Chikamatsu must have acquired in his youth a thorough practical training in the dramatic techniques of his day. He worked both for the narrator-and-puppet theatre (*bunraku*) and for the live-actor theatre (*kabuki*). *Bunraku*, which had an early period of vigour in Edo in the seventeenth century, was eventually perfected in Ōsaka, where it remained. *Kabuki* theatre, on the other hand, reached its peak, and flourished as nowhere else, in Edo in the second half of the eighteenth century. By then, it had emerged to some extent from its original aura of disrepute as a façade for prostitution and worse, and could hold its own as an established form of dramatic art. *Bakufu* interference, especially the ban on women or seductive youths appearing on the stage, actually assisted the transformation, as certain actors came to specialize in feminine roles. *Kabuki's* close association in its early stages of development

[5] Sargent (translator), *The Japanese Family Storehouse or The Millionaires' Gospel Modernised*, p. 39.

with the more refined *bunraku* worked towards the same end, and traits like a concentration on dancing and an omnipresent stylization had even deeper roots in the medieval *nō*. Yet the Edo *kabuki* completely lacked *nō*'s general air of austerity and overriding concern with metaphysical religion.

The purpose of *kabuki* was simply to give pleasure by entertaining the audience in a full-blooded way. Fairly large orchestras, consisting of clappers, drums, flutes and the three-stringed *samisen*[6] provided the plays with a variety of musical accompaniment occasionally augmented by vocal recitative. The theatres were large and rather sumptuous permanent buildings, containing very wide stages with a section that could be pushed round like a turn-table to allow for rapid changes of scene or the simultaneous playing of two separate scenes. A long, raised gangway stretched from the left-hand corner of the stage as seen by the audience to the back of the auditorium, and important entries and exits were made along it at the eye level of the spectators. The essential strength of *kabuki* lay in its visual appeal. Elaborate scenery, costumes, and make-up combined with the formal poses (*mie*) of the actors to produce a series of brilliant and compelling spectacles, and an undercurrent of almost sensual excitement. This fleshed picture-effect derived from a non-naturalistic style of acting that relied heavily on bravura and required years of training, and Chikamatsu often wrote with the virtuosity of a particular actor in mind.

There is a total Chikamatsu repertoire of about one hundred and thirty plays falling into the three categories of historical, domestic, and love-suicide. The domestic plays, which have contemporary settings, are more realistic than the historical plays and the greatest are 'love-suicide pieces' (*shinjū-mono*), which have relatively few characters and an action which is completed within three acts. Invariably the theme is ill-starred love and, as in classical tragedy, the protagonists move almost inevitably to their doom. The stage is bare of kings and queens, lords and ladies, and other conventional heroes. In their place come members of the petty bourgeoisie: shopkeepers and their wives, clerks, commission agents, maid-servants and prostitutes, and low-ranking samurai and their families.

---

[6] The *samisen* (or *shamisen*), is a banjo-like instrument covered with catskin and played with a plectrum. Reputedly from the southerly Ryūkyū Islands, its prototype was improved in Japan by *biwa* players in early modern times. Given this background, its subsequent use in narrative accompaniment called *jōruri*, harking back to the romances about Yoshitsune, is not surprising. Its twangy tone evokes for modern Japanese the world of entertainment and accompanied song.

As has often been pointed out, the essential conflict in Chikamat-su's works is between a sense of duty (*giri*) and human feeling (*ninjō*). A reasonably happily married family man falls hopelessly in love with a prostitute; a lonely samurai wife indulges in an illicit affair while her husband is away in Edo; a girl whose parents have already betrothed her gives her heart elsewhere. In none of these cases can the persons concerned satisfactorily reconcile their emotions with their duties to society. They come to realize this and finally set out on a last journey:

Farewell to this world, and to the night farewell.
We who walk the road to death, to what should we be likened?
To the frost by the road that leads to the graveyard,
Vanishing with each step we take ahead:
How sad is this dream of a dream![7]

Giri and *ninjō* undoubtedly sustain the plays, but it is wrong to suppose that this aspect is unique. Did not Macbeth feel a definite *giri* sense of revulsion at killing Duncan, who was his kinsman as well as king and a guest under his roof at the time of the murder? Yet the 'human feeling' of ambition, coupled with his susceptibility to his spouse, drove him on. Similarly, Cordelia suffered because, although full of deep human affection for her father, she was personally too upright (or as Japanese might say had too strong a sense of *giri* to herself), and perhaps too public-spirited, to pander to the whims of his old age. True, Chikamatsu gives a specifically Confucian-samurai flavour to his treatment of these situations, and the concern for personal honour goes further than most Western dramatists would allow. Nevertheless, his ethic, in its *giri-ninjō* essence at any rate, is by no means peculiarly Japanese; by regarding people in this fashion he tapped one of the mainsprings of tragedy the world over. This enhances his claims to be considered a dramatist of universal importance.

Concentration on *giri* and *ninjō* risks losing sight of Chikamatsu's other great talents as a playwright. A superb verbal craftsman in verse as well as prose, his plays glitter with puns and with allusions to not only Buddhist Sutras and classical literature, but also the literature of the streets—popular ballads, proverbs, and so on. His

[7] The opening lines of the celebrated *michiyuki* (journey sequence) in the play *Sonezaki Shinjū* (*The Love Suicides at Sonezaki*), from Keene, *Major Plays of Chikamatsu*, p. 51.

audiences needed to be familiar with general political conditions and with the outlines of Japanese and Chinese history. At least one of the plays has for its background Mt Kōya with its aura of Shingon mysteries, and in most of the others he introduces an element of Amidism. Yet, so far as Chikamatsu had a conscious didactic purpose, it was Confucian. He was too good an artist to stoop to undiluted propaganda, but play after play stresses the pre-eminent virtues of loyalty, filial piety, and conjugal fidelity. Benevolence and forgiveness also figure, but less obviously.

Other qualities command attention. The plays excel in swift changes of mood; even the grimmest tragedy has its humorous moments. In addition, the playwright portrays women as forceful personalities in their own right, and allows his tragic characters, especially the men, to grow in moral stature. Such versatility is the very stuff of drama, and since Chikamatsu also had the power to imbue his climaxes with genuine pathos, it is not difficult to see why he has been dubbed, by the Japanese at any rate, 'the Shakespeare of Japan'. In the final analysis, however, he deserves attention purely on his own merits, his works constituting 'the first mature tragedies written about the common man'.[8]

There is some reason to think that Chikamatsu Monzaemon was a *rōnin*. In the case of Matsuo Bashō (1644–94), famous for the invention of the classical *haiku* poem, the evidence is quite clear. He had been born into the samurai class, but chose to leave it when he grew up and make his way as a commoner. Similarly, *haiku* had antecedents both in the classical *tanka* of the court poets and in the comic epigrams of the common people. After 1600 the spread of literacy and the development of the townsman's culture broke down many of the traditional social barriers and restraints in the practice of literature and the arts. 'Bashō' became virtually a household word while still alive and attracted patrons, associates and pupils from all classes and both sexes. Just as the theatre could flourish only by reaching as wide an audience as possible, so the *haiku* tradition profited greatly from this initial impetus towards popularization. *Haiku* are humorous. Sometimes the humour is obvious and cutting; more often it is gentle and oblique.

Chōnai de	Throughout the town,
Shiranu wa teishu	Only her husband
Bakari kana	Does not know.

[8] Keene, Op. Cit., p. 1.

Kaze hito ni	How hot he is—
Se ou atsusa ya	The fan-seller carrying from door to door
Uchiwa-uri.	His burden of breeze!

(Kakō)

Haiku are concrete and imagistic. All the poem does is briefly sketch a picture, the implications of which are left unstated. To a quite extraordinary degree, therefore, *haiku* poetry remains embedded in the general culture and way of life of an entire people as they were some two hundred years ago; and the reader has to be aware of this wider experience, in addition to such literary conventions as season-words.

Harusame ya	A Spring shower—
Monogatari yuku	While an umbrella and a straw raincoat
Mino to kasa	Pass by chatting.

(Buson)

Chōmatsu ga	Johnny has called,
Oya no na de kuru	On behalf of his parents—
Gyokei kana	A New Year felicitation.

(Yaha)

Yaha conjures up a picture of a little boy, dressed in his best and full of self-importance, who is paying a formal new year visit literally 'in the name of his parents'. *Chōmatsu* is a familiar term used in the Edo period for a boy or an apprentice. Typical of the colloquial language generally favoured for *haiku*, it contrasts strongly and humorously with the stiff *gyokei* (felicitations).

Haiku are evocative and emotive.

Haru no umi	The Spring sea—
Hinemosu notari	All day long it rose and fell,
Notari kana	Rose and fell.

(Buson)

Natsugusa ya	The summer grasses—
Tsuwamonodomo ga	All that has survived from
Yume no ato	Brave warriors' dreams.

(Bashō)

Okite mitsu	Getting up and lying down,
Nete mitsu kaya no	Lying down and getting up—
Hirosa kana	How wide the mosquito net!

(Ukihashi)

Tsuyu no yo wa	The world of dew
Tsuyu no yo nagara	Is the world of dew,
Sarinagara	And yet, and yet.
(Issa)	

Japanese mosquito nets are suspended from the four corners of a room, giving plenty of space for other activities besides sleeping. Ukihashi made use of this fact to indicate her impatience while awaiting her lover. Issa struck out at a Buddhist platitude when replying to condolences on the death of a beloved baby daughter; and Bashō composed his verse during a visit to the site of Minamoto Yoshitsune's suicide in 1189, when, in his own words, he 'wept bitterly till I almost forgot time'.[9]

Shizukasa ya	Such stillness—
Iwa ni shimi-iru	The cicadas' cries penetrate
Semi no koe	The very rocks!

Umi kurete	The sea darkens,
Kamo no koe	And the voices of ducks
Honoka ni shiroshi	Are faintly white.

Ara umi ya	A rough sea,
Sado ni yokotau	And stretching to Sado
Ama no gawa	The Milky Way.

Tako-tsubo ya	A lobster in a pot,
Hakanaki yume wo	Dreaming awhile
Natsu no tsuki	Under the summer moon.

This last group of *haiku* consists entirely of verses by Bashō. In his maturity, he sometimes achieved heightened effect by 'transposing' from one semantic or sense plane to another. Silence and sound are made to convey a predominant impression of heat. Similarly, the ducks' voices in the dusk are faintly white. Buddhism, especially that of the Kegon school which had flourished in Nara times, taught that all phenomena were fundamentally one and interchangeable. The *haiku* on Sado expresses this philosophy by making that island the unseen point of meeting between the rough sea and the tranquil Milky Way. The poem is really a magnificent statement about the

[9] Yuasa (translator), *Bashō—The Narrow Road to the Deep North and other travel sketches*, p. 118.

tension of opposites and the Buddha's capacity to reconcile them. Diction skilfully complements meaning: the words *ara umi ya Sado ni* are naturally spoken in a staccato manner, but with *yokotau* there is a notable change of rhythm, the vowels becoming long and peaceful. The double use of water imagery, as the Japanese name for the Milky Way (*Ama no gawa*) means literally 'river of heaven', seemingly adds yet another dimension of depth and complexity, but in fact strengthens and clarifies the poem's basic statement.

Interchangeableness—the idea that 'many', however different, are somehow 'one'—is linked in the last poem with the even more pervasive Buddhist notion of transience. Bashō felt reasonably happy when he wrote it, enjoying an evening boat trip on Akashi Bay. He looked down at the trapped lobster and realized that it, too, was was still content with its situation, lying in the warm and pellucid sea that was its accustomed environment. Man and lobster! The doom of the latter is quite predictable; in the morning he will be raised to the surface and sent to market. But is the outlook for the former any more reassuring?

The achievement of all three men—Saikaku, Chikamatsu and Bashō—lay in their ability to innovate. In the novel, in the drama, and in poetry, respectively, they created new forms that incorporated the experience and interests of ordinary people, in the great cities primarily, but also in the smaller towns and villages of the countryside. Hitherto literature, like life's other rewards, had been largely the preserve of civilian, military and religious aristocrats.

The new developments began in the Kinai where both Saikaku and Chikamatsu were content to spend their days. Bashō, however, though born not far from Kyōto, left his native district for Edo in 1672 when, serving a kind of poetic apprenticeship, he travelled there with his instructor who had been summoned to teach the reigning *shōgun* the art of *haiku*. Necessity forced him to work for a few years as a minor waterworks official, but subsequently he managed to live independently as a successful teacher and writer of poetry. Long, reflective journeys on foot, back to the western provinces and northwards into Mutsu, became part of the pattern of his life:

> *Yoshino nite*   Come, my old hat—
> *Sakura mishō zo*   Let us go and see
> *Hinoki-gasa*   The flowers at Yoshino.

Nevertheless he continued to make his home in Edo; and this choice foreshadowed a general trend. For after about 1750 Edo was sufficiently large and mature to be pre-eminent culturally as well as politically.

Intelligent connoisseurs, dilettante samurai as well as rich merchants, accounted for the rise of *kabuki*, and also for Edo's other great contribution to Japanese, and world, culture: the wood-block print. *Ukiyoe* ('floating world pictures') showed aspects of contemporary life, rather than the traditionally sanctioned 'flowers and birds' or scenes drawn from Chinese and Japanese classics and history. Contemporary life being what it was, at any rate in the imagination of the average townsman, many pictures have as their subject the inhabitants and frequenters of the amusement quarters. Along with the prints, paintings on paper and on silk are an important part of the general *ukiyoe* tradition and include such masterpieces as the Kaigetsudō school's pictures produced in Edo in the early 1700s. It was in Edo, not Kyōto (where simple black and white block illustration had come into fashion in the seventeenth century) that the techniques of multi-coloured wood-block printing eventually matured. The crucial artist was Suzuki Harunobu (c. 1725–70), who in the last ten years of his life designed notable colour prints. Of course, in this field credit does not go to the artist alone: engraving the blocks, one for each colour to be used; preparation and mixing of dyes; and the actual printing, were all highly skilled occupations. The importance of custom is shown by the fact that the first 'brocade' or multi-coloured prints were commissioned as distinctive new year greetings cards by a group of wealthy art lovers.

In his prime Harunobu concentrated on pictures of young girls, whom he drew in a variety of situations but always in a wistful, childlike manner. He was followed by other artists who specialized in human figure pictures of women and actors. Toshusai Sharaku (fl. 1794), Torii Kiyonaga (1752–1815) and Kitagawa Utamarō (1753–1806) were three of the most outstanding of this group. After 1800 or so, the quality of figure prints sharply declined. For the first time they became genuinely plebeian, and were marred by mass production and increasing crudity of design to meet popular tastes. In the nineteenth century the speciality of prints was landscape, in particular the justly famous works of Katsushika Hokusai (1760–1849) and Andō Hiroshige (1797–1858). Views of Mt Fuji and scenes along the Tōkaidō highway connecting Edo and Kyōto were perennially favoured.

Ukiyoe was by no means the only notable artistic tradition of the Tokugawa period. Official patronage went to the Kanō school, which lost its initial exuberance as its patrons' demands switched from magnificence to edification. Nevertheless, in Kanō Tanyu (1602–74) the school had yet one more artist of outstanding talent and it remained perfectly capable of supplying the great with proficient, and suitably decorous, works of art. Its leaders moved from Kyōto to Edo. The Tosa school, a medieval development of *Yamato-e*, continued into the seventeenth century with the support of the imperial court, whose distant glories it recalled in a less than vital manner. There was also a new and largely amateur 'literati' (*bunjinga*) school. Initiated by visitors from China in the seventeenth or early eighteenth centuries, it specialized in careful brush-work and produced gentle and refined pictures in the 'southern' Chinese manner. But real freshness was blown into the art world (for such an independent, secular world was becoming distinguishable) by decorators in the native Japanese tradition stemming directly from the artist-craftsmen Honami Kōetsu and Tawaraya Sōtatsu. Their younger relatives, the brothers Ogata Kōrin (1658–1716) and Ogata Kenzan (1663–1743), were decorators of vitality with distinctively Japanese qualities. Kōrin's bold patterns in dress materials and design—his painting in purple and green of irises on a folding screen of gold is a National Treasure—were matched in quieter vein by Kenzan's decorative painting on tea bowls, cake dishes and plates.

In literature, with the exception of great *haiku* poets like Yosa Buson (1716–83) and Kobayashi Issa (1763–1827), the second half of the Tokugawa period on the whole failed to live up to the achievements of the late seventeenth and early eighteenth centuries. The Ōsaka writer Ejima Kiseki (1667–1736) wrote in the realist-humorous manner of Saikaku, but lacked the latter's verbal dexterity and underlying sympathy with humanity. His 'character-books', the most celebrated written with style and wit, ostensibly condemn irregular behaviour especially on the part of the young, but in fact condone it. The third outstanding practitioner of the humorous sketch was Shikitei Samba (1776–1822) who made a lively and interesting portrait-gallery collection of Edo 'types' in such books as *The Floating World at the Bath-house* and *The Passing Parade at the Barber's*.

The novel, as opposed to the humorous sketch or 'character-book', fared particularly badly after Saikaku's death. One of its leading exponents in the later Tokugawa period was Jippensha Ikku (1765–1831), who wrote a long picaresque novel which was published in serial form and widely read at the time. Commonly called *Hizakurige*, it is the story of two Edo working-class friends, Kita and Yaji, who decide to leave their home town more or less for their home town's good, and make a leisurely journey along the great Tōkaidō highway as far as Kyōto. Their low comedy adventures along the way, coupled with an interminable flow of repartee, constitute the essential ingredients of *Hizakurige*. But the humour is too obvious and the protagonists too commonplace. Written in anticipation of popular demand, this book, like the late figure prints, is doubtless a case of a mass market destroying true art.

Takizawa Bakin (1767–1848) was another writer who enjoyed a wide readership in his own lifetime, and who possibly had more innate literary talent than Jippensha Ikku. His early stories in the picaresque tradition—for example *The Vendetta of Mr Fleacatcher Managorō, The Fifth*—are genuinely funny.[10] Unfortunately, however, for most of his life Bakin chose to write deliberately respectable novels and the wildly improbable situations encountered therein do not in any way compensate for their excessive length and interminable moralizing along Confucian lines.

Ueda Akinari (1734–1809) stands apart from the general run of Tokugawa period authors. He lived in Ōsaka and Kyōto, working as a professional writer and at times as a doctor. Early years of comfort, affection and pleasure gave way to disappointment and bitterness; and Ueda's most famous book, *Ugetsu Monogatari* (*Tales for the Rainy Month*), seems to have been written at about the time his circumstances began to change. This perhaps helps to account for its intensity, although its technical skill owes more to a writer's mastery of his craft than to the onset of any personal misfortune. The *Ugetsu Monogatari* consists of short, sometimes whimsical stories drawn from diverse sources in folk-lore, legend, and authentic history. Extremely slight in construction, they hold the reader's interest remarkably well, partly because they are often built around a genuinely interesting idea and partly because of the story-teller's ability to evoke a by-gone age. In choosing to ignore his own time and its class structure in favour of a kind of literary eclecticism within the national tradition, Ueda exemplifies an important general characteristic of middle and late Tokugawa

[10] Cf. Zolbrod, 'The Vendetta of Mr Fleacatcher Managorō, The Fifth', in *Monumenta Nipponica*, Vol. XX, Nos. 1–2, pp. 123–34.

culture: its tendency toward amalgamation of basically different traditions, trends and interests.

Intellectual Life and Education

Following the secular trends of the sixteenth century, Japanese intellectual life came to be dominated by Confucianism. Buddhism still had a hold over the masses, and received official endorsement as the approved alternative to Christianity. Moreover, a system of compulsory temple registration by families had administrative uses. The taking of a regular national census after 1720 would have been impossible without it. But intellectually, Buddhism stagnated, though its traditions continued to be a vital force in aesthetics and literature.

Tokugawa Confucianism divided into a number of distinct schools, all of which, however, agreed in stressing the individual's role in society and, in particular, relations between rulers and ruled. In most cases, therefore, it represented a markedly conservative political ideology reflecting the interests and professional requirements of the emergent samurai bureaucrats. Even so, Confucian teachings on loyalty and filial piety became standards of conduct in all walks of life and at all social levels.

Other traits common to all Confucianists were a strong bias in favour of study, especially the study of history, and a general rationality of outlook. These characteristics led to the publication by the Mito *han* of the great multi-volume *History of Great Japan* (*Dai Nihonshi*) on the one hand, and to the career of Ogyū Sorai (1666–1728) on the other. One of the most illustrious of all Tokugawa Confucianists, Ogyū occasionally advised the reforming *shōgun*, Yoshimune. He came close to making the crucial distinction between the natural, moral, and political orders, and was exceptional in this; most Confucianists throughout the period adhered doggedly to the notion that the three orders were inseparable. For them, man stood at the centre of things and among men, the sage should be king. In other words, they saw the universe as an organic, moral whole and were reluctant to study nature bereft of moral connotations and for its own sake, as in the natural sciences.

Confucian notions about time and the past made it very difficult for even the best of Confucian-trained historians to conceive of progress as an advance to a totally new and generally better condition. To the orthodox of all schools, change or novelty was inherently dangerous and bad and the only feasible socio-political improvement was some kind of 'restoration' of a legendary golden age supposed to have existed thousands of years earlier.

Despite such defects and limitations, the dissemination of Confucian studies in the Tokugawa period gave Japanese society an intellectual liveliness that seems to have been lacking at the time in Confucianism's homeland in China. As early as the last quarter of the seventeenth century, scholars were appearing who, although definitely in the Confucian tradition, could not be identified with any particular school. The most eminent of these independent thinkers was Arai Hakuseki (1657–1725), whose achievements in politics and scholarship alike were impressive. Arai seems to have sensed the basically evolutionary nature of history, and his writings include a short but extremely interesting autobiography.

Apart from this increase in rationalism and independent thinking within the general Confucian tradition, the eighteenth century gave rise to two new fields of scholastic enquiry. Both had their roots in the Confucian-inspired revival of learning, but both soon came to stand quite apart from Chinese learning, or *kangaku*.

The school of National Learning (*kokugaku-ha*) concentrated on Japanese, rather than Chinese, history, literature, and religious traditions. Its leaders were Kamo no Mabuchi (1697–1769), who made a detailed study of the *Manyōshū* with the aim of making that ancient anthology intelligible to eighteenth century readers; Motoori Norinaga (1730–1801), who succeeded in the even more difficult task of up-dating and interpreting the *Kojiki* chronicle and who also wrote valuable commentaries on the Heian classics; and Hirata Atsutane (1776–1843) whose speciality was Shinto. Philology was basic to *kokugaku*, and Motoori's signal achievements in this field still command respect. Unfortunately, he allowed his not unnatural enthusiasm for things Japanese to carry over into a quite unreasonable hostility towards Chinese culture. Hirata went even further and, though not without some genuinely religious insights, was so anxious to demonstrate the inherent racial superiority of the Japanese that he became completely xenophobic, holding up what he knew of the West as well as China to general ridicule.

These excesses, together with the fact that their attitude was a precursor of modern ultra-nationalism, have earned the scholars of the National Learning a bad name. Yet a few things can be said in their defence. Nationalism has been a force for good as well as evil in the emergence of modern States, and though the *kokugaku* scholars over-reacted to the prestige of Chinese studies in their own times, their valid premise was that the national society in which they lived and for which they wrote was Japan, not China. In purely literary terms they launched a telling and praiseworthy attack, in the name of genuine human feeling, against the passionless sterility with which Confucianists sought to defend themselves against the claims of great literature. Finally, with regard to ideology, though the neo-Shinto attitude to history was distorted by acceptance of national and racial myths as articles of faith, it left the future more open than did the detailed prescriptions emanating from an imaginary Confucian golden age in the past. So long as the throne was preserved and the *kami* honoured, no change in the polity's structure—for example, industrialization or the widespread adoption of Western political and intellectual culture—was too great for them to contemplate.

Kokugaku received a measure of both official and private support, but never threatened the ideological supremacy of Chinese learning. The same may be said of *rangaku* or Dutch (i.e. Western) Learning, which slowly developed, with some initial encouragement from Tokugawa Yoshimune, into the third great field of academic enquiry. As a result, in the first half of the nineteenth century most highly placed or highly educated Japanese knew that in some respects—notably medicine, geography, navigation, astronomy and calendar-making, and gunnery—contemporary Western practice was ahead of traditional Chinese and Japanese lore.

The point of contact was the Dutch trading settlement at Nagasaki, a place visited by the majority of *rangaku* scholars at some stage in their careers. The regular Dutch embassies to Edo provided opportunities for acquiring further knowledge. But probably the most important single source of information was accounts of the West given in Chinese books. Yoshimune permitted the importation of such works provided that they did not deal specifically with Christianity. The obstacles confronting the *rangaku* scholars were considerable, due more to the intrinsic difficulties of their task than to any official or Confucian opposition. At best, contacts were spasmodic. There was also a constant problem of trying to understand what the foreigners said or wrote: it took years to make even a very imperfect Dutch-Japanese dictionary. Nevertheless, slow progress was made. To the end, *rangaku* kept its emphasis on scientific and practical subjects. Yet even though Western thought and politics neither were nor could be studied to the same extent, the newness of the United States and the antiquity of Egypt were both being written about by 1800 and there is a somewhat inaccurate outline description of the British parliamentary system under George IV in a book written towards the end of the 1820s.

The broad development of school and college education in the second half of the Tokugawa period proved ultimately to be of greater significance than the evolution of any particular branch of academic learning. By 1800 all members of the samurai class had long been literate. Daughters received their education in their own or relatives' homes as did sons until their mid-teens, when they might be expected to enrol in the local *hankō*, or *han* college. The majority of the *han* had established such institutions for the higher education of their samurai by the early nineteenth century. Courses lasted for several years and were largely given over to *kangaku* in its least exciting variants. Instruction in warlike exercises such as fencing and archery must have relieved the tedium for most students. At the very end of the period, some colleges began to include Western subjects in their curricula, especially gunnery.

Commoners were not generally admitted to the *hankō*, their educational needs being met by local community schools (*terakoya*). These taught children how to read and write in Japanese (as distinct from the *hankō* concern with Chinese), simple mathematics, and the basics of filial piety and loyalty. Young children of the lowest samurai grades often attended *terakoya*. By the first half of the nineteenth century perhaps eleven thousand *terakoya* were scattered throughout the country, and they continued to bear the brunt of popular education even after the fall of the Tokugawa in 1868.

It has been calculated that the literacy rate for the total population, including the samurai, was over thirty per cent in the last part of the Tokugawa period. If the calculation is done for males alone the figure rises to about fifty per cent. Such a high degree of literacy is quite extraordinary for a pre-modern society, and the 'mass' aspects of Tokugawa education certainly helped shape the country's future after 1868.

Qualitatively speaking, however, the most interesting and fruitful element in Tokugawa education was neither the *han* colleges, the fundamental aim of which seems to have been to give the samurai a nodding acquaintance with the letters and thought of a dead Chinese past, nor the modest though worthy *terakoya*, but the various private academies (*juku*). These schools specialized in a single branch of learning or in the military arts, at a fairly advanced level. Their students, invariably young men, included commoners as well as samurai. They came from all over the country and often boarded at the school. Being private enterprises the number of *juku* fluctuated, but there were probably more than a thousand in existence at any one time after 1780, scattered through the country but normally to be found in the cities and larger towns. Many Tokugawa period scholars were intimately involved in *juku* education and an academy often disappeared when its principal teacher died. This appears to have been the case with Motoori Norinaga's establishment at Matsuzaka (Mie prefecture). On the other hand, the Kogidō, founded in Kyōto by the *kangaku* philosopher, Itō Jinsai (1627–1705) was a famous centre of learning for well over two hundred years.

Socially, *juku* indicate the existence of a semi-independent national intelligentsia after about 1750, one that had little to do with the conventions of class and regional differentiation. Intellectually, they embraced the whole range of available learning, and some concentrated exclusively on Western studies. Their general air of vigour and diversity stemmed from the initiative and capacity for hard work of their founders, who were frequently pioneer scholars in their respective fields. The *juku* are also interesting because many of the scholars who ran them were samurai, often *rōnin*. If the word 'culture' is taken to mean literature, music and the fine arts, then the Tokugawa centuries do seem to have been a time of growing bourgeois and commoner influence, with the samurai making but little contribution. Yet as soon as the definition of culture is extended to include education and intellectual life, to say nothing of administration, the picture radically alters. The samurai take the lead in effecting changes and fostering developments which, more than any other factors, were to account for the nation's future greatness.

The Japanese 'Family System'

With the exception of *rangaku* and later 'practical' studies, education in Japan from Tokugawa times has been linked with ideas and problems of moral indoctrination. For most Westerners, traditional Japanese morality is summed up in the term *bushidō*, a word meaning 'way of the warrior' and tarnished by misbehaviour of Japanese troops. Though the constituent virtues of courage, loyalty and frugality have been real enough guides, both the term *bushidō* and the degree of formalization it denotes are Edo-period inventions, and have not had the transcendental importance sometimes ascribed to them. A more comprehensive approach to the ethical norms of modern Japan is provided by the alternative concept of the 'family system'.

Unlike *bushidō*, the family system of early modern Japan took account of the widest possible range of classes and ages. It was not restricted to samurai men. Nevertheless, one of the most apt models of the system is a sociologically 'typical' Tokugawa samurai family. Such a family had no source of livelihood other than the hereditary stipend paid by the *shōgun* or a *daimyō* to its recognized head, and out of this fixed family stipend the head had to provide for a range of dependants. The number of dependants was obviously not fixed, but it could include such people as the head's aged parents, his eldest son's wife and his eldest son's children, and his younger unmarried brothers and sisters. A rather full household might be as follows:

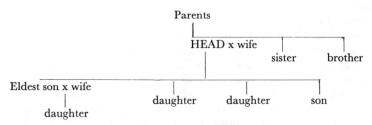

Three important points emerge from even this simple description.

In the first place, because the family lived on a fixed income it was obliged to have a 'nuclear' organization that covered immediate kinsfolk only and did not really extend to aunts, uncles, and cousins. To keep numbers down, only the head or prospective head was permitted to marry and stay within the family. Younger sons and daughters in each generation, if they wished to have children of their own, had to be adopted or married away from under the parental roof. The ideal was that of a smallish household perpetuating itself through a succession of family heads.

Secondly, relations within the family were ideally conducted in a spirit of 'hierarchical wholism'. The family head's responsibilities were heavy, and the system gave him proportionate authority and privileges. In theory, and to a considerable extent in practice, family relationships were coloured by Confucian standards of propriety between parent and child, husband and wife, elder brother and younger brother: on the one side (benevolent) authority, on the other (loyal) service. Even though there was a well-defined

rank-order based on differences of age and sex, the system's fundamental objective was the ongoing welfare of the group as a whole, not
the temporary aggrandizement of any member of it. Consequently, those vested with authority were expected to use it circumspectly, and subordinates had implicit 'rights' to minimal standards
of welfare and human dignity. Incompetent elder sons could be
passed over in the succession to the family headship. Informal
consultations within the family appear to have been the rule, and
on occasion the head would seek the help of more distant relatives
in resolving major family problems.

Thirdly, there was a marked emphasis on the principle of steward-
ship or management. Nobody had absolute rights in property apart
from customary personal possessions, for in the case of the samurai
no other property had existed. There was only a life interest in the
family stipend and the obligations that went with that interest,
above all the obligation to preserve the family's income and good
name for coming generations. This managerial aspect of the
samurai's private and domestic circumstances fitted very well with
their public and administrative responsibilities in the shogunate and
domain governments. The relatively small and compact *han* could
be easily envisaged as the family writ large. In the same way, after
1868 the centralized nation-State was to be envisaged as the family
on a larger scale still, with the emperor occupying for the country as
a whole the symbolic, integrative position formerly held by the
daimyō in their various domains. Although the samurai were gradually destroyed as a class by the Meiji Restoration, it was perhaps
easier for them than for most other ruling classes to accept the
challenges of revolutionary transformation. At least they did not have
extensive estates or big business interests at stake, and the large
numbers of them who were concerned with devising and administering the new order were fulfilling a traditional managerial role.

Mention has been made of the family system's relevance to the
other two great Tokugawa classes of merchants and peasants. But it
has to be reiterated that this section so far has been written in terms of
abstractions. Of course, though, the family system was not just a
sociological model. It involved real people, with all humanity's
capacity for love and hatred, gratitude and resentment. For instance,
neither Ōkuma Shigenobu nor Fukuzawa Yukichi, two of the great
men of the Meiji period, seems to have got on very well with his
elder brother. On the other hand, hierarchy was often softened by
consideration and ties of genuine affection.

It may well be that most of the virtue of the family system lies strictly in its capacity as a *family* system, and that its defects can be most readily found in wider social and political applications. It is obviously particularist in that it assumes a flow of moral obligations up and down a single vertical line of authority (grandfather-father-son; ruler-official-subject) or within a small parochial group (village, urban ward, school class), rather than a general diffusion of morality regardless of status or location. As a result, it has been remarked that modern Japanese have plenty of patriotism and local community attachments, but are relatively lacking in a sense of citizenship. Similarly, though Tokugawa and modern Japan have had their share of good Samaritans, the accepted ethic has done little to encourage them. Finally, it is undeniable that the family system is a basically collective ethic. Individuals are expected, if need be, to sacrifice their personal interests for whatever may be considered the good of the group.

Despite its failings the Tokugawa family system proved surprisingly resilient, and much of it survives at the present time. There arises, then, a paradox. Late traditional *baku-han* Japan had a socio-political structure which was markedly pluralistic and potentially 'open'. Its values and ideology, however had a strong corporate, collective bias. Tension between these two opposed sets of conditions has produced much of the dynamism, the play of dark and light, in modern Japanese history.

A portrait of Hideyoshi

Himeji castle, built in the first decade of the seventeenth century, when the country was almost at peace; it is the most splendid surviving example of castle-building

The rice harvest: a scene from the nineteenth-century scroll *Rōno Yawa* (*Veteran Farmer's Evening Talks*)

Terakoya: the local school of early modern times that spread literacy among the mass of the Japanese people

PART V

Modern Japan

CHAPTER FIFTEEN

The Meiji Era and Policies for Modernization

Against the background of three hundred years of early modern Japanese history, Emperor Meiji's reign (1867–1912) stands out as a time of deliberate modernization. During the Tokugawa period, certain pre-conditions for modernization had developed. Though vitally important, these pre-conditions were accidental in that concepts like modernization and progress were never consciously adopted as social and administrative goals. In the Meiji era, however, Japan's government and people set themselves the ambitious task of deliberately catching up with the technologically advanced nation-states of the West, and in striving to achieve this aim, they absorbed sufficient Western civilization to profoundly affect society at all levels. The change from unthinking acceptance of traditional attitudes to deliberate espousal of new goals marked a decisive break with the past.

To the Japanese, being 'modern' in the second half of the nineteenth century meant having an economic system of industrial capitalism and a political system of liberal or quasi-liberal constitutionalism as in the United States and a number of European countries. Japanese domestic policies were guided by these aspirations, which gave the Meiji era a certain simplicity: the goals, though awesome, were few and clearcut, and authority remained in the hands of a small number of people enjoying widespread support.

Foreign relations, an increasingly perilous area of public concern after 1912, possessed a similar simplicity of basic aim and method. The central objective, for government and people alike, was negotiated revision of treaties which the *bakufu* had been forced to sign with Western countries during its last years, and which relegated Japan to an inferior status. Full revision did not occur until the end

213

of the Meiji reign. However unfortunate and irritating the delays may have been, they enforced a valuable unanimity of opinion on the nature and importance of the tasks confronting the nation's diplomats.

The Meiji era then was a time of transition and of deliberate transformation in response to the West. During its forty-five years, national life went through a period of intensive and extensive reordering, which brought it to the threshold of the next stage, when affairs moved of their own momentum, with governments attempting to keep pace with, rather than instigate, change. Generally speaking, the Meiji statesmen did well, working diligently and boldly to lay the foundations of a modern nation-state. It was their achievements, not their mistakes, that gave rise to an increasingly complex social, political and diplomatic situation not long after their departure from the helm.

The Restoration

The Meiji Restoration of 1868, quite apart from its importance for the history of Japan, has proved to be a major event in modern world history. As a result it has attracted much scholarly interest both inside and outside the country, so that there are almost as many interpretations as there are scholars. The truth is that no one explanation will suffice, since the inter-relation of events makes the Restoration's history as labyrinthine as it is portentous.

In so far as it can be said to have been a single happening, the Restoration was a return to effective rule by centralized monarchy, and its rationale was the idea of restoring the emperor to his rightful position which had been usurped by the Fujiwara and a succession of *shōguns*. The person ostensibly benefiting from this was the young Emperor Meiji (1852–1912) who had just succeeded to the throne. But the real sponsors of the Restoration were 'loyalist' samurai from the western *tozama han* of Satsuma (Kagoshima prefecture), Chōshū (Yamaguchi prefecture) and Tosa (Kōchi prefecture). These *han* were among those which had successfully implemented major military, administrative and fiscal reforms in and subsequent to the Tempō era (1830–1843), and as a result were in a good position to intervene in national politics, given the opportunity and sufficient determination. The conspirators' first objective was the overthrow of the *bakufu* that stood between them and their dream of forming a national government under the throne. For a number of years the shogunate had been subjected to physical as well as moral pressure; and in November 1867, the reigning *shōgun*, Tokugawa Keiki (1837–1913) voluntarily stepped down from his office, refusing to nominate a successor and saying in his letter of resignation:

> Now that foreign intercourse becomes daily more extensive, unless the government is directed from one central authority, the foundations of the state will fall to pieces. If, however, the old order of things be changed, and the administrative authority be restored to the Imperial Court, and if national deliberations be conducted on an extensive scale, and the Imperial decision be secured, and if the empire be supported by the efforts of the whole people, then the empire will be able to maintain its rank and dignity among the nations of the earth . . . it is, I believe, my highest duty to realize this ideal by giving up entirely my rule over this land.[1]

Tokugawa Keiki's gesture took the Court by surprise and it was obliged to instruct the *bakufu* to continue administering the country for the time being. Then, late in December 1867, Ōkubo Toshimichi (1830–78), a strong-minded retainer from Satsuma *han*, persuaded the group of radical court nobles that the emperor should be promptly restored. In addition to Ōkubo's political associates from Satsuma, the effective ruler of Satsuma, Shimazu Hisamitsu (1817–87), his counterpart in Tosa, Yamanouchi Toyoshige (1827–72) and the chief minister of Tosa, Gotō Shōjirō (1838–97) also knew of the plan, as did representatives of the *han* governments of Aki (Hiroshima prefecture), Echizen (Fukui prefecture) and Owari (Aichi prefecture). More importantly, a large body of Chōshū troops and their fervently loyalist leaders were near Kyōto, poised to re-enter the city from which they had been expelled a few years earlier in the course of the political and military skirmishing that preceded the Restoration.

Matters came to a head in the early morning of 3 January 1868 when Iwakura Tomomi (1825–83), the most forceful of the radical court nobles, took charge of a draft statement proclaiming the Restoration, which was to be read forthwith by the emperor. Despite confusion at the palace gates, troops under the command of Saigō Takamori (1828–77), a Satsuma samurai, secured the palace, and the formal proclamation of the Restoration was heard by a small

[1] McLaren, 'Japanese Government Documents' in *Transactions of the Asiatic Society of Japan*, Vol. XLII, p. 2.

band of courtiers and *daimyō*. Keiki's resignation as *shōgun* was accepted for the second time, in his absence, and the high offices of the *bakufu* abolish. Still later in the day, the extremists prevailed once more. Intent on keeping the Tokugawa and their closest adherents out of any new system of government, they decided to demand the surrender of the former *shōgun's* territories (the *tenryō*). These actions, which terminated the *bakufu* as an institution of national government, were taken by a handful of far-sighted plotters with only very limited support; at this stage the Meiji Restoration seemed little more than a palace revolution.

Tokugawa Keiki tended passively to accept the loyalists' actions. However, many of his vassals, especially in the northern provinces, did not give in so easily, and a War of the Restoration, which had begun near Kyōto in January 1868, continued until the final surrender of Tokugawa forces in Hokkaidō in June 1869. Despite the fighting, the new government was able to embark at once on an important re-structuring of the country's administration, which included the removal of the emperor to Edo, now renamed Tōkyō or the Eastern Capital.

Behind these successes lay *baku-han* pluralism which permitted

✓ Kyōto Court	× Edo Bakufu	× Fudai han	✓ Some *tozama han*, i.e. Satsuma, Chōshū, Tosa and Hizen	× Senior retainers	✓ Junior retainers	× City merchants	✓ Rural merchant	× Chinese Learning	✓ National Learning	✓ 'Dutch' Learning

✓ indicates institutions or groups that initiated or directly profited from the Restoration

× indicates institutions or groups that were destroyed or eclipsed by the Restoration

changes to be made from within the existing structure and its traditions, rather than from outside. In other words, the Meiji Restoration was neither a Norman Conquest nor a French Revolution. The preceding figure shows how, as the dominant elements in the old *baku-han* regime weakened, subordinate or alternative elements replaced them to prepare the way for what would follow. In general, the proponents of change both before and after 1868 came mainly from the middle and lower samurai ranks and from the rural merchants. The merchants of the cities and towns stood on the sidelines; and although Meiji society was destined to acquire bourgeois traits, for many years the bourgeoisie itself deferred to the other *élite* groups. All the active groups were, of course, in a sense one upper class. The great mass of the population, ninety per cent or so, had little or nothing to do with the national politics of the time. Surprisingly, the Kyōto Court, under Meiji's father Emperor Kōmei (1831–66), was generally antipathetic to the idea of a Restoration and only a small minority of courtiers actively intrigued against the *bakufu*.

Ideologically, the Restoration was propelled neither by an upsurge of spontaneous loyalty to the imperial house, nor by a sudden revulsion of feeling against the shogunate as an institution. Its main impetus before 1868 was nationalist xenophobia, felt first by young samurai and spreading to politically minded landlord-entrepreneurs in the villages. This *sonnō jōi* ('revere the emperor, expel the barbarian!') movement had been triggered by the unequal treaties, and the *bakufu* came under increasingly severe attack for being unable to stand up to the foreigners.

The importance of foreign policy as a factor in the Restoration has been under-played by modern historians both in the West, where people do not care to dwell on their own imperialism, and in Japan, where it runs counter to the preconceptions of nationalists and Marxists alike about the primacy of internal evolution and motivations. Probably something like the Restoration would have occurred by the end of the nineteenth century even if there had been no Western aggression, as knowledge of Western industry and the opportunities it offered became more widespread in Japan. Yet the fact remains that the most proximate cause of the Restoration was the failure of the *bakufu's* seclusion policy which dated from the pre-industrial age.

The industrial revolution, even in its early iron and steam phase, gave the West enormous technological superiority over the rest of the world and at the same time made the pressure for markets and resources ever more urgent. In Japan's case, the United States took the lead in opening up a hitherto unexploited region. The motivation was not so much a desire for trade with Japan, considered at the time a relatively poor country, as a wish to use Japanese ports for provisioning and sheltering American ships engaged in trade with China. There was also the problem of castaways, a category of persons not really catered for by the seclusion policy. Stranded Americans were closely confined before being shipped out of the country at Nagasaki, and rescued Japanese were difficult to repatriate. Finally, protestant nineteenth century America, that strange mixture of philanthropy and intolerance, was ready to resume the missionary tasks which seventeenth century catholic Portugal had been forced to relinquish.

American initiatives resulted in the despatch of a naval squadron of ten ships commanded by Commodore Matthew Perry. He carried a letter from President Fillmore to the Japanese emperor requesting trade and diplomatic relations, and approaching the shogunate directly, steamed unopposed into Edo Bay in the summer of 1853. The authorities in Edo, though forewarned by the Dutch king, were far from being forearmed, especially at sea. Perry delivered his letter, and promised to return for a reply the following year. The visit had been brief and polite, but there was no mistaking the menace of the 'black ships', and when Perry returned in 1854 the shogunate signed a preliminary treaty committing it to direct relations, but not trade, with the United States. In 1858, a full treaty of amity, commerce and navigation was concluded after much arduous negotiation by the first American consul, Townsend Harris. Treaties granting similar privileges were signed with Holland and the other European Powers, who tended to dominate Japan's relations with the outside world in the 1860s as the United States tore themselves apart in their first civil war.

In those days even major strokes of international diplomacy often had a rather leisurely air, and their domestic repercussions could take even longer to mature. Moreover, the shogunate generally kept control over external and internal developments until the assassination of its chief minister, Ii Naosuke (b. 1815) in 1860. Yet although fifteen years elapsed between Perry's first visit in 1853 and the Restoration of 1868, the foreign treaties were a kind of slow poison which gradually destroyed the *bakufu* by depriving it of its powers of independent decision.

Resistance to foreign demands was clearly foolhardy, as nothing could prevent the bombardment from the sea of Edo and other coastal towns. However, the humiliation and cultural shock arising from the sudden breaching of the seclusion policy, and even more from the one-sided nature of the treaties, exposed foreigners and *bakufu* alike not only to verbal wrath but also to the physical hostility of the *sonnō jōi* advocates. There were instances of murder, arson and open warfare, the most notorious being the 1862 killing of an Englishman, Richardson, by the samurai escort of the Satsuma *daimyō* on a highway just outside Yokohama, and the 1863 bombardment of foreign shipping in the straits of Shimonoseki by Chōshū batteries. The diplomatic repercussions included huge indemnities and direct reprisals by the Powers against the offending *han*. But they were hardly less damaging than domestic consequences; and the nadir of *bakufu* fortunes was reached when armies it raised to cow Chōshū in 1866 failed miserably, mainly through lack of zeal.

In order to placate domestic critics as well as strengthen their hand against foreign adversaries, the Edo authorities not unnaturally sought a national consensus in favour of either their decision to sign the treaties or a long-term policy of self-strengthening and ultimate opposition to the West. Consensus, however, implied consulting with the court and great *daimyō*, and treating them as relative equals in the making of decisions. This was something that had never happened before, and neither the courtiers nor the more assertive of the *daimyō* were slow to take advantage of a changed situation. The court, in fact, refused to confirm the treaties and at times argued for their abrogation. The shogunate found itself caught between two conflicting sets of pressures, foreign and domestic, neither of which it could resist on its own over a period of time. The dilemma was cruel, and one from which there was to be no escape.

Meiji Foreign Policy

Even before 1868 the loyalists in control of the western *han* had made contacts of one kind or another with the Powers, and one of the first actions of the Meiji government was to guarantee the existing treaties pending revision. Thus, with the Restoration, loyalist policy changed from the negative and introverted *sonnō jōi* stance to an acceptance of foreigners in Japan and a resolve 'to base actions on international usage'.[2] Helpful though this change of attitude was, it did nothing to solve the basic problem of the treaties.

[2] A legitimate rendering of the fourth clause of the Meiji charter oath. See p. 236.

The treaties were unequal because they prevented Japan from levying more than token customs duties on foreign imports, and because they removed resident foreigners from Japanese jurisdiction, subjecting them to their own country's laws as enforced by special consular courts. These provisions, as much a threat to Japan's economy as they were a violation of its sovereign rights, were concessions no Western State would have made to another Western State.

Consequently, for reasons of national prosperity and pride, treaty revision loomed large in Meiji era diplomacy. In its dealings with the Powers, the government tried a variety of approaches, and the crucial break-through was achieved when the British government agreed to a new and equal treaty in 1894. The other Powers quickly followed suit, thus terminating a situation of inequality and injustice that had lasted for more than forty years.

As a piece of history, treaty revision amounts to more than protracted diplomatic negotiations. Against all temptation and pressures the Meiji government stuck to its original aim of properly negotiated revision, rather than unilateral denunciation of the existing treaties. This showed its seriousness in abandoning the seclusion policy, and its commitment of Japan to open diplomacy and an appropriate place in the existing Power system. Moreover, although modernization would have occurred anyway, it must have been a powerful incentive to know that treaty revision could be accomplished only if Japanese legal and political institutions resembled those in the West.

The new attitudes were symbolized by the Rokumeikan (Hall of the Baying Stag), a pleasure pavilion which the government erected in the 1880s, and where the prime minister Itō Hirobumi (1841–1909), and his friend Inoue Kaoru (1835–1915) who was foreign minister, took the lead in entertaining Westerners. At this time Inoue was holding a series of general conferences on treaty revision, and the Rokumeikan and kindred festivities were meant to convince all concerned, in as agreeable a way as possible, that Japan was already sufficiently westernized to be treated as an equal.

The Prime Minister gave a fancy-dress ball in his own residence. Over four hundred guests took part. The Prime Minister appeared as a Venetian nobleman, Prince Arisugawa as a medieval European warrior, Inouye as a strolling musician, the Director of the Legislative Bureau as a mendicant Buddhist monk, the Chancellor of the University as a pilgrim to Buddhist shrines, the chief of the Metropolitan Police as Bingo Saburo, a loyal knight of early feudal history. The wives and daughters of these high officials appeared as romantic or poetic characters in Japanese legend and were much sought after as partners by the young foreign gentlemen, many of whom appeared in Japanese dress.[3]

As Sansom goes on to make clear, many people in and out of public life strongly disapproved of Rokumeikan diplomacy. In fact, Meiji foreign policy was always subject to pressures arising from dissentient opinion either within the government itself or in the country at large. Such opinion frequently turned out to be ill-informed or mischievous or both at once.

In addition to treaty revision, Meiji foreign policy concerned itself with frontier demarcation and national security, questions which affected relations with the three neighbouring countries of Korea, China and Russia. There was a desire, particularly in the second half of the era, to make economic as well as strategic use of Korea, and economic penetration was destined to extend beyond the peninsula into Manchuria, and into other parts of China. Quite apart from any strategic or economic considerations, both the people of Japan and their government realized that possession of an over-seas empire had become one of the badges of national greatness. In all these matters, the Meiji ministers showed good sense, if no particular virtue.

Negotiations led to a frontier agreement with Russia in 1875 whereby Japan surrendered its claims to Sakhalin in return for the Kurile Islands. Hokkaidō's territorial status had never really been disputed, but this agreement implicitly confirmed Japanese sovereignty over that island. About the same time, in 1879, the Ryūkyū (Okinawan) Islands, which had been a dependency of Satsuma since early in the seventeenth century but also maintained a tributary relationship with China, were incorporated in mainland Japan by having the prefectural system extended to them. The local king, Shō Tai, whose family had ruled the islands since the fifteenth century, was brought to Tōkyō and made a pensioner of the Japanese court. The Meiji government had already notified the world of its possessive attitude towards Okinawa, when it sent a punitive expedition to Taiwan in 1874 to exact vengeance for attacks by Taiwanese natives on Okinawan fishing vessels.

Relations with Korea were put on a formal footing by the treaty of Kanghwa in 1876, agreed on only after Japan had used a certain

[3] Sansom, *The Western World and Japan*, p. 389.

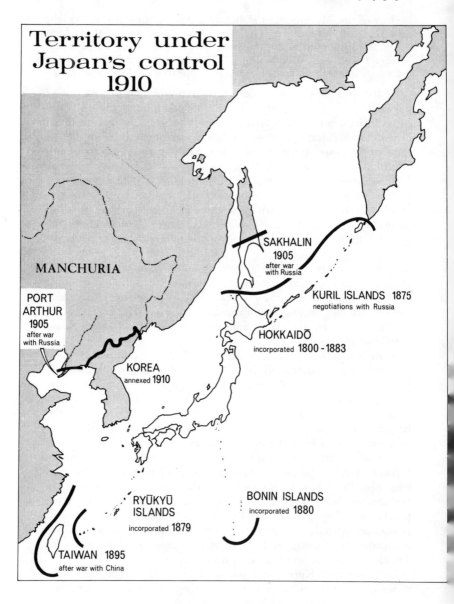

Territory under Japan's control 1910

MANCHURIA

PORT ARTHUR 1905 after war with Russia

KOREA annexed 1910

SAKHALIN 1905 after war with Russia

KURIL ISLANDS 1875 negotiations with Russia

HOKKAIDŌ incorporated 1800 - 1883

RYŪKYŪ ISLANDS incorporated 1879

BONIN ISLANDS incorporated 1880

TAIWAN 1895 after war with China

amount of force. Thereafter Korean domestic politics, truly those of an impoverished and backward country, were given over to struggles between a conservative, China-leaning faction and a progressive, Japan-oriented faction. In 1894, Japan, having sent troops of her own to the peninsula, denounced the presence of a Chinese army in Korea, and Chinese reluctance to co-operate in reforming the country's administration. China refused to conciliate her rival, and in the ensuing war was rapidly and soundly defeated both on land and at sea. Under the treaty of Shimonoseki, signed in April 1895, Japan received a handsome indemnity and the large and potentially productive island of Taiwan. It looked for a while as if the victor would also obtain strategically important concessions on the mainland; but in a diplomatic manoeuvre known as the triple intervention, Russia, Germany and France prevented Japan from making territorial gains at China's expense while they themselves did so.

Meanwhile Korea, now free from overt Chinese influence and nominally independent, found itself exposed to Japanese economic exploitation and political guidance. The latter was often ham-fisted and occasionally gave rise to acts of brutality like the murder of a recalcitrant queen in 1895, plotted by senior Japanese officials in Seoul without the knowledge of the Tōkyō government. Anti-Japanese elements in Korea, having been disappointed by China, turned for possible succour to Russia. That country, with the building of the trans-Siberian railway in the 1890s, had been following an aggressively expansionist policy in north-east Asia and was by 1900 the dominant Power in Manchuria. The tsar and his advisers showed themselves equally eager to extend their influence into Korea but, not unnaturally, this development was keenly contested by the Japanese. Negotiations having failed, war broke out in 1904.

The Russo-Japanese War of 1904–5 was far more sustained and serious than the conflict with China had been ten years previously. Two hundred thousand Japanese and some three hundred thousand Russians lost their lives or were wounded in the land fighting, which took place in Manchuria. The Japanese troops, led by General Nogi Maresuke (1849–1912), gradually won the upper hand. After capturing the great Russian stronghold at Port Arthur in January 1905 following a seven month siege, they went on to their final triumph at Mukden in central Manchuria. Throughout the hostilities, the seas between Japan and the mainland were dominated by the Japanese navy, which won a historic victory when Admiral Tōgō ʻHeihachirō (1847–1934) intercepted and destroyed a Russian relief fleet near the island of Tsushima in May 1905. The American president, Theodore Roosevelt, acted as an intermediary in the subsequent peace negotiations. In the treaty of Portsmouth (New Hampshire) Russia agreed to cede southern Sakhalin and Port Arthur, together with its surrounding territory, to Japan. Korea now became a Japanese protectorate, with Itō Hirobumi as the first resident-general, and was eventually annexed outright in 1910.

Thus, the Meiji era ended on a note of resounding diplomatic success. Treaty revision had been accomplished; the national frontiers were clearly defined and made secure. Japan's army and navy had acquitted themselves well in two major wars, and it was generally recognized that Japan had a 'natural' sphere of influence in north-east Asia. This recognition lay behind the Anglo-Japanese alliance of 1902, whereby Britain acknowledged Japan's interests in Korea in return for Japan's acceptance of British predominance in the Yangtze valley and, when the alliance was renegotiated three years later, British rule of India. To both Powers, Russia loomed as a mutual enemy. In its progress to Power status, Japan had acquired two important colonies: Taiwan (Formosa) and Korea. The former, whose inhabitants were hardly conscious of themselves as a nation, was governed bureaucratically but on the whole justly and benefici- ally. The latter received the economic and educational infra- structure of modernization from its new masters, but at a heavy price in terms of political oppression and frustrated nationalism. Meanwhile, north of the Yalu river, the spacious and sparsely populated land of Manchuria lay open to Japanese commerce and industry.

Yet all that glisters is not gold. Though in retrospect it looked as if the Meiji statesmen had been following a carefully conceived, long-term plan with regard to Korea, this was not in fact the case. They often reacted to, rather than anticipated, events, and in general vacillated between contradictory policies of firmness and conciliation. Moreover, the government always had to deal with public opinion several times more bellicose than it cared to be itself. The terms of both the Shimonoseki and Portsmouth peace treaties, for example, caused deep dissatisfaction in Japan, and Tōkyō had to be put under martial law when the latter were announced because of popular disturbances.

Most serious of all, however, was the fact that Japan had come of age in a Great Power civilization which, though outwardly stable and brilliant, was riddled with national hatreds and rivalries. Given this global community and the fact that the Chinese and Russian empires continued to weaken rapidly, the emergence of a new Power necessarily created new tensions. Moreover, from Meiji times Japanese diplomacy had a background of unquestioned nationalism in theory and a marked tendency toward opportunism in practice. Neither of these factors did anything to ease the tensions of a world where war was still thought to be a legitimate extension of diplomacy.

Economic Policies and the Beginnings of Industrialization

In terms of the future, the most important decisions of the Meiji leaders were taken in the field of economic policy. Within a few years of the Restoration the new government had expanded the limited Tokugawa experiments with foreign technology into a pervasive and self-perpetuating programme of economic modernization. In so doing, it rejected the essentially defensive mentality behind the early efforts at shipbuilding and gun-casting in favour of a broader industrialization virtually for its own sake, to the detriment of the traditional social and political ordering of society. A few other countries—notably China and Turkey—were in the same position as Japan in the mid-nineteenth century, but none set out to remedy it so boldly or with such effect. Even in the case of Japan, it is hard to believe that the Meiji leaders at first understood all the implications of what they were doing. They saw industry and a modern economy as roads to national security and national greatness, but their policies were to carry the country far beyond these objectives.

Whatever the degree of their personal commitment to modernization, the samurais' traditional managerial functions made them ideal sponsors of the changes contemplated. History has probably had no class better suited for the task of planning deliberate economic transformation. Yet samurai guidance, however talented, would have been frustrated if the common people had been incapable of following; and the role of the latter in promoting economic modernization, though more difficult to trace in detail, should not be minimized. The development in Tokugawa times of towns and a system of manufacture and commerce that extended throughout the countryside was crucial. As well as fostering devices like credit and bills of exchange and semi-permanent business connexions between principals who might never see each other, Tokugawa development had endowed the general populace with what was, for a traditional society, a high degree of literacy and an abundance of the kind of manual skills associated with handicrafts. Moreover, and perhaps most importantly, the Meiji Japanese inherited a spirit of entrepreneurship which was particularly strong among the richer peasants. Indeed, rural villages remained the main source of production until the late nineteenth century.

More immediate factors also operated as spurs to economic modernization. There was a problem of adverse foreign trade and consequent outflow of gold and silver, as the Japanese soon developed an irrepressible liking for foreign goods. Given Japan's inability to impose protective tariffs, the only remedy was to develop modern industries and so enlarge the range of goods available for export. In addition, only modern methods could save domestic handicraft industries from obliteration by cheaper Western machine products. Finally, the government showed itself anxious to start new industries in order to help the samurai. On the one hand it had decided, correctly, that it could not afford to go on paying hereditary pensions and that samurai everywhere would have to engage in gainful employment. On the other hand, it had no desire to bring about the complete ruin of a class to which the majority of its own members belonged and which it regarded, again correctly, as the hope of the nation.

The government, having decided in principle on a modern economy, had to assume responsibility for the introduction both of new industries and of new methods in old industries like agriculture and textiles. The requisite techniques were entirely foreign, and only the State could afford to pay the princely salaries of the foreign experts hired as advisers, and to arrange for the regular despatch of Japanese students abroad. Either approach would have tapped a plentiful supply of expertise, but this was not an age when a backward country could expect free aid from more advanced societies, with the exception of missionary services. Apart from the special problem of actually importing knowledge, shortages of domestic capital led to a situation in which the new technology, in its early stages, had to be largely financed as well as planned by the bureaucracy. The great merchant houses which had survived from Tokugawa days were reluctant to supply money for projects such as railways. The rural merchants were more venturesome but lacked funds.

Hokkaidō stands out as the prime example of government initi-

Tōkyō–Yokohama railway, built 1873

Emperor Meiji on his way to open the first Diet, 1890

Children with paper carp streamers for soldiers at the front, March 1943

Kōbe under the Occupation, 1946

ative. Hitherto it had barely been exploited outside its southernmost district around Matsumae. The Meiji government encouraged settlers, especially from northern Honshū, and samurai were given considerable financial inducement to emigrate with their families as *tondenhei* (soldier-settlers), dividing their time between routine military training and agricultural labour. At the same time, the government developed Hokkaidō's mineral resources (especially coal), its timber, and its fisheries, and it sought not only to extend the zone of rice-growing as far north as climate and improved seed would allow, but also to make use of the island's pastures for a dairy industry along Western lines. The responsibility for laying the foundations of Hokkaidō's economic future, as well as for the territory's day to day administration, were entrusted to a special public authority, the Hokkaidō Development Board (*Kaitakushi*). The *Kaitakushi* went to work with a will under the able supervision of one of the more important ministers of State, Kuroda Kiyotaka (1840–1900). When its ten year charter expired in 1881, roads and harbours had been built, a great deal of land cleared, and the city of Sapporo founded as headquarters of an effective local government. Immigrants had begun to arrive in appreciable numbers, and thereafter the island's population and supporting economy grew of their own momentum. Before long, a particularly delicious brew of beer (barley-based and new to Japan) figured in its list of noted products.

Elsewhere, though the government intelligently planned the country's modernization and was prepared to finance it generously, the concrete results on a scale large enough to affect the overall situation only came slowly. In the field of communications, the electric telegraph was the first widespread innovation. By 1885, the government was operating a system that virtually covered the country, making it possible, for example, for newspapers to relay news from all districts. In the same year the Mitsubishi Company formed the *Nihon Yūsen Kaisha* (Japan Mailship Company), with strong official backing. Mitsubishi had its origins in shipping in the early 1870s and already ran regular services to certain Chinese ports and to Vladivostok. *NYK* was destined to grow into one of the world's biggest shipping firms; its chief rival, the *Ōsaka Shōsen Kaisha*, had been founded two or three years earlier.

Despite these promising developments in the early 1880s, the total tonnage of merchant ships under the Japanese flag did not grow very markedly until about the turn of the century.

Year	Modern Ships (in thousand gross tons)
1872	26
1880	66
1890	143
1896	363
1903	657
1913	1,514

Modern vessels for the imperial navy as well as the merchant marine were nearly all purchased overseas. The spectacular rise of modern ship-building had to wait for the establishment of a modern steel industry, just as the mechanization of hundreds of thousands of fishing craft followed the development of the internal combustion engine. However, the Meiji government was able to forge ahead with an unobtrusive but vital programme of harbour improvements and navigational aids.

The first Japanese railways had to be government planned, owing to a lack of private capital or technological skills. In 1872 the emperor opened an eighteen-mile line between Yokohama and Tōkyō which had been built by British engineers with a loan raised in Britain. Twelve years later, Japan still had only seventy-six miles of track, the new sections connecting Kyōto with the ports of Kōbe, to the west, and Ōtsu, on Lake Biwa, to the east. The Kyōto-Ōtsu line, all ten miles of it, built in 1880, was the first constructed without foreign help. In 1879 the government decided to sponsor a private company, the *Nihon Tetsudō Kaisha* (The Japan Railway Company) to share the expenses of railway development. However, the first *NTK* line did not open until 1884. It connected Tōkyō with Maebashi, sixty-six miles away across the Kantō plain at the foot of the Japan Alps, and was built by government engineers, with the help of a government loan. Thereafter a number of successful private companies were formed, and a boom in railway construction occurred as they took over from the government. By 1891, it was possible to travel by rail all the way from Aomori, in the far north of Honshū, to Tōkyō, and on to Kōbe. Nevertheless a truly national network did not come into existence until the first decades of this century.

Year	Mileage of Track
1872	18
1883	240
1887	640

1894	2,100
1904	4,700
1914	7,100

Mines were in private as well as government hands, but private companies tended to be small and not very productive. The government had inherited many of its enterprises from the *bakufu*, but by 1868 places like the Sado gold and silver mines were badly run down. With foreign advice, the situation gradually improved.

Year	Gold	Silver
	in kilograms	
1868	85.6	1,680
1890	204.8	3,370
1911	572.6	5,266

Total production of gold, silver and lead never amounted to very much by world standards, but at the beginning of this century Japan ranked fourth in world copper production. One of the most important sources of copper was the Ashio mine (Tochigi prefecture), not far from Nikkō. At the time of the Restoration it was virtually abandoned, and soon passed into the hands of Furukawa Ichibei (1832–1903). Furukawa, reputed to have started his working life as a street pedlar, proved to be a businessman of genius. Installing modern machinery and pumps and later electrifying the mine, he increased its annual production from fifty-three tons in 1877 to six thousand four hundred tons in 1901. About 1917, production stood at approximately fifteen thousand tons *per annum*.

Coalfields in northern Kyūshū and central Hokkaidō were also exploited for what they were worth. The coal was not of particularly good quality, but was used for railways, ships, and a variety of industrial purposes, and its existence in workable quantities persuaded the government to begin iron and steel production in areas where it was found, after the turn of the century. This industry eventually grew to be one of the pillars of the new economy, though it was slow to start and encountered all sorts of difficulties in its early years.

While iron and steel and the industries they made possible had a bright future as a result of initiatives taken in the Meiji period, textile manufacture was the dominant industry of the era itself. A quick change occurred in silk-making, where the transition from hand to machine reeling was well under way by the 1880s, a result as much of private enterprise as of official guidance. Traditional sericulture was well established and its product cheaper than foreign thread and as easily used in a modern mill. Domestic cotton yarn, on the other hand, was relatively expensive and unsuitable for machine spinning, and it took time to organize regular imports from India and America. Moreover, while the technique of machine silk-reeling was similar to traditional methods, the skills needed to operate cotton-spinning machinery were totally unfamiliar. However, in 1878 the government raised a domestic loan to buy cotton machinery in England. Most of this machinery was resold to Japanese entrepreneurs on easy terms, but two thousand spindles were kept for two model mills which the government opened in 1881 at Ohira (Aichi prefecture) and 1882 at Kamiseno (Hiroshima prefecture). In order to accelerate modernization through importing machinery, the government organized a general conference of cotton-spinners in 1880. Thereafter the number of modern factories and spindles began to increase: the latter from 8,000 in 1877 to 77,000 in 1887; to 971,000 in 1897; and to 2,415,000 in 1913. By way of contrast, woollen cloth remained a luxury import throughout the Meiji period. The one government mill at Senjū (Tōkyō, 1877) and the few private mills in Tōkyō and Ōsaka relied heavily on government orders for such things as uniforms and army blankets.

Economic modernization in the Meiji period did not just consist of the discrete importation of separate industries and techniques. An entire society was about to be radically changed; such things as fiscal reform and the development of modern banking were also involved.

Fiscal reform meant unification of the currency, which was in a chaotic state by the time of the Restoration, with *han* paper notes and new and old *bakufu* coinage all circulating. The government minted standard coins to replace the Edo period issues; and after 1885 only the Bank of Japan (established by the government in 1882) could print notes, with the result that other types of paper money gradually disappeared.

A second aim of fiscal reform, full convertibility of paper money into gold and silver coin, was harder to achieve. The government constantly spent more than it received in revenues, and specie left the country to pay for imports. Both these conditions gave rise to rapid inflation and depreciation of government paper money, a condition made even worse by the financial strain of defeating armed uprisings. However, after 1880 a new finance minister, Matsukata

Masayoshi (1835–1924), followed a rigorous policy of retrenchment and deflation, withdrawing much of the paper money the government had been forced to print a few years before. As a result, the value of notes remaining in circulation rose in terms of gold and silver until they stood at par. In 1886, paper yen were made convertible into silver yen, and eleven years later, with the help of the post-war indemnity from China, Japanese currency was made fully convertible into gold, in keeping with the best economic theories of the time.

Inevitably, tax reform also figured as a major preoccupation of the early Meiji period, and a new, uniform system of land and other taxes replaced the various *baku-han* imposts. The government had all taxable land surveyed afresh, giving each plot an assessed value that was rather arbitrarily related to its supposed yield. Taxes were then levied as percentages of this assessed value, and responsiblity for paying them rested with the owner, not necessarily the cultivator, of the plot. Land-tax was charged at three per cent of the assessed value *per annum* until 1877 and two and a half per cent thereafter. During its initial year or two, and again after 1884, the new system seems to have yielded roughly the equivalent of the old taxes. Inflation in the late 1870s hurt the authorities in a number of ways, by no means the least being a sharp reduction in the real value of taxes based on a fixed assessment. Conversely, farmers prospered when the price of their produce rose but not their taxes. The land-tax paid for most of Japan's early modernization, and was the largest single source of revenue until the turn of the century.

Period (fiscal years)	Land-tax as Percentage of Ordinary Revenue
1868–1881	78
1890	50
1897	30

The efforts to establish a modern banking system largely depended on policies for currency reform and underwent similar vicissitudes. In 1872, new regulations were promulgated setting up national banks. This was the result of a recommendation from Itō Hirobumi, who two years before had been sent to the United States to report on the national banks recently introduced there. The Japanese institutions were to be indirectly under official control, but their working capital was to come from private individuals and concerns, and they were authorized to issue their own convertible bank-notes.

The system of national banks was sound enough on paper, but was soon overtaken by the political and economic turbulence of the 1870s. Revision of the regulations, allowing the national banks to exchange their notes for unconvertible government notes and so conserve their reserves of the precious metals, helped save the situation. So did the government's commutation of all *daimyō* and samurai pensions into interest-bearing bonds, a measure which substantially increased the amount of private wealth available for deposit in banks. Following these changes, which took place in 1876, national banks flourished. Though many of the ventures were too small to be viable, by 1882 there were one hundred and forty-three of them in operation.

Private banks, which were not subject to detailed official regulation but could not issue their own notes, also developed fairly quickly after the Mitsui Company founded the first in 1876. There were several hundred in existence in 1890, when the government issued regulations within which they could operate on a trustworthy basis. These regulations, which also affected the national banks, were enforced from 1893. At about the same time the government decided not to renew the charters of the national banks as they ran out towards the end of the century. As a result, by 1899 most of them had been converted into private banks, and the rest were dissolved.

Banking, currency, textiles, mining, railways, shipping, all show the same basic features. First, the tempo of development was slow. The foundations, but no more than the foundations, of an industrial economy had been securely laid by the end of the century. It is easy, but mistaken, to think that Japan industrialized overnight.

Secondly, government leadership in planning, financing, and operating early ventures was probably crucial to the success of industrialization. The Meiji period established a close and enduring relationship between the bureaucracy and modern business which in many ways anticipated twentieth century trends in other industrialized countries. Yet Meiji authorities never envisaged permanent State ownership of industry. They saw it only as a temporary device to hasten the development of privately owned industries. Whenever possible (and perhaps in some cases sooner than they would have done had they had more cash at their disposal) they transferred factories, mines, and public utilities like the *Kaitakushi* to private hands.

Thirdly, the new industries, whether State or privately owned, for many years hardly paid their way. They had to be massively supported by funds collected from the traditional or agricultural sector of the economy, which already directly sustained about eighty per cent of the population. There has been some controversy recently about the exact extent of increases in rural production.[4] Whatever the case, and despite the collapse of markets for such major traditional cash crops as cotton, dye-plants, and vegetable oils, total output in the Meiji period was sufficient to pay for the new industries, and to provide people in the cities as well as the villages with food and other necessities. Furthermore, although the population grew from approximately thirty million in 1868 to approximately fifty million in 1912, its standard of living also rose, albeit slowly and unevenly.

With holdings remaining small and mechanization virtually non-existent, agriculture continued to be a matter of hard labour with hand and foot. In view of the prior claims of secondary industry, the government could do little to alleviate this situation by diverting large sums into primary industry for subsidies or expensive research stations. However, it did set up properly staffed agricultural bureaux down to the prefectural level, and using these to propagate relatively inexpensive means of improving production, it generally and effectively sought to have the peasants help themselves.[5] Villagers tilled more land; bought more effective, imported fertilizer; planted their rice in straight lines to make cultivation easier; and selected better strains of seed. Above all, the more enterprising continued to diversify to products other than rice, and to enlarge the scope of local business to include such things as banking, insurance, and local railway building. Fishing and forestry showed a similar capacity for expansion. In all this it is easy to see the continuing importance of the traditional village *élite* of big farmers and rural merchants.

Individual responsiveness to the general economic advance was true of Meiji secondary industry as well; Furukawa Ichibei, the copper king, was no solitary monument to entrepreneurial success. Other members of the new industrial and business *élite* were Iwasaki Yatarō (1838–85) and Shibusawa Eiichi (1840–1931). The former, a country samurai from Tosa, founded the Mitsubishi Company more or less single-handed, and his business was destined to grow into one of the world's biggest. The latter was a farmer's son, with

[4] Rosovsky, 'Rumbles in the Ricefields. Professor Nakamura vs. the Official Statistics', *Journal of Asian Studies*, Vol. XXVII, No. 2.
[5] Cf. Dore, 'Agricultural Improvement in Japan: 1870–1900' in *Economic Change and Cultural Development*, Vol. 9, No. 1, Pt. II.

a flair for banking, who introduced modern business techniques to Japan, including the joint stock enterprise. Shibusawa naturally took the role of persuader, and most of his business positions were advisory or honorary. Iwasaki, on the other hand, had more than a touch of masterfulness; he gloried in overcoming opposition, and doggedly kept Mitsubishi under his close personal control. The careers of both men helped make big business respectable by showing how it could be of service to the State. They were also alike in combining the new techniques introduced by the opening of Japan with a marked reliance on traditional ethics: in Iwasaki's case, the samurai urge for personal distinction and utter commitment to the job in hand; in Shibusawa's case, a Confucian concern that private enrichment should enhance, and not conflict with, the general welfare.

In the last analysis, however, modern Japan was not the creation of statesmen and business tycoons. The people finished what their government and other leaders had started and the innumerable innovations, however small, made by individual citizens, helped materially to push their society into its new age. Professor Lockwood has drawn attention to this, suggesting that local, piecemeal improvements were every bit as significant for national development as large-scale plans.[6]

Domestic Politics and the Transition to Constitutional Rule

In politics, as in economics, the Meiji era was characterized by openness, willingness to experiment and innovate, and its rewards to men of exceptional ability. Though the technology and underlying ideas of the Western civilization to which Japan was so powerfully attracted already existed, it was left to the Japanese to discover how they could be absorbed into a non-Western society. Since theirs was the first country to attempt such modernization, they had no model except, perhaps, dim memories of a distant Taika Reform. From this point of view, the assimilation of Western ways was as much creative as imitative.

The inauguration of constitutional forms of government in 1889 is both a notable illustration of this process, and the focal point of the era's political history after the initial upheaval of the Restoration. By creating a national Diet (parliament) and an independent

[6] Lockwood, *The Economic Development of Japan*, pp. 17–18. Also Ward and Rustow (eds.), *Political Modernization in Japan and Turkey*, p. 119.

judiciary, the ruling officials in effect agreed to share their hitherto untrammelled powers. In the courts, they now had to defer to the decisions of professional judges with whose appointments they could not tamper. In the legislature, they had to win the approval of law-makers who owed their positions to accidents of birth or public election. Most onerously, they had to take account of the activities and attitudes of political parties, already formed in anticipation of the developments of 1889.

In themselves, of course, and in the wider context of European civilization, respresentative assemblies and the separation of judicial power from the other functions of government were nothing new; and because their beliefs and practices do have a certain universal value, Westerners have often thought they are somehow natural and easy to adopt. However, the experiences of countries which have become independent since the second world war, to say nothing of older States like Turkey and the nations of Latin America, show that this is not so. Indeed, the inherent difficulty in transplanting the ideas of liberty and parliamentary democracy, together with the appropriate legal systems, into an alien environment underscores Meiji Japan's achievements in this respect. Even in this case, the record was not without fault, and the end result imperfect. But it should be remembered that the Meiji leaders, often for reasons that lay outside the field of constitutional policy, wished to preserve as well as to liberalize. Moreover, they saw that to endure, Japanese constitutionalism had to be adapted to Japanese antecedents and conditions.

Meiji society's political life contended with many pressures, including violence. Pressures arose from the legacy of traditional thought and institutions; from a sense of competition with the West; from conditions newly generated within the country as the great transformation got under way; and, last but not least, from the fact that the government was never a solidly unified *bloc*, but always a coalition of different and sometimes competing interests.

Compositeness and a mood of expediency were particularly marked at the very beginning of the era, when the loyalist politicians from Satsuma, Chōshū, Tosa and Hizen had little to unite them or rally the rest of the country. Their government lacked funds and was fighting a war. Moreover, its own structure represented a strange mixture of improvisation and antiquarianism, since the Restoration had brought into fresh prominence not only the throne but an array of court titles and institutions that went back to the Nara period. Most of the senior posts in the new administration were filled in a purely ornamental way by members of the imperial family, aristocrats, and *daimyō*. However, membership of the Council of State (named but not exactly patterned after the old *Dajōkan*) quickly came to include all the important, and relatively young, retainers from the western *han* who had been the real power behind the Restoration. With ability beginning to replace birth as the chief criterion for high public office, these men before long were appointed titular as well as effective ministers of State.

The Meiji government, ever conscious of its weaknesses as of its strengths, was usually anxious to conciliate opponents, actual or potential. As early as April 1868, in a solemn ceremony in the palace in Kyōto, it had the emperor issue what turned out be one of the major State documents of the reign. This took the form of an oath, sworn by the monarch to the gods (*kami*), which foreshadowed in a general but pertinent way the basic trends and crucial policies of the next four or five decades. Deliberative assemblies, freedom of residence and occupation, abolition of hereditary classes, and full cultural contact with the West were either explicitly or implicitly promised. Because of its literally epoch-making qualities, the pronouncement of April 1868 has come to be called the 'charter oath' by Western writers. Japanese works refer to it by the more modest title of 'the five article oath'; and it is possible that it was originally intended to do no more than provide general reassurance in conditions of widespread uncertainty. However, this does not explain its subdued but unmistakably revolutionary tone; and after political strife broke out it acquired all the portentous authority of a charter, as both government and opposition used its pledges to justify their respective standpoints.

By 1870, the government's situation had improved. Six months earlier it had won the War of the Restoration, formal relations with the Powers were cordial, and it was circumspectly going ahead with revolutionary plans to replace the *han* with prefectures and to recruit commoners for its army by means of conscription. Domains that had not already been voluntarily returned to the throne were eventually abolished by decree in August 1871, and conscription regulations went into force from 1872. Together, these two measures effectively buried the old order of local autonomy and samurai privilege.

That times were changing was brought home to the former ruling class by laws forbidding the warrior hair-style and the wearing of swords in public. Deprived of their traditional privileges as a martial

and bureaucratic *élite* and outraged by the government's westernizing proclivities, the samurai then had to accept commutation of
their hereditary pensions. Not only were they deceived and dis-
honoured in their own eyes, but the threat of destitution hung over
them.

In all these actions the government was acting in the interests of
the nation as a whole. But its policies inevitably aroused the resentment of most of the two million or so members of the samurai class.
Matters came to a head with the decision, taken in the summer of
1873, not to go to war with Korea over that country's contemptuous
refusal to enter into diplomatic relations with a westernizing Japan.
Saigō Takamori, the leader of the pro-war party in the Council and
a man widely considered to be the embodiment of military virtues,
resigned in disgust, and left Tōkyō for his native Satsuma. There he
became ever more deeply associated with samurai reaction and local
defiance of the central authorities. Another important figure in the
government, the Hizen retainer Etō Shimpei (1834–74), similarly
withdrew to his former *han* which recently had become Saga
prefecture.

The rising of dissatisfied samurai, which Etō led in Saga the
following year, was a small-scale affair and quickly suppressed. But
it was one of a number of similar disturbances that culminated in
the full-scale Satsuma rebellion from February to November 1877.
Twenty thousand or so Satsuma *shizoku* (former samurai) set out to
march to Tōkyō under the leadership of Saigō Takamori, intending
to take over the administration and revert to the traditional order
and attitudes. They got as far as Kumamoto in central Kyūshū,
where the castle garrison under General Tani Kanjō withstood a
siege of four to six weeks. Meanwhile, the government's conscripts
entered the fray with their rifles and gradually drove the two-
sworded rebels back to Kagoshima, finally crushing them at the
battle of Shiroyama. The Satsuma rebellion was by far the most
severe ordeal the Meiji authorities had to face, and they emerged
from it greatly strengthened, in that the futility of armed opposition
to their rule had been clearly demonstrated. On the other hand,
victory had cost much in time and treasure.

Itagaki Taisuke (1837–1919), Gotō Shōjirō, and a few other Tosa
officials had also left the government in protest against the failure
to take a strong line on Korea. This group of highly placed malcontents decided to launch a political campaign, rather than an
armed attack, on their erstwhile colleagues. In this way the Liberty

and Popular Rights Movement (*Jiyū Minken Undō*) was born, publishing its first demand for a written constitution and a national assembly early in 1874. Tosa had· been the scene of mounting interest in French and English political philosophy since the early 1860s, but Itagaki himself was a somewhat late convert to a Liberalism which he never ceased to regard in a nationalistic and collectivist manner. Nevertheless, once converted, he remained true to what he understood to be its basic principles, bringing to the cause considerable gifts of intellect and a marked capacity for political leadership.

Using Tosa regional and *shizoku* discontents as a nucleus, he and Gotō built a national association of Liberal groups which they called the *Aikokusha* (Patriotic League). The *Aikokusha* had its headquarters in Ōsaka. In addition to its original *shizoku* sponsors, it attracted support from the rural landlord-entrepreneurs who had to pay the land-tax, and from the small but growing modern business and professional urban middle class. The Liberals campaigned ardently for a constitution and national assembly through speeches, journalism and direct petitions to the throne. They were often in trouble with the authorities, but this did not deflect them from their course. It was appreciated in all political quarters that the strength of the government's opponents came from their *élite* support and the Western modishness of their doctrines. They also derived moral sustenance from the first article of the charter oath, which ran: 'assemblies widely convoked shall be established, and all matters decided by public opinion'.

The Liberty and Popular Rights Movement was active and influential. But it is wrong to think that the government's decision to inaugurate a constitution came about solely as a defensive response to Liberal pressure, even though this is the guise in which Meiji political history has frequently been presented. Immediately after the swearing of the charter oath a makeshift written constitution (*seitaisho*) was introduced, together with deliberative assemblies of *daimyō* and *han* samurai representatives (*kogisho*). But this proved to be premature, and the first stages of modernization too revolutionary for such devices to work, and they were soon allowed to lapse.

After the departures of 1873, since Iwakura came to spend most of his time in his villa in Kyōto, the two most prominent ministers were Kido Kōin (1833–77) and Ōkubo Toshimichi. The former resigned, however, in 1874 because he disagreed strongly with the expedition his colleague had arranged against inhabitants of Taiwan who interfered with Japanese fishermen. Ōkubo's real motive was to appease the martial ardour of discontented samurai, and he had sufficient strength of will to go ahead, regardless of opposition. Yet he was never a despot in the sense that he wished to govern forever in Bismarckian isolation. No Japanese in the Meiji period or afterwards entertained such ambitions.

In general, Ōkubo laboured to increase the power of the Tōkyō administration, and in particular the authority of the home ministry of which he was head, by policies of fiscal and bureaucratic centralization that tied the provinces to the metropolis. He also firmly believed in economic modernization. Ōkubo's basic philosophy of government had been formed during his period of high office in Satsuma immediately before the Restoration. But the particular policies he followed in the later period of his life, when responsible for the whole of the country and not just a part of it, were confirmed, if not actually conceived, as a result of the personal experience of Western civilization gained in 1872 and 1873 as one of the large party of senior officials who accompanied Iwakura Tomomi on an extensive tour of North America and Europe.

During his travels, Ōkubo had been specially impressed by England's combination of industrial and commercial energy with political strength and stability. This happy state of affairs he attributed to Liberalism which, he felt, allowed Englishmen to feel individually responsible for the welfare of their country and to enhance its general good while pursuing private interests. Consequently, Ōkubo returned home favouring an eventual written constitution for Japan that would clearly define and delimit political authority, in order to provide the people with legal protection against bureaucratic arbitrariness and the incentive to co-operate actively with their government. Though this seemed a somewhat revolutionary idea, Ōkubo's concern clearly sprang from an interest in administrative and social efficiency rather than any deep philosophical conviction about individual rights.[7]

While Ōkubo was putting his ideas about the nation's future political structure on paper sometime in the years 1873–4, another member of the Iwakura mission, Kido Kōin, reported to the throne his view that the country should not only have a written constitution but gradually prepare itself for a parliament as well.

In enlightened countries, though there may be a sovereign, still he does not hold sway in arbitrary fashion. The people of the

[7] See Beckmann, *The Making of the Meiji Constitution*, pp. 111–19.

whole country give expression to their united and harmonious wishes, and the business of the State is arranged accordingly.[8]

Kido's reasoning resembled Ōkubo's, and Itagaki's for that matter, in that it was basically statist. Liberalism appealed as a means of building a strong State based on a loyal, because contented, population. Nevertheless, behind his words it is also possible to detect on occasion a concern for purely individual ends and interests.

Ōkubo's and Kido's memoranda preceded by several years the burgeoning of the Liberty and Popular Rights Movement; and it is clear that the government, as represented by two of its most senior ministers, of its own volition and independently of the Liberals, was coming to the conclusion that Japan should eventually have a Western-type constitution. Ōkubo, in fact, felt his political isolation after 1873 and, with the help of some younger members of the Council of State, attempted to reconcile himself with his former colleagues. Saigō proved obdurate, but his differences of outlook with Kido had never been very deep and at a series of meetings in Ōsaka in February 1875 known as the Ōsaka Conference, Ōkubo came to an agreement with both him and Itagaki. The result was a rescript, dated 14 April 1875, in which the emperor solemnly declared that he intended to abide by the charter oath and to establish a constitutional form of government 'by degrees'.[9]

Yet after 1876 there was another period of pause and uncertainty. Kido was dying; Itagaki resigned once again in protest against the government's determination to hasten slowly on the question of a constitution, and over everything hung the threat of Saigō's hostility and Satsuma truculence. The great rebellion took up most of 1877, and Itagaki had difficulty in restraining his more radical followers from joining in. The next year Ōkubo himself was dead, assassinated because he had 'monopolized power' and, ironically, while he was preparing legislation to permit elected local government assemblies.

Events took a new turn with the resignation of Ōkuma Shigenobu (1838–1922) from the government in the autumn of 1881. For some time previously a revived *Aikokusha* had been vociferously demanding popular rights. In 1879, Iwakura suggested that the emperor ask each of his ministers for a written opinion on the question of future constitutional developments. Virtually all the replies favoured persisting with the existing '1875' policy of gradual advance to full

[8] McLaren, 'Japanese Government Documents', p. 572.
[9] Mason, *Japan's First General Election, 1890*, p. 215.

constitutionalism. In particular, both Itō Hirobumi and Yamagata Aritomo (1838–1922) expressed themselves cogently on the inevitability of some form of liberalism in Japan, though arguing that the government should continue to give itself plenty of time to prepare.

Ōkuma delayed his memorandum and when he did submit it, his colleagues were stunned to read that he proposed the election of a national assembly within two years and the transfer of powers of government to the leaders of its largest party. Iwakura and the others regarded such views as extreme and their author as little better than a renegade. At the same time, Ōkuma was estranged from his fellows in the Council, because as finance minister he opposed the proposed sale of *Kaitakushi* installations in Hokkaidō at a low price to a company with which Kuroda Kiyotaka was associated. News of Ōkuma's standpoints on the constitutional and *Kaitakushi* issues became public. He found himself a popular hero, and the Liberty and Popular Rights groups intensified their efforts, organizing demonstrations and political meetings in Tōkyō and elsewhere. The impasse was eventually resolved by a plan of Itō Hirobumi's, by which Ōkuma left the government, but simultaneously the *Kaitakushi* sale was called off, and on 12 October 1881 the emperor announced that a parliament would be summoned in 1889, ordering Itō to make the necessary preparations.

Early in the following year, Itō left Japan with a small party of advisers to study at first hand European political theory and constitutional practice. He spent some time in Britain and Belgium, but his chief mentors were conservative professors at the universities of Vienna and Berlin. However, it must not be thought that the Meiji constitution was made in central Europe. What Itō and his group found there was no more than a useful, because up to date and unimpeachably Western, amount of theoretical justification for a statist outlook they already had.

He returned home in August 1883 to the busiest and most resplendent six years of a long public career, becoming prime minister in 1885 when a modern Cabinet system replaced the *Dajōkan*. The previous year he had arranged the creation of a new peerage consisting of court nobles, *daimyō* and men of more recent distinction like himself. This peerage was needed primarily to form the nucleus of an upper house in the proposed parliament. A third innovation for which Itō made himself responsible took the form of new civil service regulations. In time, these gave rise to a modern bureaucracy, recruited and organized in terms of aptitude and scholastic talent. Meanwhile, Yamagata, who was home minister in the first Itō Cabinet, spent the mid 1880s constructively revising the entire system of local government. His labours bore fruit in the shape of the Municipal Code and the Town and Village Code of 1888. Though the home ministry continued to carry a great deal of weight in local affairs, the general effect of these codes was to consolidate the element of popular self-government. They remained the basis of Japanese local administration for the next sixty years.

Momentous though these developments were, they had only a subsidiary role in relation to the main task of drafting the new constitution. As Itō became busier with this, he handed over the post of prime minister to Kuroda in 1887. The actual drafting was done in secret with the help of a small committee, and he often sought the advice of Hermann Roesler, a German professor of jurisprudence at the Tōkyō Imperial University. In the course of 1888, the final draft was deliberated and ratified at meetings of a specially convened privy council, consisting of members of the government and other high dignitaries. Itō had had his fair share of youthful recklessness and political adventuring in the days before the Restoration, but had become a convinced gradualist, and in 1888 was certainly no believer in full-blooded democracy. Nevertheless at the privy council meetings he vigorously defended the wording of sections in the draft that gave the people 'rights' as well as 'duties' and empowered an elected legislative chamber to veto government bills.[10]

The arduous processes of drafting and ratification at length completed, the Meiji constitution, was promulgated by the emperor on 11 February 1889:

> The rights of Sovereignty of the State We have inherited from Our ancestors and We shall bequeath them to Our descendants. Neither We nor they shall in future fail to wield them in accordance with the provisions of the constitution hereby granted. We now declare to respect and protect the security of the rights and the property of Our people. . .[11]

It was one of the great occasions of the reign, and the date chosen, national foundation day, was the anniversary of the legendary accession of Emperor Jimmu to the throne of Yamato in 660 B.C.

[10] See Pittau, *Political Thought in Early Meiji Japan 1868–1889*, p. 178–81.
[11] Itō, *Commentaries On The Constitution Of The Empire Of Japan*, 3rd edition, p. 1.

Formation and Development of Political Parties

The constitution had been a triumph for the men in power. On the opposition side of the political fence, Itagaki and his supporters immediately after the issue of the 1881 rescript had re-formed their *Aikokusha* into a Liberal Party (*Jiyūtō*) professing liberty, rights and general happiness. In March 1882, Ōkuma Shigenobu founded the Constitutional Progressive Party (*Rikken Kaishintō*), which was solidly in favour of constitutional and parliamentary rule, but less doctrinaire than the *Jiyūtō*. In the same month, some of Itō's political friends, chiefly in the newspaper world, organized a Constitutional Imperial Party (*Rikken Teiseitō*), also dedicated to constitutionalism, but constitutionalism as understood by the government. For a time all these parties, together with their affiliates and other political groups, actively sought public endorsement, and Liberals and Progressives alike continued to berate the authorities. Yet by 1884 another of those oscillations so characteristic of Meiji political life had occurred. Both the Liberal Party and the Imperial Party had been formally dissolved, and the Progressives were quiescent following the resignation of Ōkuma Shigenobu from the post of party president.

The early 1880s were a time of agricultural distress in Japan, as the effects of Matsukata's deflationary policies were worsened by poor harvests and near famine in the north. As always, these conditions gave rise to peasant unrest and scattered outbreaks of violence. Certain radical Liberals, frustrated by having to wait so long for a constitution not of their own making, were implicated in the disturbances. As a result, Itagaki decided to dissolve his party for the time being, to avoid having it held responsible for the actions of a few of its members. These years also saw a hardening of the government's attitude towards its Liberal opponents. Itō harassed them by restricting public meetings, censoring the press, and so on. As part of their general campaign against the parties, the authorities wound up their own Imperial Party. Nevertheless, Inoue Kaoru, who almost certainly acted as a kind of advance scout for Itō in this matter, never abandoned altogether the idea of forming a pro-government party.

As for the popular parties, they revived spectacularly following Gotō Shōjirō's launching in 1886 of a campaign against the government's handling of the treaty problem. This resurgence was not really affected by the government's promulgation of a seemingly draconian peace preservation ordinance at the end of 1887. The police were now empowered to order leading politicians to leave the centre of Tōkyō. For a time they used these powers to the full, with the result that the capital's political temperature fell but that of the provinces rose. The first general election for the lower house (House of Representatives) of the new Imperial Diet was held at the beginning of July, 1890. Progressives fought as one party; Liberals as three factions, though agreed on reunion after the polls.

The election itself had been efficiently organized by the government, which did not interfere with the voting. The electorate was restricted to a tiny fraction of the adult male population. The results were a win for the popular parties, which secured about one hundred and sixty of the three hundred seats in the House of Representatives. Under the terms of the constitution, however, the upper house, which was known as the House of Peers and composed of hereditary and appointed members, had the same powers as the lower house. Moreover, there was no direct mandate for party government in the constitution. Cabinets could continue to be made up of the cliques of officials that had run the country ever since the Restoration, as ministers of State were formally chosen by the emperor and not by means of a popular vote.

The first decade of constitutional government was taken up with inconclusive struggles between a succession of bureaucratic Cabinets, manned by the old guard statesmen, and a Liberal-Progressive majority in successive Houses of Representatives. Neither side had the power to overrule, but each could seriously obstruct and frustrate the other. Particular issues usually ended in compromise. Sometimes, it seems, bribery helped to bring about this result, but the government's use of force in the second general election in 1892 did not secure a pliable majority. The annual budget never failed as a subject for prolonged dispute, but, on the whole, the most controversial topics concerned foreign policy. The governments of the day also had to withstand a good deal of criticism from independents and right-wingers in the House of Peers.

War with China in 1895 brought about an easing of this confrontation, but it was no more than a temporary lull. Consequently, when Itō resigned from his third term as prime minister in 1898, he persuaded his fellow bureaucrats to let Itagaki and Ōkuma form the next Cabinet. This first party Cabinet soon failed, however, because the Liberals and Progressives were unable to agree for long on a division of posts.

The next major development occurred in 1900. Itō, about to

serve his fourth and final term as prime minister, took the Liberals under his wing, forming them into a new party which he called the *Rikken Seiyūkai*. This manoeuvre opened the way to greater domestic stability. The other dominant political figure of the late Meiji period, and Itō's rival and temperamental opposite in many respects, was Yamagata Aritomo. Yamagata had had links from the beginning of the era with the military, whereas Itō had made his way as a leader of the civil bureaucracy; he was somewhat slower than Itō to appreciate the need for a basic understanding with a major group in the House of Representatives. Eventually, however, even the conservative and autocratic Yamagata came to see that constitutional government could not be expected to operate properly unless the political parties were given a chance to share executive power.

By 1900 concessions of this nature probably came more easily to Itō and Yamagata, because they themselves were getting too old for the day to day activities and strains of Cabinet office. Their ambition now was to be 'elder statesmen' (*genrō*), who from formal retirement could hope to continue to wield influence when necessary through a system of nominees. Consequently, the 1900s saw an alternation of *Seiyūkai* Cabinets headed by Saionji Kimmochi (1849–1940), a court noble associated with Itō, with spells of government by a reasonably capable Chōshū army general, Katsura Tarō (1847–1913), who was a protégé of Yamagata.

Political party activity had from the first been marred by factionalism, opportunism, and petty violence. Moreover, parliamentary life in the Saionji-Katsura period and earlier had its full quota of corruption. On the other hand, enduring systems of parliamentary government elsewhere have had these faults at one time or another; and in the case of Japan, by the close of the Meiji era the Imperial Diet had already become an accepted and effective element in the national administration. Its parties had ceased to be mere coteries of malcontents, and changes in the franchise had enlarged the electorate from a mere half million in 1890 to one and a half millions in 1912.

Some writers have gloomily referred to the 'settlement' between government and opposition that came about with the formation of the *Seiyūkai* as the 'bureaucratization of the political parties', seeing it as either the final treason of an always fragile Liberalism, or else as the supreme guile of an incorrigibly illiberal Itō and Yamagata. This is perhaps too pessimistic a view, and developments over the twenty or so years after 1890 can just as truthfully be described as the politicization of the bureaucracy. To oppose the idea of the politicization of the bureaucracy to the until recently more fashionable notion of the bureaucratization of the political parties is, of course, to raise the whole question of the fundamental nature of political change in the Meiji period. Opinions legitimately differ; but the position taken here is that change took place as a result of a process of interaction. Interaction occurred in the first place between the individuals and interests which composed the government throughout the Meiji era. It also occurred between that government as a whole—in other words a bureaucracy equipped with a great store of skills, political advantage and staying power—and, principally, Liberal-Progressive opposition groups which had their own sources of strength. Furthermore, this interaction, in turn, had grown out of the pluralist, cellular structure of the old *baku-han* regime.

Even after the weakening of its court noble component (principally Iwakura, Sanjō Sanetomi), of its Hizen component (Ōkuma, Etō Shimpei), and of its Tosa component (Itagaki, Gotō), the inner cadre of Meiji leadership continued to represent at least two distinct and equally powerful interests: Satsuma and Chōshū. Consequently, one of the premises of government was that positions had to be filled and policies devised by a process of continuous mutual adjustment between a Satsuma interest and a Chōshū interest, each of which had a powerful base and a characteristic political style. Moreover, figures like Itagaki and Ōkuma, or for that matter Saigō, did not leave the government for the complete obscurity that usually accompanies political retirement. Quite the contrary; these opposition leaders, too, had their bases from which they could fairly safely launch counter-attacks against the authorities.

Bases for both the government and the opposition were, of course, to a large extent regional. Thus, both Itō and Yamagata throughout their careers kept up the closest possible political links with their native Chōshū, while there was a Saigō for the reactionary element in Satsuma, and an Itagaki for the liberal and regionalist impulses of Tosa. Beneath the regionalism lay a nation-wide complex of parochial loyalties to district and village, to town and urban ward. Localism, like regionalism, influenced all political quarters. In particular, however, it provided the Liberty and Popular Rights Movement with a vital initial impetus and, later, helped to produce Diet lower houses that were representative in fact as well as name

The idea of a political base or stronghold has social and class, as well as geographic, implications. Here, once again, it would be wrong to exclude the government and bureaucracy from the picture. They, too, had sizeable *blocs* of supporters in certain occupations and at certain social levels. However, at the risk of over-simplification, one may say that three great classes, at one time or another and to some degree, came out against the Meiji government: the *shizoku*, the rural entrepreneurs, and the new business and professional class of the towns and cities. The *shizoku* were to be found in all political camps, ranging from ultra-conservative to militant radical; the rural entrepreneurs and land-tax payers in general supported the Liberals; and the urban middle-class tended to favour the Progressives.

All of these classes were numerous, widely dispersed, and self-confident. None of them could have been forcibly eliminated by the government, even if it had wished to take such a drastic step. Indeed, they were all vital in one way or another to the maintenance of political stability at the time and the successful achievement of modernization in the future. Moreover, two of them at least—the *shizoku* and the rural entrepreneurs—were but perpetuating and expanding in the Meiji period a leadership and strong personality role which they had acquired during the Tokugawa era as local *élites* at the *han* and village levels, respectively. When this finding is set beside a knowledge of the fragmented and diversified political system before 1868, it is not difficult to see how Meiji interaction grew out of Tokugawa pluralism.

The Constitution and the Ideology of Kokutai

The creation and operation of the Meiji constitution are not wholly attributable to the old regime's pluralist structure; traditional values also played an important role. The era's early years lacked a strong official ideology, except for an intense concern with westernization that at times went to culturally ridiculous, if not harmful, extremes. This state of affairs began to change in the 1880s, and by the time of the emperor's death in 1912, an official ideology was firmly established. Known as *kokutai*, it supplied a working philosophy to bureaucrats and party politicians alike, and was deliberately propagated by educationists and sections of the intelligentsia, by the press, and by the armed forces. The new system of compulsory primary education gave ample opportunity for its indoctrination, and the military, in particular, had contact with every able-bodied male during his term of conscription.

The term '*kokutai*' means something like 'the distinctive character of Japan's institutions and processes of government'. The most authoritative Meiji statement of the word's connotation is to be found in the imperial rescript on education, issued in 1890 and thereafter regularly read to school children all over the country:

Know Ye, Our Subjects:
Our Imperial Ancestors have founded Our Empire on a basis broad and everlasting and have deeply and firmly implanted virtue; Our subjects ever united in loyalty and filial piety have from generation to generation illustrated the beauty thereof. This is the glory of the fundamental character of Our Empire and herein also lies the source of Our education. Ye, Our subjects, be filial to your parents, affectionate to your brothers and sisters; as husbands and wives be harmonious; as friends be true; bear yourselves in modesty and moderation; extend your benevolence to all; pursue learning and cultivate arts, and thereby develop intellectual faculties and perfect moral powers; furthermore, advance public good and promote common interests; always respect the Constitution and observe the laws; should emergency arise, offer yourselves courageously to the State; and thus guard and maintain the prosperity of Our Imperial Throne coeval with heaven and earth. So shall ye not only be Our good and faithful subjects, but render illustrious the best traditions of your fore-fathers.
The Way here set forth is indeed the teaching bequeathed by Our Imperial Ancestors to be observed alike by their Descendants and their subjects, infallible for all ages and true in all places. It is Our wish to lay it to heart in all reverence in common with you, Our subjects, that we may all attain to the same virtue.

As expressed here, and as generally understood in the Meiji and subsequent Taishō eras, *kokutai* was clearly conservative in inspiration. Yet it was hardly the dogma of extreme nationalism mixed with totalitarianism that it came to be after 1930. Its values have, in fact, had the general effect of promoting national solidarity in good causes as well as bad.

Not all the attributes of *kokutai* stemmed solely from the native past. Indeed, one of the most important of them—nationalism—has been very much to the fore in nineteenth and twentieth century societies the world over. Japan, however, was particularly susceptible to the excesses of nationalism. Apart from being caught up, both as victim and participant, in Great Power competition, the country embarked on its tremendous and pioneering effort at self-transformation, resulting in many decades of cultural and racial isolation. Seeking to escape from the decay of traditional east Asian civilization, it looked to, but failed to gain full acceptance from, the West. In these circumstances, nationalism seemed the supreme justification for public policy. This secular attitude was not tempered by the more ecumenical viewpoints of Buddhism and Confucianism, both of which were in decline as ideologies of universalism.

Other important elements of *kokutai* were a sense of the State as a hierarchically ordered family, and the practice of having its senior members make decisions by a process of mutual consultation and consensus. Much more than nationalism, these two traits had a direct link with Tokugawa conditions;[12] but, like nationalism, they found their ultimate sanction and symbol after 1868 in the person and office of the emperor, whom the constitution of 1889 deemed 'sacred and inviolable'.

The Meiji emperor, his son, and his grandson were given a dual role by the builders of modern Japan. On the one hand, these sovereigns were theocratic patriarchs; on the other, they were constitutional monarchs. Their theocratic antecedents went back to Yamato legends celebrating the divine descent of the ruling house, and to traditional world-wide, semi-magical concepts of kingship as the linchpin of the moral and natural order as well as the socio-political world. During the Meiji era, these aspects of the imperial institution were modernized in the official cult of State Shinto. By creating this new form of worship, the government divested the shrines up and down the country of their centuries-old Buddhist connections. It then linked local and national cults in a single, albeit complex, organization aimed at the inculcation of patriotism and loyalty to the throne. This policy developed the idea that the emperor was an exceptional, semi-divine being.

The constitutional aspects of the modern sovereign were, of course, embodied in the 1889 constitution. This document remained in force until after the Pacific War, and underwent re-interpretation during its period of authority, yet its contents reveal well enough what was meant by *kokutai* in the mid-Meiji period, and how these principles were expected to work out in practice.

[12] See pages 207–10.

Both the manner in which the constitution was promulgated, and the document itself, made it quite clear that sovereignty resided in the person of the emperor alone. From the point of view of the further development of liberal institutions, this theory of unmitigated imperial sovereignty was of disservice, in that it contradicted the idea of natural rights. As has been noted, in practice the constitution allowed room for individual rights, but in the last resort these had to be thought of not as inherent and inviolable, but as a gift from the emperor. As a result, the people were to be at a serious disadvantage in their dealings with the State. On the other hand, imperial sovereignty was fully in keeping with national traditions, and reflected the outlook of a family system that liked to have its hierarchies regulated, ostensibly at least, from the top. Moreover, a measure of authoritarianism may well have helped to preserve constitutional government through its early stages. Certainly, other monarchies in the process of becoming constitutional retained some or all of the attributes of sovereignty; and in Japan's case, too, this formulation alone was not sufficient to thwart the evolution of government by parliament and parties.

Habits of consultation and consensus made it inevitable that the principal issues raised by the constitution turned on the locus of power, not the locus of sovereignty. The emperor was supreme, but his supremacy was purely formal. Article LV of the constitution illustrated this quite dramatically. It read:

> The respective Ministers of State shall give their advice to the Emperor, and be responsible for it. All Laws, Imperial Ordinances and Imperial Rescripts of whatever kind, that relate to the affairs of the State, require the counter-signature of a Minister of State.

and so effectively prevented the sovereign from taking any independent action whatsoever. Other articles transferred the emperor's judicial powers to a system of courts 'to be set up by law'; his legislative powers to the Diet; his executive functions to the Cabinet; and his command over the armed forces to their respective chiefs-of-staff and ministers of State.

In effect, the Meiji constitution recognized the need for a practical, though not theoretical, separation of powers, and proceeded to set up a system of checks and balances. The innate danger of these arrangements was that they would lead to deadlock, because separate centres of authority—the Cabinet, the two houses of the Diet, and the armed forces—were all entitled to about the same amount of power. This diffusion of responsibilities accounts for the prolonged struggles between non-party Cabinets and opposition majorities in the House of Representatives in the 1890s, and for Itō's eventual decision in favour of bringing about through the *Seiyūkai* a gradual shift in the power structure from bureaucratic Cabinets to party Cabinets. It also accounts for the significance after 1900 of the little group of retired elder statesmen. These men, the *genrō*, formed a completely extra-constitutional but vital co-ordinating element, to whose views other sections of the establishment usually deferred in moments of major decision making.

The *genrō* were a living monument to the principle of consensus. Relations between bureaucrats and party politicians had to be founded on this same principle if minimal requirements for a coherent and forward looking administration were to be met; and it was even more important for relations between the armed forces and other elements of State authority. In fact, there came to be a considerable difference in the degrees of autonomy enjoyed by the civil bureaucracy on the one hand, and the services on the other. In the case of the former, the long-term trend was towards permanent association with the Diet parties. In the case of the latter, however, the constitution had said nothing at all about the primacy of civilian rule. Moreover, at the beginning of the twentieth century Yamagata Aritomo had secured quasi-constitutional ordinances to the effect that only serving officers could fill the posts of army or navy minister. Yamagata's actions sprang from a determination to protect the nation's fighting strength from encroachment and, as he saw it, corruption by the political parties.

The actual terms of the constitution, its underlying principles, and its first twenty years of operation all combined to make the emperor function essentially as a symbol. He was head of State; the various ruling entities and factions governed in his name, and his presence was at least a reminder of their final responsibility to compose their differences and carry out a concerted policy. Moreover, though circumscribed politically, his role was of tremendous moral and ideological importance to the smooth running of the entire system. In the first place, the throne subsumed, in a way no other institution could, general feelings about Japan's identity and destiny as a nation. It served as a reminder to the nation that they had existed as a people from the remote past, and seemed to guarantee that they would go on so existing until an equally remote future. This was of the very essence of *kokutai*, and inevitably attracted much tawdry mysticism and febrile nationalism. Yet, at the same time, this conservationist function must have given psychological reassurance and direction to millions in times of stress and sweeping change.

Secondly, the Japanese emperor, through the family system and ties of religion, was linked with his subjects in a peculiarly close moral relationship. He was commonly regarded as the head of the senior household, distantly related to all the petty households that composed the nation and so endowed with an indefeasible right to the loyalty of his subjects. Again, to write in this fashion is to risk echoing the worst of ultra-nationalist propaganda; but the better side of the relationship can be detected in rescripts like the one on education, and was to be displayed most tellingly at the time of national surrender and humiliation at the end of the Pacific War.

Meiji Society

Whatever their difficulties with the political forms and spirit of full-blown Liberalism, the Meiji leaders acted quickly and decisively in implementing related concepts of social and legal equality. Distinctions of wealth and poverty did not disappear, and private property rights linked with the capitalist system of production were to be one of the mainstays of the new nation-State and an essential element in its internal sharing of power between bureaucrats and other *élites*. But the old, hereditary class divisions were abolished once and for all; women, whose position had never been completely servile in Japan, took the first steps along the path to full emancipation; and the law, especially after it had been codified along Western lines in the 1890s, was no respecter of persons. Moreover, with careers opened to talent, bright but socially handicapped youths achieved positions of distinction in academic life, in journalism, in business and industry, in the public service, or in the armed forces.

This was the situation at the beginning of the era; but leadership in its early decades naturally came primarily from groups of former samurai. Many of them occupied government posts while others formed the backbone of an emergent upper middle-class consisting of industrialists, large rural landlords, professional men including politicians, and educationists. Though often at odds with itself over details of policy, this *élite* was sufficiently small and cohesive to give effect to the Meiji government's plans for modernization.

Lower down the social scale, peasants, craftsmen and unskilled labourers were completely free from about 1870 to change their jobs and places of residence. That they did so in their tens and hundreds of thousands is part of the crucial but largely unnoticed popular aspect of Meiji history. The way the latter is usually written, and usually has to be written, gives an impression that Japanese rulers for nearly fifty years were at liberty to mould a docile populace into whatever shape they pleased. 'Revolution from above' sums up this misleading point of view. Clearly, there was revolution. Equally clearly, it was *instigated* from above, but no more: the masses were by no means simply raw material in the process of social transformation. Personal choice combined with official directives to change their lives, and while the authorities continued to guide the flow of events, that flow itself was increasingly determined by innumerable individual decisions of a private nature.

Transport, information, and formal education were all staples of the new society and, coupled with the modernization of small businesses which were entirely in private hands, reveal very well its popular dimension. After all, administrative action in favour of social equality would have led to no more than á series of paper reforms if the bulk of the people had continued to lack the means to move around easily, access to new ideas and the chance to be trained for new jobs. Roads remained poor owing chiefly to difficulties of topography, and mass transport depended on railways and local shipping services. Printed matter included numerous Western publications, imported or translated; and newspapers, which by 1890 were being published all over Japan, often attained a very high standard.

In the sphere of public education, announcements as early as 1872 anticipated the establishment of a uniform system for all the country's children. However, serious administrative difficulties ensued, and it was left to Mori Arinori (1847–89) to devise a viable system in the 1880s. Mori centralized ruthlessly, and by 1910 children of both sexes all over the country attended local co-educational schools between the ages of six and twelve. This achievement took forty years. It had no equivalent in Asia, and paralleled developments in the most advanced societies in Europe.

Mori and his successors in the education ministry provided facilities for further education at the middle school (ages 12–17) and high school (ages 18–20) levels. Vocational schools and colleges were an important adjunct of the system; and imperial, that is,

State, universities were set up in five centres: Sapporo (Hokkaidō), Sendai (Tōhoku), Tōkyō, Kyōto, and Fukuoka (Kyūshū). Education beyond the primary level was non-compulsory and more specialized, and it catered for far fewer children. This was the situation in 1910:

Primary school enrolments	6,335,261
Middle school level enrolments	219,203
High school and college enrolments	66,300
University enrolments	7,239

The paucity of children going on from primary to middle level schools is a reflection of low *per capita* income, rather than an effect of government policy; in fact, the numbers grew dramatically in the next three decades. Entry at the higher levels, however, was deliberately restricted, with an imperial university course being the greatest prize of all. General economic conditions also affected the situation here and the day when advanced societies can afford full education for all their citizens has only just dawned; but no doubt the prevalent *élitism* of Meiji times was just as strong an influence. Post-Tokugawa *élitism* had at least the virtue of being linked to merit, not birth; and students' expenses at high schools, colleges and universities run by the State were kept to the minimum.

Apart from the State system of education, there were numerous private schools and colleges, which depended for their finances on endowments and student fees. Christian missionaries were particularly active in the field of higher education for women; but the most famous private foundations were two secular, male, and entirely Japanese-financed and administered universities in Tōkyō: Keiō (founded by Fukuzawa Yukichi in 1858) and Waseda (founded by Ōkuma Shigenobu in 1882).

Keiō and Waseda still flourish as respected institutions of higher learning in Japan. Their success is indicative of the general enlightenment with which Japanese of the Meiji era remodelled their society's education. Transformation, here as elsewhere, came about as a mixture of governmental and private initiatives and through policies of trial and error. The main framework was, of course, the State system, but *élites* outside the bureaucracy made valuable additions, and the general public for its part paid its taxes and sent its children to school. Children did their lessons; students were students. Everybody—bureaucrats, benefactors, teachers and pupils—sensed the opportunities provided by a time which, outside the confines of recondite constitutional theory, was pragmatically and insistently open to new ideas and foreign influences. Horizons lay unobscured; maps remained to be filled in; progress appeared as a goal in itself. As a result, and despite the teaching on *kokutai* which featured prominently in the primary school syllabus, the Meiji period saw education largely abandon its traditional, narrowly conservationist function, and assume a new role as one of the chief vehicles for the importation of the substance as well as the forms of modernity.

CHAPTER SIXTEEN

From Consensus to Crisis, 1912–1937

Emperor Meiji died in 1912, to be succeeded by the Taishō emperor who reigned until 1926. This dynastic event denotes more than a change in the year-period chronology.[1] In the Taishō era it was realized that modernization had acquired a pace of its own that was sometimes exhilarating, sometimes terrifying. In complete contrast to the leisurely absorption of mainland civilization by the tiny Yamato *élite* thirteen hundred years previously, Western political ideas and cultural values had rapidly become familiar to a large proportion of the population. Mass literacy and opportunities for foreign travel opened the world to the inquiring minds of a Japanese intelligentsia drawn from all social classes. Moreover, this was happening at a time when the philosophy of Liberalism, together with the political, legal and property rights sanctioned by the constitution, was strengthening and extending the promptings of individuation, that process whereby the individual comes to see himself, and demand acceptance by others, as an end in himself. Whereas the concept of individual rights is outward and public, individuation is inward: psychological and necessarily slower to develop. Yet despite its less obvious nature, it has been an important element in the modernization of Japan.

It would be wrong to discount the continuing appeal of material incentives and concern for Japan's national interests, summed up so effectively in the Meiji slogan 'enrich the country, strengthen the army', or to think that technology and science[2] ceased to dominate the list of imports. Nevertheless, because of the short time-span and great numbers of people involved, and because of the existence of

[1] Since 1868, year-periods have corresponded with the reigns of emperors.
[2] Science, as a system of ideas, has not received the treatment it clearly deserves in this or any other account of the modernization of Japan.

interior forces like individuation, there has been another side to the story of Japan's response to the West. From the Meiji period onwards, individuals not directly concerned with, or even alienated from, the political and economic order have emerged as proponents of cultural change. These men made their mark, especially in the effervescent metropolis of Tōkyō, by challenging or modifying accepted cultural and social values.

Painting

It is against a background of many centuries of painting in what is broadly called the Japanese style, and the beginnings of an interest in Western-style painting in the Tokugawa period, that painting in modern Japan is best seen. Both styles of painting have become 'modern' in this century as the hold of traditional schools over individual artists has weakened and the impact of the West has increased. It is misleading to think of Japanese-style painting as tradition-bound and static and Western painting, in contrast, as experimental and original.

The first important group of men dedicated to the revival and reform of traditional Japanese painting came forward in the wake of the early Meiji enthusiasm for all things Western. Of the leading figures in this group, Okakura Tenshin (1862–1913), an educator and polemicist, is known in the West through books that he wrote in English, especially *The Book of Tea*, published in New York in 1906. Curiously, the artists whom he encouraged, like Yokoyama Taikan (1868–1958) are not as well known outside Japan. Taikan's most famous work (1923) is a scroll, forty metres long, on the theme of the vicissitudes of life, a grand composition tracing a stream's course from mountains to the sea and, at last, into the clouds. He painted many pictures of the Pacific Ocean and of Mount Fuji. Although his style is linked with that of the Kanō school, he reacted against his inheritance, subordinating the old insistence on strong line to his preference for subtle shading. The painter Shimomura Kanzan (1873–1930) worked on other lines. A Kanō-school product from boyhood, he tried to revive some of the even more ancient techniques of the Heian period. Two other artists drew on *Yamato-e* traditions, with Okakura Tenshin's encouragement, but developed contrasting personal styles. Yasuda Yukihiko (1884–   ) created a gentle and dreamy effect; Maeda Seison (1885–   ) had a command of line which produces sharp delineation of physical form and character.

Traditional elements in modern Japanese painting are not confined to modified *Yamato-e* and latter-day Kanō. At least one notable modern artist recalls the vigour and urge for display of Momoyama days. Kawabata Ryūshi (1885–1966), in his youth a student of Western painting, was converted to an approach which he and the critics insisted is traditional because it involves the use of ink and water colours on silk or paper. However, even in maturity, he was sufficiently unconventional to introduce the nude as a subject for Japanese-style painting, and to design his works for hanging in places where they would attract the maximum of attention. It is typical of Kawabata's bold and independent turn of mind that he should have quarrelled with existing institutions, which he thought too purist and pretentious in their promotion of Japanese-style painting. From 1928, he ran his own organization, the *Seiryū Sha*, still one of the many groups exhibiting to the public.

One artist, perhaps the most remarkable of all, Tomioka Tessai (1837–1924), seems to have survived from the Tokugawa era as a singular scholar-painter in the Chinese *literati* tradition.[3] Although he is greatly admired, no one has succeeded in following him. To the end of his long life he retained a vigour and a dashing use of ink and colour which gave his work an individual distinction. Some critics say that he is Japan's finest *modern* artist.

While Tessai tramped the Japanese countryside, painting as only he knew how, younger men went abroad. One of the earliest to succeed was Kuroda Seiki (1866–1924), who set out for France as a law student, and returned nearly ten years later in the 1890s, a competent painter in the Western style. In the years to come he played an important part in establishing the acceptability of painting in oils in a representational manner; his painting 'Lakeside', which depicts a Japanese woman in a blue kimono and is dated 1897, is important in this respect. Even representational painters could create a stir in those days by their choice of new subjects, as Kuroda showed by painting a standing nude.

Many ambitious young artists chose, like Kuroda, to study in France. Once there, to varying degrees, they were caught up in the latest style of painting. As the post-impressionists reacted against impressionism, introducing fauvism, cubism, and abstract painting, Japanese students were drawn to these challenges, and took back to Japan a command of the techniques as well as finished canvases. What happened after their return, in terms of the individual's

[3] See p. 201 above.

relation to his own society and the style in which he continued to paint, has not yet received adequate attention in books for Western readers. For example, Yasui Sōtarō (1888–1955) returned in 1914 after eight years abróad. A picture of a seated woman washing her feet that he had painted in Europe attracted wide attention when it was exhibited in 1915. With its dark blue colours and heavy style, it was reminiscent of Cézanne. It was not until a long time after his return that he developed a personal style, distinguished by studied control of composition and a skill in representing volume which is notably lacking in Japanese-style painting. Some of the many artists exhibiting their work in this period possessed real ability, but turned from one style to another, never settling down. In the process however, they widened the range of acceptability among the viewing and buying public. Others simply copied, the school of Western painting, and even the individual European master, being easily recognized.

It was otherwise with Umehara Ryūzaburō (1888–   ), who also went to France, at the age of twenty. Studying under Renoir, he passed beyond his master's style, developing a bold use of colour. Critics' remarks suggest that comparison of Umehara's works with those of Rouault, Cézanne, Van Gogh and Gauguin would reveal his particular powers within the general ambit of Western painting and also his debt to native Japanese traditions. Artists like Umehara raise the difficult problem of distinguishing clearly between what is modern-Japanese and what is Western in their painting. This distinction is of importance in Japan where Japanese and Western styles have been placed in separate categories based on differences in materials and in formal training. The schematization that results from these categories has at any rate the doubtful merit of making the critics' task easier, enabling them to search for a truly Japanese style. Meanwhile, twentieth century artists have continued to paint as best they can, in a world that is constantly becoming aware of new sources of artistic inspiration and the means to express them.

Music

Though for Western opera-goers Japan has been immortalized in Puccini's 'Madame Butterfly', it is not well known that within eight years of its first performance in 1907, a Japanese soprano trained in Japan was singing the title role of Cho-Cho San in London. In the same year of 1914, Yamada Kōsaku (1886–1965), then a young man studying composition in Berlin, returned home to collect costumes for an opera of his own composition. With the outbreak of war, and Germany an enemy, Yamada stayed in Japan. His own operatic work has not become popular but as a song-writer he remains without peer in modern Japan, and the inspiration he gave to other opera composers is important.[4] Yamada's influence after 1914 extended to purely instrumental composition and orchestral music. He organized and conducted the earliest fully professional symphony orchestras of Japanese musicians, and his long-term importance may well lie in this area, despite his success in writing for the human voice. Though the weight of Japanese tradition has made music a subordinate element in ritual, drama and plebeian entertainment, it is difficult to imagine that audiences are obeying mere social imperatives when they flock these days to the fine new concert halls in Tōkyō, Kyōto and elsewhere to hear symphony orchestras play programmes of purely instrumental music that often include modern compositions.

Various influences have combined to create a widespread liking for Western-style music, instrumental and vocal, whether composed overseas or in Japan. Until recently it was the only form taught in State schools, where the singing of folk-songs of diverse origins has always been an important and cheerful part of the curriculum. The leading institution in promoting Western classical music was the government's Tōkyō Music School, where Yamada studied before going overseas. In a literate society, sympathetic music critics exerted an influence in forming taste, and the music magazines to which they contributed became popular. Records came down in price when they were produced in Japan after 1914, making it possible to hear some of the world's finest performers; and before long the latter began to include Japan in their recital tours. Finally, radio has had an incalculable influence. Broadcasting came to Japan almost as soon as it did to the most advanced countries in the West, and the official corporation (*Nihon Hōsō Kyōkai*), set up in 1926, had all the powers and privileges of a public monopoly. Like its counterparts elsewhere, the *N.H.K.* has promoted its own orchestras, which are without peers in their homeland.

Official encouragement and improvements in communications have helped also to keep alive an interest in Japan's traditional

[4] In 1952 the Yamada Prize was awarded to the young composer Dan Ikuma (1924–   ), whose opera *Yūzuru* ('The Twilight Crane') has been acclaimed as the country's first truly successful opera, using dramatized Japanese folktales.

Japanese instruments and styles of music. *Gagaku*, which had barely survived until the Restoration, was refurbished and given new status in the official and religious ceremony of a revitalized court. The bamboo *shakuhachi* was not heard so often in public after the beginning of the Meiji era, when official recognition was withdrawn from a *bakufu* espionage service whose members had roamed the streets of Edo playing this recorder-like instrument. In private, however, the *shakuhachi* experienced something of a revival. The *koto*, a stringed instrument going back to the Heian Court, became popular in middle class households in the twentieth century. Its principal exponent, the blind virtuoso Miyagi Michio (1894–1956), made numerous recordings and gave frequent recitals, some of them in Europe. Besides playing works from the established repertoire, Miyagi blended traditional and Western elements, the *koto* and violin for example, to produce fresh pieces of traditional music. The *koto*, with its impeccable cultural associations, was sometimes combined with the *shakuhachi* and the *samisen* to form a trio in compositions of the chamber music type.

Such innovations, like Yamada's opera, lacked intrinsic merit, but may have been a necessary preliminary to fuller cultural exchange. Certainly, the *samisen* never lost the popularity it had acquired in the Edo period as the main instrument for both private and public entertainment. Modern Japan has produced countless hit songs in which it figures, and it is at this popular level that the combination of Japanese with Western instruments has been free and unselfconscious and most evidently successful. Moreover, the best of the ephemera have, along with their verve, a topicality which makes them faithful echoes of the passing moods of the past. The following example dates from the time of the Versailles peace conference in 1919, when Japan was awarded a League of Nations mandate to administer the Marshall Islands.

Watashi no lover-san	My lover
Shūchō no musume	Is a chieftain's daughter
Iro wa kuroi ga	Her colour is black
Nanyō ja bijin.	But in the South Seas she is a beauty.
Sekidō chokka	There, just near the equator,
Marshall guntō	In the Marshall Islands,
Yashi no kokage de	In the shade of a coconut tree
Dobuzake nonde. . . .	Drinking toddy. . . .

Dramatic Entertainments

The traditional dramatic arts have been preserved with varying degrees of vigour, despite the introduction of new forms of theatre and the development of a major film industry. *Nō* had been the official drama of the *bakufu*, and Iwakura Tomomi thought it worth encouraging as an entertainment proper for distinguished persons, with the result that imperial patronage helped to tide actors through a difficult period. In more recent times, the main support for *nō* has come from private citizens and amateurs keen to learn one or other of its skills, singing in particular. As a result, *nō* occupies a secure, if modest, place in the cultural spectrum. *Bunraku*, on the other hand, has barely survived even with official help.

Kabuki continues to flourish as basically commercial theatre. Adaptation to changing circumstances began in the Meiji period when, as with so many of Japan's 'worlds', the theatre produced its own remarkable innovator. Ichikawa Danjūrō (1838–1903), the eleventh of a distinguished line of actors bearing that name, played a dual role in theatrical history. With others, he successfully established the social respectability of *kabuki*. He also staged a distinctive kind of historical drama in which, free from official constraints, he essayed authentic recreations of past situations. From the mid-Meiji period a new school of *kabuki*, called *shimpa*, presented plays dealing first with contemporary politics, then with Japan's wars in Asia, crimes, other newsworthy items, and dramatizations of contemporary fiction—but ultimately without great success. For the traditional *kabuki*, new plays with pre-Meiji settings have come from men in touch with the wider world, men like Tsubouchi Shōyō (1859–1935), a late figure of the Meiji enlightenment, translator of Shakespeare and theatre reformer. The list of modern playwrights for traditional Japanese theatre includes at least one foreigner, the German missionary and academic, Hermann Heuvers. His five-act play on the violent death in 1600 of the Catholic lady, Gratia Hosokawa, was first staged in 1940 and has been regularly performed since then. On the technical side, lighting has changed with the coming of electricity, and the stage itself has been altered with the rebuilding of theatres, so that while *kabuki* remains traditional theatre, it is not played in the same style as during the late Edo period.

Contact with the West soon led to a realization that both *kabuki* and *shimpa* were too attached to the sensational and the spectacular to serve as effective media for the dissemination of ideas. Therefore, since late Meiji times there has been a persistent interest in Western-style theatre (called *shingeki* or 'new drama'), which deliberately cuts itself off from all traditional dramatic forms in favour of an intellectual and realistic approach that frequently entails social criticism. Tsubouchi Shōyō was the leader of one group of amateurs working for a more 'cultivated' theatre. Another group was headed by Osanai Kaoru (1881–1928) who, with the progressive *kabuki* actor Ichikawa Sadanji II (1880–1940), set up the Jiyū Gekijō ('Freedom Theatre') with professional actors. Sadanji himself appeared in the theatre's first play in 1909, a translation of Ibsen's *John Gabriel Borkman*. It had been rehearsed, so we are told, with the help of 'clippings and observations sent by a friend in Munich who had seen a performance of *Borkman*'.[5]

As if to retain its links with *kabuki*, this, perhaps the first *shingeki* play, had some women's roles played by men and some by women! In the years that followed, the public has come to see plays by modern Russian, Swedish, Irish, German and English playwrights and by Japanese writers. Since the appeal of such plays is to the intellectual, like that of the little theatres in the West, the direct challenge to *kabuki's* box-office has been negligible. As with Western-style art, it is easy for the foreigner to regard this Western-style drama too lightly, as something familiar and far less interesting than the exotic *kabuki*, thereby misjudging the impact it has made on an influential and growing group of Japanese—the intelligentsia. The theme of *John Gabriel Borkman*, for example, the relation of a genius to society, raises that universal fantasy of the intelligentsia—unfulfilled genius. Its treatment in Western-style dramatic form represented a new and important artistic departure.

The greatest challenge to the attraction of *kabuki* came from films, a new field for artistic endeavour, and the true mass theatrical entertainment in the first half of the twentieth century. The break with existing theatrical traditions in terms of actors, acting techniques and scripts was neither sudden nor complete, but the speed with which film makers seized on the capabilities of the new medium was remarkable. Some of the earliest films were scenes from *kabuki* and excerpts from *shimpa*, or short movies by *shimpa* actors, with men continuing to take female roles. Silent films were enlivened by running commentaries from men called *benshi*, who practised a new

[5] Komiya, *Japanese Music and Drama In The Meiji Era*, p. 302.

set of skills but obviously owed much to the ancient craft of the professional story-teller.

The first proper cinema theatre was built in 1903, and by 1918 Japanese film-makers were looking to foreign films rather than the traditional theatre for their inspiration. Close-ups as well as long shots, continuous action, simple mobile camera techniques, artificial lighting, shots on location, sub-titles, and actresses for women's roles helped to free films from the aesthetic standards of the past. One of the earliest films showing an understanding of movies' technical potentialities was *Sei no Kagayaki* ('The Glow of Life'), made in 1918 by a young man of twenty-five, Kaeriyama Norimasa, a great admirer of D. W. Griffith. He believed that acting should be realistic, and in this he was not alone. In 1921 a group led by Osanai Kaoru, still a leading figure in the 'new drama' movement, produced *Rojō no Reikon* ('Souls on the Road') using two stories, the first of which was by Maxim Gorky, 'The Lower Depths', and 'Child of the Street', to create an early example of the 'mood movie'. This style is considered to be a special kind of Japanese cinematic art, and it is a far cry from the world of *kabuki* in presentation, though not in the power to evoke feelings.

> The directors particularly sought to capture the components of what were for them the greatest forces in the world: love within a family and comradeship between men. These they preferred to examine not in the uncommon moments of high emotion, as in a plotted film, but rather during those characteristic moments of an enduring period of hardship . . . filmed on location during early winter among the mountains in central Japan, *Souls on the Road* placed its characters far apart from the crowded world, in a country of dead landscapes and overcast skies, where the men and women moved almost aimlessly, harshly outlined against the sombre mountains and the dark forest.[6]

Film companies in search of commercial successes to outdo their competitors produced a great variety of films: melodrama in *shimpa* style; light 'nonsense' comedies; films about everyday life in serious and comic vein; sentimental 'mother' films; the equivalent of the 'western' with sword-play instead of gun fights; and from the late 1920s, films of social criticism, both in contemporary and period settings. *Zanjin Zamba Ken* ('The Man-slashing, Horse-piercing Sword'), made in 1929 about a masterless samurai who leads a hard life in opposition to the feudal system, well exemplifies a whole

[6] Anderson and Richie, *The Japanese Film: Art and Industry*, p. 44.

group of movies designed to stir the emotions of audiences over social inequities. Ideologically slanted movies declined in number as censorship became more rigorous in the 1930s. By this time the talkies had come, and the *benshi* went the way of the female impersonators ten years before, but not without protest.

The rising number of talkies in the 1930s coincided with a greater interest than ever before in producing movies based on literary works. It is a measure of the film-makers' maturity that the best of these films are commonly regarded as outstanding products of a new art, and not simply as celluloid novels. Among the best of the literary films of the day, highly realistic and not very cheerful, were *Hadaka no Machi* ('The Naked Town') about a man who is cheated and rejected by the world; *Naniwa Ereji* ('Osaka Elegy') about the darker side of the life of an attractive telephone operator; and *Gion no Shimai* ('Sisters of the Gion'). It is interesting to read what Anderson and Richie have to say about this the last of these, made in 1936 and hailed by some critics as the best pre-war sound film.

The title was *Sisters of the Gion*, the sisters being two geisha from the well-known Gion district of Kyoto. The younger is a *moga*— a derogatory portmanteau of the English 'modern girl'—and thus is inclined to ignore the traditions of both her profession in particular and Japanese traditional society in general. The elder possesses all the virtues of the legendary geisha. Despite the geisha code which authorises a girl only one patron, the younger sister jumps from one man to another in search of ready cash. She also decides that her sister needs a new patron since the old one has lost all of his money, and so she tells him that her sister is no longer available; and all the while she herself is going up the ladder of success from one man to that man's boss. . . . If the director's own sentiments occasionally and by default go to the elder sister, his ending leaves her condemned. The situation is such, however, that the spectator too must make a choice, because, for a Japanese at any rate, the problem suggested by the film is a very vital one and by implication goes far beyond the narrow world of the geisha. . . . To project regional atmosphere is no easy task in a country where smallness and centralization conspire to make differences extremely subtle, yet never have the narrow Gion alleys and the backrooms of its teahouses appeared more inviting. To the Japanese this picture was more than merely slice-of-life. It went beyond documentation and projected the other-world atmosphere of the Gion itself.[7]

[7] Anderson and Richie, pp. 103–4.

Clearly, the film was in the hands of makers who were fully aware that it could surpass other media in the creation of 'psychological space'.

Literature

Writers were frequently harbingers of individuation, in Japan as elsewhere. Even in traditional society, individuation had never been entirely absent. Authors, together with artists, saints, scholars and military heroes, were customarily regarded as exceptional beings deserving a certain independence of thought and life. Yet, in Tokugawa times at any rate, most writers had a story-teller's and not a romantic poet's view of the individual. They saw him as but one element in a wider mosaic of nature and society.

Unassuming individuation of this traditional type marked the work of two early and mid-Meiji writers: Masaoka Shiki (1867–1902) and Higuchi Ichiyō (1872–96). Shiki was of samurai parentage. He made his living as a journalist but came to be ranked with Bashō, Buson and Issa as one of the four great masters of the classical *haiku* tradition.

Hibari ha to	On how to sing,
Kaeru ha to uta no	The skylark school and the frog school
Giron kana	Are arguing.
Izakaya no	The tavern quarrel
Kenka mushidasu	Persists
Oborozuki	Under a hazy moon.

Higuchi, a woman writer of great talent, was fated to live in poverty and to die early, but not before she had given a perceptive, lyrical account (*Takekurabe* or Growing Up) of the capital's famous Yoshiwara amusement quarter, near which she ran a small shop for a while. In keeping with its subject, her book is in true Edo style— episodic, and painting a *genre* picture of an entire floating-world district and its way of life, as seen through the eyes of a group of adolescents. In other works, notably the short stories *Nigorie* (Muddy Bay) and *Jusan'ya* (The Thirteenth Night), Higuchi was more directly concerned with the circumstances and sufferings of a single individual; had she lived longer, this is a theme she might well have come to exploit.

Threshing rice: a contemporary scene

Civic Hall, Kagawa city, designed by Tange Kenzō

Tomioka Tessai's *Children Piling Up Stones to Make a Stupa*. 'Even children who, in play, gathered sand for a Buddha's stupa [have] attained to Buddhahood'. (Lotus Sutra)

Shimomura Kanzan (1873–1930): a six-leaf screen painted in 1916

Tōgō Seiji's *Saltimbanco*:
a Cubist work painted in
France in 1926 during the
artist's ten-year sojourn
abroad

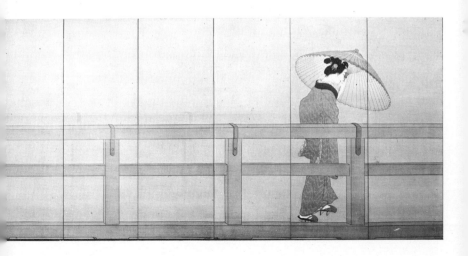

Tōkyō commuters

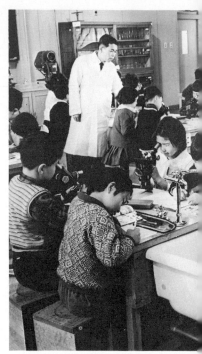

Science class, Tōkyō elementary school

National Indoor Gymnasium, Tōkyō. Architect: Tange Kenzō

By the end of the Meiji period, and as a direct result of European influence, the fate of the individual was beginning to be almost a literary commonplace. In Natsume Sōseki (1867–1916) Japan had already produced one master of a new literary form: the modern novel. Sōseki eventually held a professorship at Tōkyō Imperial University, which he later left to work for the *Asahi* newspaper, and he was in the forefront of the literary renaissance. He wrote many novels, which were short, well-contrived and reflective. His preoccupation was the role of the individual in society, and while his earlier books have a light, satirical tone, he became increasingly pessimistic about individuals achieving any real happiness. In short, with Sōseki the process of individuation had gone far enough to be frightening.

Sōseki's only peer in the late Meiji literary world was the novelist and short story writer, Mori Ōgai (1862–1922). Mori was an army surgeon, and so resembled Sōseki in being a member of the new professional upper middle-class, with good opportunities to travel and study abroad. He was an extremely proficient translator, especially from German, and his own original writings, acclaimed in their own time and since, are polished compositions in a psychological-realist style which he did much to make popular. Mori saw modernization as an awkward, but on the whole promising, necessity. In this he was at one with most of the age's intelligentsia. Alienation was a thing of the future, perhaps first revealed in the blacker moods of Natsume Sōseki.

Natsume and Mori, each in his own way, wrote the sort of 'naturalistic' novel which has dominated modern Japanese fiction. Though the term 'naturalism' has by now been so over-worked as to be virtually useless as an aid to appreciation, when it was first invented around the turn of the century it did signify an important and definite break with the past. Late Tokugawa habits of writing prose fiction either as light satirical sketches or as moralistic tracts continued well into the Meiji period. Denying the validity of both these approaches, naturalism stood for an emphasis on reality which was completely serious in intent and which expressed the whole range of human emotions, noble or otherwise. The new view was pioneered by the renowned critic Tsubouchi Shōyō, and by the novelist Futabatei Shimei (1862–1909). Both these men used their excellent knowledge of European literatures (primarily French, Russian, and English) to condemn prevailing Japanese vogues. In Europe the nineteenth century produced a maturing of the novel as an exploration of human personality. This made it the West's major literary form, and ensured that before long it would retrieve among the Japanese the standing it once had in the age of Heian.

As elsewhere, concentration on realism in Japan was linked with the use of unvarnished prose; the Japanese naturalists cannot be acclaimed as polished stylists, though they did establish a solid and worthwhile convention of writing novels in the colloquial. Japanese writers diverged most markedly from their European counterparts in their relative lack of objective concern with society. Reality for them was primarily what happened to *them*, however trivial. As a result, though unadulterated naturalism did not last very long as a literary movement, it set a persistent trend not only for writing in everyday speech but also in the autobiographical, confessional style of what is commonly called the 'I-novel'. Fiction was downgraded along with fine language, and loosely structured emotional subject-ivity has been the main ingredient of many a Japanese novel since 1900. In part this was a baffled, semi-Romantic and 'internal emigrant' reaction to what some regarded as the unwholesome speed of modernization, coupled with the pressures of *kokutai*. It is possible also to detect overtones of the ancient traditions of journal (*nikki*) and miscellany (*zuihitsu*) writing.

At its worst, the 'I-novel' is vapid and unartistic, but only at its worst. In fact, Japanese culture owes a great debt to its early exponents of naturalism and to a galaxy of later writers like Shimazaki Tōson (1872–1943), Nagai Kafū (1879–1959), Shiga Naoya (1883–   ), Tanizaki Junichirō (1886–1965), and Akuta-gawa Ryūnosuke (1892–1927). Between them, these and lesser talents have produced a great body of literature, which inevitably varies in quality but is indisputably modern, and undeniably Japanese. Moreover, in a society shot through with Confucian disdain for the novel and its begetter, they have succeeded in asserting the artistic integrity of the one, and the social respectability of the other. Most important of all, however, their efforts bear witness to the vehemence and versatility of Japan's modernization, which affected all areas of life and all sections of the population in a thoroughgoing, and often painfully bewildering, fashion.

Ideology

With the exceptions of the film and Western popular music, the initial impact of exotic cultural forms was limited. The fact that they were minority tastes, however, does not detract from their significance, because the same urban intelligentsia which interested itself in new developments in the arts and literature also took the initiative in scholarship and political commitment. The urban intellectuals were influenced in all their activities by the same dynamics of innovation and individuation, with the same potential for disruption or outright rebellion. In general, from the early Meiji period onward, Japanese authorities had tolerated, even promoted, cultural diversity. Nevertheless they were always wary of those who openly advocated radical change in the political order and at times rigorously suppressed them; by 1937, politics and culture were demonstrably one in the official ideology setting out the essentials of Japan's national entity, i.e. *kokutai*.

To a large extent, the seriousness with which ideology was officially regarded in the 1930s was a defensive reaction to left-wing agitation in the previous decade. This proletarian movement had roots in international events following the upheavals of the first world war and the trauma of the Bolshevik capture of power in Russia, as well as in such domestic conditions as an expanding industrial work-force, relative impoverishment of the peasantry, and a general growth in class consciousness. In its rawest form, leftist radicalism was mouthed, and on occasion implemented, by professed communists and anarchists who totally rejected the idea of a family State, proclaiming the need for its forcible destruction together with capitalism. On a somewhat different plane, the proletarian movement encouraged scholars and writers to infuse their work with social criticism and, specifically, Marxist ideas of class struggle. Individual professors, like the brilliant and unselfishly resolute Kawakami Hajime (1879–1946) at Kyōto Imperial University, turned to the propagation of the ideas of Marx and Lenin, as did lesser men with a flair for writing. In time, the principal concern of some of these others was the application of their theories to the situation as they perceived it in Japan. Much polemic ensued.

Governments in the late 1920s and early 1930s acted strenuously in defence of the national entity and private property. Nearly three and a half thousand people were arrested in 1928 for suspected violations of a peace preservation law. Thereafter there was an increase in the numbers affected each year by this legislation, which was aimed not at acts of terrorism or sabotage but at the organized expression of revolutionary views, until they reached a peak of more than fourteen and a half thousand in 1933. By 1937, success in crushing communists and their sympathizers in the intellectual and cultural worlds was reflected in a falling off in arrests to under fifteen hundred. Only a very small proportion of those arrested were actually made to stand trial for 'thought crimes' and then punished by imprisonment; but the danger of falling foul of the law had been made plain enough, and after 1932 many of those released without trial were placed under a sophisticated system of surveillance with which they themselves had to co-operate.

A few writers had joined issue with the government with such phrases as 'poems are bombs' and, while they do not seem to have set high artistic standards in their magazines, they did produce some fierce combatants. Kobayashi Takiji is one of the few proletarian writers still taken seriously as a writer. He attracted attention with a story entitled 'March 15, 1928', about the first severe suppression of radicals in 1928, but his success with the general public was even greater with *Kani Kōsen* ('The Crab-Canning Boat') written in 1929, which described in highly ideological terms the shocking treatment of the (proletarian) crew of a vessel in northern waters by the (capitalist) superintendent. Kobayashi's commitment to the illegal communist cause forced him underground. He was caught by the police, tortured terribly and died in prison in 1933, at the age of twenty-nine.

Ideological and political extremism was partly a by-product of 'Taishō democracy', the somewhat illusory strengthening of the ideas and forms of political liberalism between the years 1912 and 1926. The institution of party cabinets from 1919, through pragmatic convention rather than constitutional amendment, and the introduction of full manhood suffrage in 1925, were the two most notable manifestations of 'Taishō democracy'. Its leading exponent in the theoretical field was Yoshino Sakuzō (1878–1933). Yoshino, a professor at Tōkyō Imperial University, published a number of moderately pitched articles on politics in serious journals. A growing minority of Japanese with some education beyond the compulsory six years, in the cities especially, made a ready market for this type of journalism. As a result, even though it appeared before allied victory in the first world war kindled widespread enthusiasm for its subject, an article Yoshino wrote 'On Democracy' (*Mimpon Shugi Ron*) for the January 1916 issue of the Central Review (*Chūō Kōron*) was enormously influential. In it he advocated an extension of voting rights and a larger role for popular representatives within the existing constitutional system as the solution to the essential problem posed by Japanese politics as he saw it: 'How was the benevolent Emperor to know what was the general welfare?'

Just as some artists had combined traditional Japanese patterns of thought or technique and Western ideas to resolve their problems, so Yoshino drew on many sources for his synthesis.

> From Confucianism he took the concept of benevolent rule but attempted to set it upon a democratic base by the use of Utilitarianism. From the English liberals he took proposals for limiting powers of the old establishment (the Genrō and the bureaucracy, in the case of Japan) through enhancing the Diet, and for restricting the influence of the new plutocracy through popular suffrage. He even borrowed slightly from the German organicists . . . for he accepted the analysis of the functioning of the Meiji Constitution as in fact limiting the powers of the Emperor while leaving the locus of sovereignty legally in the Emperor. . . . The foreign elements were carefully used to reinterpret the traditional symbol of the Emperor.[8]

Yoshino, a committed liberal of the Taishō era, was never publicly arraigned in the reaction that followed. Yet, in the process of making it more abundantly clear to the nation what was meant by the *kokutai* or national entity, zealous nationalists made free speech and enquiry more difficult over the wide range of subjects brought to the fore in the period of Taishō democracy. Marxists of an academic turn of mind, who carried rational enquiry into the workings of society further than any other group, were suppressed. Others who were not Marxist were also driven from public life. In particular, Minobe Tatsukichi (1873–1948), retired head of the law department of Tōkyō Imperial University, higher civil service examiner and member of the House of Peers, came under damaging criticism because his views on the constitution, which had been staple establishment-bureaucrat fare for decades, became incompatible with the strict theories of unfettered imperial sovereignty. The humiliation in 1935 of such an eminently respectable personage as Minobe, accompanied as it was by a great deal of publicity, deflected less well known scholars from airing opinions which might get them into trouble. Inevitably, intellectual life became impoverished in the mid-1930s as ultra-nationalism grew in influence.

In their pursuit of ideological conformity, governments had at their disposal techniques at once more subtle and more pervasive

---

[8] Totten, *Democracy in Prewar Japan—Groundwork or Facade?*, p. 37.

than either mass exercises in police intimidation or the solitary hounding of distinguished individuals. Because Japanese children at school for the compulsory six formative years had used the same official textbooks from the first decade of the twentieth century, they were presented with one view of their nation's identity. History lessons, as much as the formal ethics (*shūshin*) course, were lessons in moral education, on how to behave in a unique family State. More specifically, a comparison between the national history textbook of 1920 and its successor issued in 1934, reveals a measurable intensification of the moral, semi-religious aura attaching to the imperial house. The 1934 publication contained a completely new final chapter called 'The People's Creed'. This expounded in simple form what were thought to be essential features of the national order: continuity of the imperial line; the sun goddess' charge to her descendants to rule over the country as recorded in the *Nihon Shoki*; the compassion of emperors down the ages and the loyalty of illustrious subjects; and the bond between sovereign and subject which is likened to the relationship between parent and child.[9]

Of course, Japan was not alone in using history lessons to sustain the existing political and social order, but what was remarkable was the thoroughness with which the official viewpoint was purveyed to the masses, on the one hand, and the mounting vigilance against dissent on the other. Official efforts were matched by a certain aptness for uniformity in social and intellectual matters.

The most ambitious re-statement of traditionalism, prepared by the bureau of thought control in the ministry of education, was published in March 1937. Entitled *Kokutai no Hongi* ('Cardinal Principles of the National Entity of Japan'), it was intended for use by teachers and older students throughout the country. It was an attack on individualism, which was regarded as being the cause of 'ideological and social confusion and crisis' and ultimately the basis of socialism, anarchism and communism. It was also an affirmation, in elevated language, of the values already described in relation to the teaching of history. By affirming these values, the government proposed to fit Japan's youth with an outlook which made them instruments of the emperor's will. In avoiding rational explanation of the economic processes and political mechanisms which were transforming society, *Kokutai no Hongi* may have offered emotional comfort.

[9] Cf. Caiger, 'The Aims and Content of School Courses in Japanese History, 1872–1945,' in E. Skrzypczak (ed.) *Japan's Modern Century*.

Our national economy is a great enterprise based on His Majesty's great august Will to have the Empire go on developing for ever and ever, and is a thing on which the subjects' felicity depends; so that it is not a disconnected series of activities aimed at fulfilling the material desires of individual persons, a doctrine expounded by western economists.[10]

More seriously, *Kokutai no Hongi* set out to elevate the figure of the emperor in the minds of Japanese youth, while deliberately neglecting to draw attention to the real forces that manipulated his authority. In so doing, it ignored the latter-day plight of political life under the Meiji constitution when the grand consensus that document assumed had finally broken down.

Politics and the Economy

Government by consensus is difficult even in the best of circumstances; it is almost impossible in times of massive, unplanned change. The authoritarianism in the Meiji constitution bespeaks its authors' awareness of these facts. At a deeper level of motivation, their handiwork has a markedly static quality, almost as if the new nation had been an old *han*, something small, largely self-contained, and hierarchically ordered. But, of course, it was not; and by 1912 economic change alone would have been sufficient to put serious strains on traditional methods of political control. Moreover, whereas 'old Japan' had been a closed country, the 'new' was part of an international maelstrom of political and social currents. It would have needed a clear head and firm hand to steer the country safely through the turbulent backwash of Bolshevik revolution and Chinese warlordism, even if there had been no desire to take advantage of neighbours' misfortunes.

In fact, although national leadership continued to be exercised by the elderly and the experienced, it was certainly less secure, and perhaps less perceptive, after 1912. Able men rose to power late in life after having made a timely switch from the senior ranks of the civil bureaucracy to a career of adroit politicking in the Diet parties. But the latter still gave an appearance of being little more than loosely organized interest groups, and their leaders lacked the confidence and prestige of the Meiji statesmen. This general situation was not improved by the existence of an alternative avenue to

[10] Hall (ed.), *Kokutai no Hongi—Cardinal Principles of the National Entity of Japan,* p. 169.

Cabinet office in the armed services, nor was it helped by a cruel catalogue of assassinations.

Despite these difficulties, the general history of the years 1912–1937 is not without its successes. Moreover, some of these, like the period of party government in the 1920s or the emphasis on heavy industry in the 1930s, can now be seen to have also had a long term importance as preparatory exercises. Therefore, even though the dominating note of these times seems to have been failure, and failure all the more grievous for having often worn a mask of success, it is still too soon to pass lasting judgment. Even at the superficial level, setbacks and advances occurred in an agonizingly haphazard fashion in the two great areas of foreign and domestic policy. Japanese humanity was to find itself trapped on the shifting sands of mid-twentieth century time, with no clear idea of how it got there and no obvious route out.

The Taishō era began with a major domestic political crisis, the resolution of which can safely be regarded as having augured well for the development of responsible party government in Japan. Katsura Tarō became prime minister for the third time late in 1912 after army intransigence on a proposed budget had brought about the downfall of the second Saionji Cabinet, even though the latter enjoyed a clear (*Seiyūkai*) majority in the House of Representatives. Katsura, lacking votes in the lower house, used an imperial command to try to prevent his opponents in the *Seiyūkai* from overthrowing him. The command was rejected by the *Seiyūkai*; Katsura was ruined, having in the process called down on himself a memorably vitriolic attack on extra-parliamentary manipulation of the emperor's authority.[11]

Issues at stake had been, firstly, whether even bureaucratic cabinets should be responsive to popular opinion as represented in the Diet; and, secondly, the independence and solidarity of political parties. In this last respect Katsura's manoeuvres while the political storm clouds gathered had a beneficial, though totally unlooked for, side effect. The incoming prime minister had already foreseen the need for a large and organized *bloc* of supporters in the Diet and

---

[11] On 5 February 1913 a party politician, Ozaki Yukio, gave a speech in the House of Representatives in the course of which he said: 'Whenever they [Katsura and other bureaucratic leaders] open their mouths, it is to speak of loyalty and patriotism, as if loyalty to the Sovereign and love of country were theirs and theirs alone. But when we take a look at their actual conduct, they hide behind the throne and snipe at their political enemies. (applause) Is it not their purpose to ruin their foes by making the throne their rampart and rescripts their missiles?'

elsewhere, and set about forming a new political party shortly after taking office. Behind Katsura's actions lay a realization that the *genrō*, including his erstwhile patron Yamagata Aritomo, were fading away. Therefore second generation political leaders like himself would have to acquire new and institutionalized sources of power; and, in addition, new mechanisms would have to be devised for ensuring orderly change in a political world that still lacked fully regularized procedures for the selection of new cabinets. The party (the *Dōshikai*) that Katsura founded in these few hectic months grew in strength and in time offered a respectable, because fully parliamentary, alternative to the *Seiyūkai*.

This and other gains on the domestic political front arising from the crisis of 1912–13 had been hard fought for, and were not immediately realized. By way of contrast, the onset of the first world war in 1914 conferred on the nation great and fortuitous benefits both at home and abroad. Despite Japan's participation as an ally of Britain, the unknown soldier is not the symbolic figure of those times for the Japanese people. With the occupation of Germany's possessions in China (Shantung) and her naval bases in the Mariana, Marshall and Caroline islands north of the equator in the western Pacific, actual fighting was soon over, far from native shores and at little cost.

Spared the destruction, or even the dislocation, of war, Japan did well thanks to enterprising businessmen who seized the opportunity to sell goods in stock, to expand their businesses and move into world markets. The men who took quick fortunes in shipping at this time helped make Japan the third maritime nation after Britain and the United States. Japanese ships, besides carrying war materials for the allies, transported the products of Japan's expanding textile industry to China, south-east Asia and Africa, displacing British competitors in the process. Now that Germany could no longer provide chemical and pharmaceutical products, the Japanese turned to making their own. Iron and steel production, especially at the Yawata works in north Kyūshū, increased to meet the demand of machine shops and shipbuilding yards.

Overall industrialization forged ahead quickly, as the following figures show:

| | Percentage of Total Production | |
	1914	1919
Industry	44.4 per cent	56.8 per cent
Agriculture	45.4 per cent	35.1 per cent

| Mining | 5.1 per cent | 4.3 per cent |
| Fishing | 5.1 per cent | 3.8 per cent |

If the more spectacular changes were evident in the industrializing cities, the countryside, where most people still lived and worked, also saw change. High and difficult country from an agricultural point of view was turned to good account with the building of hydro-electric stations, as war-time conditions forced up the price of coal. Within two decades of the commencement of these schemes, Japanese industry was well served with power from this source and others, as were farmhouses in the agricultural areas, even if they had but a single bulb. Industry had begun to lighten the farmers' physical load in other ways: by manufacturing and selling chemical fertilizers, metal tools and small kerosene motors for pumps and harvesting machinery. By 1937 mechanization had begun on the Japanese farm, a slow change that is easily overlooked in the welter of spectacular events, but one of great importance in the context of Japan's long history of dependence on agriculture for its higher civilization, and, during the Meiji period, for the bulk of the funds to develop into an industrial nation.

The preoccupation of the Powers with their war in Europe also had the effect of increasing Japan's relative standing in north-east Asia, the area that mattered most in strategic as well as economic terms. The Japanese government under Ōkuma Shigenobu pressed for confirmation of former German rights in Shantung, requesting at the same time fresh Chinese assent to already existing Japanese privileges and concessions elsewhere in China and Manchuria. Such was the relatively innocuous core of the 'twenty-one demands' made on China in 1915; but the Japanese minister in Peking was also instructed to relay as 'wishes of the Imperial Government' suggestions that Japanese political, financial and military advisers be appointed to the Chinese administration. The far-reaching nature of this last set of proposals, together with the generally inept handling of the matter by Ōkuma's Cabinet, brought resentment not only from China and from Western countries with interests in the area, but also from the elderly *genrō* Yamagata, who had not been properly consulted. Ōkuma then resigned as prime minister, to be succeeded by Terauchi Masatake (1852–1919), an army officer and governor-general of Korea.

The Terauchi Cabinet (October 1916–September 1918), after mending relations with China and the Western nations, suddenly faced a new and severe test of its powers of decision in the field of foreign affairs. The Russian revolution opened up an extraordinarily fluid situation in Siberia. Should Japan intervene unilaterally to safeguard its strategic and economic interests in Korea and Manchuria by despatching a military expedition to Siberia? Close study of the events that followed has revealed the diverse forces at work behind the final and formal sanction by the emperor. At meetings of a select advisory council on foreign relations, representatives of most of the institutions of government took part: the foreign and home ministries, the army and navy ministries, members of the House of Peers and of the privy council, and two leaders of political parties in the House of Representatives.

Although outside the advisory council, the army and navy general staffs and the *genrō* played vital parts. Indeed, the person most responsible for the eventual decision seems to have been Yamagata, the strongest of the *genrō*. Having cautioned one keen supporter of intervention with the words, 'When drawing the sword, one does not grasp the handle until one has considered first how it can be sheathed', Yamagata judged that it was opportune to intervene in co-operation with the Western Powers. Such was the solution arrived at in 1918 to one basic problem of foreign policy as seen by Professor Morley: 'whether to give priority to relations with the West or to interests on the Asian continent'.[12] In contrast to the serving of the twenty-one demands, this decision was a careful compromise that took Western interests into account. Imperial sanction was given to Japanese participation in a joint operation in Siberia on a limited scale. Once the expedition had been launched, however, one division of troops was quickly increased to four or five, and Japanese forces remained behind in Siberia for two years after their allies had withdrawn in 1920. At least one man in the advisory council, Hara Kei (1856–1921) foresaw the dangers of 'military diplomacy', though he did not live to see an example of far greater consequence.

The Terauchi Cabinet fell in the midst of internal troubles brought on by war-time conditions—in short the rice riots of 1918. The figures on the following page illustrate the serious rate of inflation that lay at the root of social distress.

Restraint finally gave way when dealers managed to corner the market in rice in anticipation of a price rise. Rioting spread to the cities, especially among factory workers, after the famous attack by

[12] Morley, *The Japanese Thrust into Siberia, 1918*, p. 310

housewives on rice dealers' premises in a small town in Toyama prefecture. Thirty-six prefectures were affected within weeks of the Toyama outbreak in late July 1918.

	Price Index	Wage Index
1914	100	100
1915	103	100
1916	144	107
1917	179	127
1918	230	157

No election followed immediately on Terauchi's resignation in September 1918. Instead, the *genrō* chose Hara Kei, the leader of the *Seiyūkai*, the largest party in the House of Representatives. The new prime minister had done much to make his party a political force in its own right, and was at the same time a member of the lower house. The appointment of this outstanding party politician was an important precedent. Other qualities marked him out as a more suitable choice than any of the available high bureaucrats and top military men with political experience. Even though he had opposed the appointment of cabinets not under the control of his own party, Hara had won the confidence of Yamagata. It seems that from Yamagata's point of view Hara was the best man available—in spite of his party position. In outlook, Hara, who had once been a government official, did not differ strikingly from the men who had preceded him as prime minister. Perhaps this reassured Yamagata who must have known that it was Hara who dominated his party and not vice-versa, as indeed he was to show over the next three years.

In Hara's time in office (September 1918–November 1921), Japan achieved formal recognition as a world Power. Its delegation to the 1919 Versailles peace conference, headed by Prince Saionji Kimmochi, was treated with great respect, and Japan was awarded a League of Nations' mandate over the former German Pacific islands. However, Japanese control over Shantung was bitterly contested by the Chinese delegation, which refused to sign the peace treaty. A more lasting settlement of this question and others in the area was achieved at the Washington conference which opened in November 1921. Co-operation with the Western Powers was one element in Hara's foreign policy which shifted emphasis from military and territorial, to economic concerns—towards 'co-existence and co-prosperity'. This was in tune with the less aggressive stance of the

Western Powers after the first world war. At Washington, Japan agreed to withdraw from Shantung and from Siberia, and the next few years saw the official encouragement of investment in, and trade with, China. Critics of this policy, in the army especially, were not slow to point out that the agreements in Washington had not guaranteed Japan's position in Manchuria against a resurgent China or Russia. Yet, they at any rate provided for her own security by giving her naval domination over the western Pacific. Hara did not live to see the negotiations concluded. He was stabbed to death in Tōkyō station by a lone right-wing fanatic.

Under Hara, Japan also became a member of the International Labour Organization, which was a mark of her new stature as one of the 'eight states of chief industrial importance'. Nevertheless, enthusiasm over war-time industrial progress came to be tempered by a critical view of industry's performance in the 1920s and reservations about the harnessing of industrial progress for military purposes in the 1930s. There was a counting of the social cost of industrialization now that national political goals had been achieved. People, including foreign competitors, began to point out that government encouragement of industrialization was not matched by official legislation to secure the social welfare of the work-force. There was no restriction on the hours a man could be asked to work and no fixed day off each week, for example. The growth of the city of Yawata from three thousand people in 1897 to over a hundred thousand in 1920 was the prime example of the new city as a centre of production and a source of pride on that account, but not, at the same time, a show-case of social concern.

Yet, industrialization was inevitable and, on balance, beneficial even in social terms. In 1920 Japan took her first modern census. Returns revealed a population of fifty-six million, a figure that was to rise by a little over seventeen million in twenty years. But overall economic growth was even greater, and industrialization played the leading part in absorbing this massive increase in population after 1912, and making some provision for rising living standards, especially in the cities. As agricultural, but not industrial, production levelled off in the 1920s, the younger sons and the daughters of farming families were forced to find jobs in the cities in the comparatively small number of modern, large-scale factories and in the far greater number of smaller workshops. Consequently, the number of people who stayed in the country, with the elder sons generally carrying on their parents' work, remained about the same. Industry and the cities, by absorbing surplus agricultural population, contributed to the stability of Japanese society as a whole. Without this palliative, rural problems like land-hunger, indebtedness and deteriorating landlord-tenant relations would have been even more serious than they were. Because many young men and women entered small enterprises that were not as impersonal as huge factories, the social disruption ensuing from such a continuous, unplanned migration from the land was not as great as might have been expected.

Discontent with the state of the country, especially among the intelligentsia in the cities, focused strongly on the issue of extension of voting rights to all adult males as the key to more general social reform. Hara, like all the party politicians of his day, represented the larger tax-payers. Moreover, secure in office, he did not respond positively to the widespread but somewhat ingenuous enthusiasm for extended suffrage which surged up at the end of the world war, backed by militant workers in the heavy industries which had expanded so rapidly during the war. Some observers trace later disenchantment with party politics in general back to this formative period of government by cabinets made up of party men: first Hara's, and then that of Takahashi Korekiyo (1854–1936), former president of the Bank of Japan and Hara's successor as head of the *Seiyūkai*.

When Takahashi failed as leader of his party, not only did his cabinet fall in June 1922, but the *Seiyūkai*, which had a majority of seats in the Diet, was stricken by internal divisions. There followed three cabinets led by non-party men, two of them high-ranking naval officers. That of Admiral Katō Tomosaburō (June 1922–August 1923), an ex-navy minister, saw to the ratification of the Washington conference decisions, but fell when its leader died in office. Admiral Yamamoto Gombei (September–December 1923) and his colleagues coped manfully with the immediate distress caused by the great Kantō earthquake,[13] but resigned to accept

---

[13] There had been many severe earthquakes in the past, but the Kantō earthquake of September 1923 inflicted such loss of life and wrought such destruction of property that it stands as the greatest in the country's history. While the shocks were more severe in nearby country districts than in Tōkyō and Yokohama, the fires that broke out in their wake, burning as they did for days in both cities, did the more terrible damage. The worst single tragedy occurred in the grounds of the former Military Clothing Depot in downtown Tōkyō, where forty thousand people died as a result of the fires. Overall, nearly one-third of the houses in the Kantō area were damaged or destroyed and more than one hundred thousand people killed or posted missing. Breakdown in communications made it difficult to

formal responsibility for an assassination attempt on the crown prince. Count Kiyoura Keigo led a short-lived 'cabinet of peers' between January and June 1924. The choice of a succession of non-party leaders by the throne's senior advisers, even after Yamagata had died in February 1922, so frustrated party political leaders that they sank their differences. As a result, Katō Kōmei (1860–1926), former diplomat turned party politician, became prime minister in June 1924, chosen by the latter-day *genrō* Saionji Kimmochi.

Katō's party, the *Kenseikai*, had become the largest single group in the House of Representatives in elections held the previous month, but the implementation of its reformist platform, at the core of which was universal male suffrage, was the work of professional politicians carried out after popular enthusiasm had died down, and after the government had been forced by conservatives in the privy council and House of Peers to prove that it could control radical agitation by passing the peace preservation law. As it happened, the new electorate, which was four times the size of the old and now included industrial workers and peasants, did not transform national politics by turning élitist parties with a tenuous hold on cabinet posts into mass-based organizations with decisive power. While elections continued to confirm the supremacy of the two large, and largely conservative, parties in the House of Representatives, so sustaining the claims of their leaders to form cabinets, the workings of the constitution ensured the continued and effective participation of groups other than those to be found in the lower house of the Diet. Katō's reform had simply made it easier for some radical dissidents to work within the existing constitutional structure by organizing political parties of their own.

Katō died in office, apparently worn out, and was succeeded by Wakatsuki Reijirō (1866–1949), once an official in the finance ministry. The Wakatsuki Cabinet (January 1926–April 1927) fell when the privy council refused to give assent to a financial measure designed to curb a run on the banks. The *Seiyūkai* Cabinet that followed (April 1927–July 1929) was led by the politically-minded general Tanaka Giichi (1863–1929), vice-chief of the army general staff at the time of the Siberian intervention and, since 1925,

---

combat the panic and fear that spread quickly and seized on a number of things, including the Korean minority which was in real danger. An account of the social impact of the earthquake is not readily available in English, but a first-hand account of the physical effects can be found in: Poole, *The Death of Old Yokohama in the Great Japanese Earthquake of September 1, 1923*.

president of the *Seiyūkai*. Tanaka used the peace preservation law of 1925 rigorously for the first time to hold down the extreme left, when the first general election with full manhood suffrage, that of 1928, revealed disconcerting support for proletarian candidates. On the other hand, his cabinet proved unable to press home disciplinary charges within the army against the opposition of the general staff. Certain army personnel had assassinated the Chinese warlord Chang Tso-lin, who had become less compliant to Japanese wishes as the unification of China became more of a reality.

Tanaka's successor, from the main opposition party, now called the *Minseitō*, was Hamaguchi Yūkō (1870–1931), a party politician and former finance ministry official. He took office in July 1929 and left it in April 1931 a sick man, having been shot at and wounded by a young fanatic on 14 November 1930, just six weeks after the ratification of the London naval treaty. The time was almost at hand when senior statesmen would judge that it was not in the national interest for the head of a political party to be appointed prime minister.

Hamaguchi had succeeded in gaining imperial sanction for a treaty which curtailed expansion of the Japanese navy and permitted the United States to achieve a superior ratio in heavy cruisers, theoretically 10:6 by the year 1936. This he had done in spite of the naval general staff which considered the ratio 10:7 to be the lowest limit that would allow Japan to maintain her established position in the western Pacific. Hamaguchi's success, whatever the appearances, was not a narrowly personal one, but was based on agreement among a wide group of policy-makers. It was of crucial importance that the navy minister and vice-minister and the emperor's close advisers acted in concert with Hamaguchi and the rest of the cabinet to thwart an attempt by the naval general staff to use its 'right of supreme command' to make government policy. Hamaguchi could claim, when the treaty went before the privy council, that the imperial navy was in agreement, since the navy *minister* said so, no matter what the naval *general staff* held to be true. With that, formally speaking, the matter ended. But feeling in the navy so strongly favoured the general staff that the minister, Admiral Takarabe, was forced to resign. Thereafter, it became *more* and not less important to take navy service officers' views into consideration.

Wakatsuki Reijirō, who had led the delegation to the London conference, replaced Hamaguchi as leader of the *Minseitō* and was selected as prime minister. He took office in April 1931 but in December his Cabinet resigned, unable to cope with a major crisis in Manchuria.

On the evening of 18 September 1931, the detonation of a small bomb placed by Japanese on the track of the Japanese-owned South Manchurian Railway denoted the determination of certain Japanese army officers to make good the claims to territory which their predecessors had fought over and conquered in 1894–5 and again in 1904–5. That evening, on his own initiative, the general in command of the Japanese troops guarding the railway (the Kwantung Army) implemented plans designed to bring the whole of Manchuria under Japanese military control. These plans, which he had approved of in advance, were also known to high-ranking officers in the army general staff in Tōkyō, who deliberately refrained from intervening. However, they were not in any way part of a wider government decision on Manchuria. High ranking officers, in fact, committed their country headlong to a course of action which conflicted with its settled foreign policy, whereby for more than ten years first Hara and then the foreign minister, Shidehara Kijurō, had attempted to ease the pressure of rising Chinese national-ism by co-operating with Britain and America in resolving disputes through negotiation.

In fact, by 1931 this internationalist approach was losing support in Japan, and many people quite unconnected with the Kwantung Army were apprehensive about the future. Some party politicians, echoing these fears, saw both China and Russia as a threat. The former seemed to be gaining a new sense of national purpose, together with the appropriate political and military strength, which boded ill for the separate legal rights and economic privileges Japan had amassed in Manchuria since the beginning of the century. At the same time, communist Russia was strengthening its eastern defences. Finally, in Japan as elsewhere, regional problems in the early 1930s were compounded by the devastating effects on the national economy of world-wide depression. In this general situation of anxiety and disruption, the Kwantung Army's decisive action was widely hailed as resolute. The Wakatsuki Cabinet compromised. Troops were not to be withdrawn from south Manchuria, but they were not to advance farther northward, and an attempt would be made to bring the Chinese Nationalist government to the conference table to re-confirm Japan's rights in Manchuria. In seeking to bring the situation under the control of the Cabinet in this way, Wakatsuki and his colleagues had set themselves an impossible task, for while the war minister proved that he could hold the army in check, the foreign minister could not persuade the Chinese government to negotiate.

Wakatsuki's resignation therefore heralded the success of army efforts to force a solution in Manchuria. To focus only on civilian/ military rivalry, however, is to miss the full significance of the crisis. Within the army the small group of radical officers who had precipitated events overseas had aspirations at home which involved the destruction of big business and the political parties. These domestic ambitions were eventually to be thwarted by more conservative elements, chiefly in the army itself, but they were an important feature of the Japanese political scene in the early 1930s.

In December 1931, the *genrō* Saionji was yet again seeking a prime minister. Instead of choosing the head of the *Seiyūkai*, a politician who had supported strong action in Manchuria, Saionji chose Inukai Ki (1855–1932). The latter was a prominent member of the same party but inclined to curb army demands for unilateral action to consolidate Japan's hold on Manchuria. If Inukai's hopes lay in getting the Chinese government to the conference table, they were to be promply dashed. In January 1932, news that Japan's forces guarding her interests in the international city of Shanghai had bombed Chinese troops in the city shocked an already apprehensive public in China and in the West. The reaction to Japan's attack, limited though it was, ended Inukai's hopes of securing Japan's position in Manchuria by negotiation.

Army control of the region, recognition of a puppet state under Japanese control covering the whole of Manchuria, and close army concern with the politics of neighbouring regions of China and Mongolia became established features of Japan's policy during and after 1932. The 'Shidehara diplomacy' of combining political co-operation with the Western powers with economic expansion on the continent of Asia had been terminated by a sudden revival of military expansion, reminiscent of the Siberian intervention twelve years earlier. Closer examination, however, reveals ominous differences between the two incidents. The Siberian expedition had been arranged in concert with the Powers. Moreover, it was for all concerned a kind of side-show, a gamble for hypothetical gains which could be terminated without too much hurt to material interests or national prestige. In Manchuria, on the other hand, Japan had committed herself, fully and alone, to protect an already existing complex of interests against the likelihood of a notable resurgence in Chinese power.

Inukai lived to see just the beginning of Japan's new situation in the world. On 15 May 1932, the prime minister was assassinated by ultra-nationalists at his official residence. His death had been preceded in February and March by the assassinations of a former finance minister, Inoue Junnosuke, and of the head of the huge Mitsui firm, Dan Takuma, both by members of a small society called the *Ketsumeidan*, the 'Blood Brotherhood', bitterly resentful of the powers in the land and of economic suffering, especially in rural districts.

Ultra-nationalist violence apart, distress was real enough to bring political instability. The government had followed a deflationary policy since the late 1920s but on top of this came a precipitous drop in the price of the rice and silk on which farming communities depended. From Y28.21 per *koku* (180.0 litres) in December 1929, the price of rice fell to Y27.58, then at six monthly intervals to Y18.55 and Y18.47, the last in June 1931. An even more drastic decline in the price of raw silk thread, largely exported to the United States, also took place. From Y1,174 per hundred *kin* (or 60 kilograms) in December 1929, the price slipped to Y849.00, then Y625.00 and finally to Y527.00 in June 1931. A deflationary policy, the American depression, a good rice harvest combined with imports from Japan's colonies, and the lifting of an embargo on the export of gold all brought prices crashing down. Cataclysmic distress in rural areas was matched by the chronic troubles of smaller banks and businesses, themselves aggravated by the depression.

By way of contrast, the very largest firms did well, since their diversity made for strength. Between them, the Mitsui, Mitsubishi, Sumitomo and Yasuda combines, the four largest, effectively controlled between fifty and ninety-five per cent of copper, steel, coal, oil, electricity, ammonium sulphate, rayon, sugar refining and spinning enterprises in the country. Associated banking, insurance, shipping and trading enterprises handled the mining and manufactured products of these companies, and the general success of the huge combines (*zaibatsu*) made for resentment in hard times.

The assassination of Inukai brought the end of cabinets composed of and led by party politicians popularly identified with big business. It is a measure of the growth of military influence over the previous six months that when the voice of the armed services was raised against them, Saionji submitted the name of a non-party man,

Admiral Saitō Makoto (1851–1936), to the emperor, as suitably upright and moderate. Strongly bureaucratic in character, the Saitō Cabinet lasted from May 1932 to July 1934, when it was followed by the Okada Cabinet, of similar character and also led by an admiral known for his moderation. Okada Keisuke (1868–1952) was chosen not only by the *genrō* but also by the former prime ministers and court officials. The armed services did not have a direct say in his appointment, although he was, of course, acceptable to them. The fall of his cabinet in February 1936 came in connection with armed insurrection of the most serious kind.

Before dawn on 26 February 1936, about fifteen hundred troops in Tōkyō attempted a *coup d'état*—seen by them as a true Imperial Restoration. A small number of senior civil and military officials and politicians, including the prime minister, were marked for assassination, and key buildings, including his official residence, listed for occupation. In the morning, with snow lying thick on the ground and no radio announcements, people waited quietly to find out what was happening. Some four men, including the finance minister, the lord keeper of the privy seal, and the inspector-general of military education, had been assassinated, and buildings occupied. The prime minister himself had a narrow escape. The *coup* collapsed on 29 February, with soldiers back in barracks and their attempt to strip away wicked advisers from round the throne branded as mutiny and put down firmly by conservative army leaders, whose actions did much to restore public confidence. In fact, where violent men had sown, moderate men in the services reaped. With national security at stake, there was little prospect of going back to the principles of civilian rule and party control that so many had tried hard to establish against the weight of Japanese precedent and the ambivalence of the constitution.

The two admirals, Saitō and Okada, did not leave Japan as they found it—either in terms of the economy or of foreign policy. By budgeting for much greater government spending on capital goods, especially those of military importance, their cabinets contributed significantly to the easing of social distress and, incidentally, made bureaucratic administration more acceptable to the public. The number of jobs in industry rose spectacularly, but wages did not, because people from the countryside were able and willing to fill the vacancies. Japan was thus able to use the advantages won by the deflationary policy of Inoue Junnosuke to export goods at prices lower than those of its main competitors. Consequently, despite adverse conditions of world trade in the early 1930s and the collapse of the silk market in America, the Japanese managed to double their exports. By 1936 industries which had received their initial impetus in the exceptional conditions of the first world war, such as electricity generation, the chemical industry, machine shops and metals, had advanced both technically and in volume of production, this time to meet internal demand. For a variety of reasons the Japanese, despite a rapidly rising population, made an early recovery from the world-wide depression, through industrial production. Yet growing dependence on foreign sources of raw materials, such as cotton, rubber, oil and iron-ore, stood in stark contrast to the country's estrangement from the political world order.

In 1933 Japan left the League of Nations because of that body's disapproval of what had taken place in Manchuria. In the same year, with less dramatic impact, five senior ministers in the Saitō Cabinet together spelled out a policy which recognized, but did nothing to counter, Japan's new isolation. From the end of 1933, foreign policy was directed at securing Japan's dominant position in east Asia, unaided and unchecked by formal agreements with interested Western Powers. Japan's political and economic control of Man-churia became a key factor in a foreign policy which took more notice of strategic considerations as advanced by experts in the war ministry, than of advice offered by diplomats. This position not only disrupted relations with the West, but was highly disturbing to the Nationalist regime in China, despite Japan's projection of herself as a pan-Asian leader. Furthermore, although the army dominated foreign policy, it failed to present a consistent appreciation of Japan's strategic position on the continent through the 1930s, as factions within it were locked in dispute.

With a foreign policy which accepted Japan's isolation as a fact came greater awareness within the armed services of her economic shortcomings in the face of possible land war with Russia and sea war with the United States. In fact, the two cabinets which followed Okada's fall in February 1936, the cabinet of Hirota Kōki (March 1936–January 1937) and that of General Hayashi Senjūrō (February–May 1937), both came to grief on the issue of greater economic planning. In cabinets consisting of military men and bureaucrats, the war ministry pressed for new laws to mobilize the manpower and resources of the country. The political parties in the Diet refused. Talk of Japan's 'mission in Asia,' more fervent than ever, and adopted as national policy after 1936, did not sway the political parties. When the blunt tactics of the war minister in Hirota's cabinet failed, the gentler tactics of Hayashi were tried, but the political parties would not yield, frustrated at having their leaders kept out of the cabinet. While Japan's foreign policy had been dominated by the military since 1933, it could not be said in mid-1937 that the economy of the country was under total military control. At that time the country was not geared for war.

Conclusion

In the few years before 1937 attempts by the State to dominate national life, though of limited success in the economic sphere, were noticeably effective in the realm of personal and political freedom. From the late 1920s, internal control was achieved despite organized radicalism and the more general growth of awareness of the individual's place in society. At the same time, national consciousness was inculcated to a degree unprecedented in Japanese history. Moreover, governments of the day never had to grapple seriously with political opposition that could claim to be more truly nationalist, thanks to the capture by the Meiji bureaucratic *élite* of the supreme symbol of the nation's identity, the emperor himself, as part of the process of Restoration.

Nevertheless, the successors of the Meiji statesmen in the 1930s, though still able to assert the State's power in the name of the emperor at home, were in no position to overcome problems abroad by wielding the same symbol in the face of foreign, especially Chinese, nationalists. Their own extreme form of nationalism that in some senses served so well at home, was not effective as a tool of foreign policy; yet the government was committed to it since it justified re-shaping the world order as well as explaining the Japanese national entity.

Furthermore, the commitment of the Japanese leadership in the late 1930s to the idea that their country was truly the emperor's State, and their success in suppressing contrary ideas, made the solution of the greatest problem of political life all the more difficult. The fragmentation of political leadership was screened from view behind clouds of ultra-nationalist thought. The hard fact was that the process of modernization had thrown up new kinds of men with claims for a share in politics to safeguard the proper operation of important areas of national life: army officers, the managers of giant business combines, party politicians and high bureaucrats. In the absence of a core of responsible men to succeed the *genrō* in the weighty task of making the most important political decisions in foreign affairs, it was open to the most assertive of the newcomers to press decisions on their colleagues in the name of the emperor. Here the residual powers of the armed services under the constitution were most important, for what was done was done legally.

For some commentators on the history of the 1930s, the failure of Japanese political parties to produce figures of central importance in politics is critical; for others, the narrowly technical outlook of leaders in the army and in other groups is paramount. But a more general description of the character of political decision-making in the critical area of foreign relations, subsuming these and other characteristics, lays stress on the fragmentation of Japan's leadership, together with resultant loss of flexibility. This situation was in sharp contrast to the style of government operating in the Meiji and Taishō eras, which had been at once more relaxed and more genuinely tied to consensus. Moreover, the potential for irresponsibility in fragmented leadership was a danger Japan could ill afford in the circumstances confronting her abroad in and after 1937.

CHAPTER SEVENTEEN

Solutions Through Force

The fifteen years from 1937 to 1952 were among the most eventful in the experience of the Japanese nation. They opened with an invasion of China proper, the first in Japan's long history, followed in December 1941 by a sudden attack with sophisticated aerial weapons on the world's strongest economic power and the despatch of troops to far-flung places: Burma, Sumatra, New Guinea and the Solomon Islands. In the late 1930s and early 1940s, Japan's leaders chose force to solve problems affecting her relations with foreign nations. Inadequate appreciation of the will of foreign peoples to resist was matched by too great a reliance on the spirit of the Japanese people. The rhetoric of a new 'moral' order in east Asia and the wider region, and ultra-nationalist fervour that accompanied the first thrusts and sustained the forward momentum of Japan's armed forces, collapsed in the wake of defeat. Force had met superior force in the air, under the sea and on the ground, bringing the nation to its first outright defeat in August 1945.

Paradoxically, the central element in Japan's ideology, the imperial institution, played a vital role in reconciling the nation to defeat and to the unprecedented occupation by foreign troops that followed. The imperial institution survived to become part of a new constitutional order remade under foreign direction.[1] With defeat ending the public careers of military men and those who had publicly supported them, a new atmosphere prevailed. The rhetoric of the new order was the language of 'democracy'. Preoccupied with recovery from the war's destruction in their homeland, Japan's new leaders turned to internal reform. Foreign masters and new leaders alike used the instrument of law to remake area after area of public life, intending not to bring revolution, but to prevent it. In the aftermath of war, the people proved astonishingly responsive. Yet by way of contrast, in inter-

[1] The throne has been occupied since 1926 by the son of the Taishō emperor. His reign name is Shōwa, his personal name Hirohito.

national politics Japan was inert after 1945, prevented by foreign occupation from playing an independent, let alone a leading, role such as had been hers for fifty years in east Asia.

War in China

It was against a background of stiffening Chinese resistance, brought on by Japanese activities in the far north of China, that the so-called 'China Incident' took place. In mid 1937 Japan's military leaders were not planning to wage war. Yet on 7 July, Japanese soldiers, who were garrisoned in China under the terms of a treaty concluded in 1901 after the Boxer rising, clashed with troops serving under a local Chinese warlord at rail junctions on the southern outskirts of Peking. This was not followed by decisive Japanese action, with specific territorial aims, as in Manchuria at the beginning of the decade. When the incidents occurred, the Japanese garrison numbered about ten thousand men. Hesitation in Tōkyō, particularly among army leaders, was overcome by political pressure on the part of those who were unwilling to tolerate Chinese resistance, especially by the Nationalist regime with its capital in Nanking. The purpose of a twenty-fold troop reinforcement in three months was to bring overwhelming pressure to bear on the Nationalists for a wider settlement of Japan's affairs in China.

Chinese resistance spurred the Japanese to attempt a quick solution through force. Japanese troops from Peking and Shanghai (where troops were also legally stationed) fanned out, choosing as their objectives the larger centres of population and their connecting roads, rivers, canals and railways. In December 1937 Nanking was captured and sacked. Mere incidents had escalated into a full-scale but undeclared war, and fighting spread into southern China. Over the next eight years, the Japanese occupation of China followed the pattern established in the early years of conflict. The Japanese army controlled cities and towns linked by narrow corridors of communication within a far larger area in which a variety of Chinese forces operated. The war in China was neither won nor lost.

Konoe Fumimaro (1891–1945), the prime minister of Japan at the time of the incidents in July 1937, had been in office for about a month. A prince of illustrious Fujiwara ancestry and close to the throne, he was the hope of those who wanted to recover stability in politics and to check the dominance of military men. While the events in China did not rend public life in the way the Manchurian crisis had done five or six years earlier, they were a source of grave concern to senior army officers. Nevertheless, cautious military men were overruled, and the prospect of a quick settlement in China faded. Konoe's political skill in managing to ensure that his civilian government retained the initiative in policy-making was offset by his reluctance to negotiate with the Nationalists while the Japanese army was winning. By October 1938 the Nationalists had retreated in disorder along the upper reaches of the Yangtze River to a new capital in Chungking. They gave ground but did not capitulate.

It was at this time, in November 1938, sixteen months after the commencement of hostilities, that Konoe's government issued its declaration on 'The New Order in East Asia'. While reminiscent of the twenty-one demands, the 1938 declaration is distinguished by its fervent but unrealistic rhetoric.

> What Japan seeks is the establishment of a new order which will ensure the permanent stability of East Asia. In this lies the ultimate purpose of our present military campaign. This new order has for its foundation a tripartite relationship of mutual aid and co-ordination between Japan, Manchoukou [Manchuria] and China in political, economic, cultural and other fields. Its object is to secure international justice, to perfect the joint defence against communism, and to create a new culture and realize close economic cohesion throughout East Asia. . . . What Japan desires of China is that that country will share in the task of bringing about this new order in East Asia.[2]

In the argument that preceded the Konoe government's declaration, critics of this latest round of expansion argued that Chinese nationalism was an insurmountable barrier to co-operation in realizing the vision of a harmonious, moral supranational order in east Asia. They argued too that an attempt to bring this about through force would end in failure. In many cases, these men, who included high army officers, were just as anxious to prevent the rise of a communist movement in China as the architects of official policy, but they proved more far-seeing. In concrete terms, the New Order meant the stationing of Japanese troops in key areas, control over communications in areas where Japanese troops were stationed and special economic concessions. With the growth of Japanese demands on the local inhabitants in north China, guerilla forces under communist leadership expanded

[2] Maki, *Conflict and Tension in the Far East—Key Documents 1894–1960*, pp. 78–9.

their operations against both Japanese troops and the Chinese who chose to support them. Given rising nationalism, the use of force by what were regarded as foreign troops helped to raise the very spectre that the New Order was intended to exorcise.

Until 1941 apparent success in China had to be set against serious local tension with Russians along the northern borders of the region in which Japan claimed hegemony. Fighting that demonstrated Russia's armed strength took place in 1938 and again in 1939, particularly at Nomonhan, where Japan's satellite Manchukuo bordered Russia's Outer Mongolia. A pact with Nazi Germany and Italy concluded as an anti-communist measure against Russia had been signed in 1936; but just before Germany went to war with Russia, Japan and Russia signed a neutrality pact, in 1941. This brought stability to north-east Asia until 1945.

To the south, lack of real success in China led the Japanese government to pay particular attention to the material and moral aid lent to the Nationalist government by other Powers. These latter were prompted to help by a variety of motives including the threat to their Chinese commercial interests posed by Japan's military activities. The Japanese attributed their failure to subjugate the Chinese to foreign support for the Nationalist regime, claiming in a pamphlet issued to their troops in 1941 that 'The umbilical cord of the Chungking regime runs to England and America'.[3] Relations with the Powers were inflamed by both warfare in China and the New Order's anti-colonial aims. After the outbreak of war in Europe in September 1939, Britain, France and Holland offered less resistance to pressure to co-operate with Japan in her plans for east Asia. Anticipating a German victory, Japan concluded a pact with Germany and Italy in September 1940 which cleared the way for Japanese dominance in a yet wider sphere, in south-east Asia.

For two major reasons the Japanese people were inclined to support those of their leaders who believed that armed conflict might extricate the country from what they regarded as an intolerable situation. In the first place, anti-Japanese agitation in America since the turn of the century, and well publicized laws which discriminated against Japanese emigrants to the United States, had created ill-will in Japan even before the Manchurian Incident and the events that followed. National pride had been wounded. In the second place, while the 1930s had seen a further improvement in general living standards, the material welfare of the nation seemed to be threatened by American

[3] Tsuji, *Singapore—The Japanese Version* (trans. M. E. Lake), p. 348.

efforts to thwart its expansion overseas in search of a sure supply of raw materials. The problem of rising expectations in a hostile environment has been a more potent source of conflict than plain poverty, in Japan and elsewhere.

Events in Konoe's second term as prime minister, which began on 22 July 1940, set the scene for Japan's expansion southward. The military's role in making national policy was now generally recognized, and had already been given special prominence in foreign relations by the setting up of liaison conferences between certain cabinet ministers and the chiefs of the army and navy general staffs. On 27 July 1940 a liaison conference decided on expansion south into French Indo-China to assist the war effort in China proper, and envisaged the future use of force south from Indo-China itself. The document setting forth this important decision, so fraught with complications for Japan's foreign relations, was drawn up by military men mindful of strategic considerations.

Before the year 1940 was out, a liaison conference had recommended securing bases in the southern part of Indo-China to achieve access to Thailand. In July 1941 substantial numbers of Japanese troops moved into Indo-China although America, fully aware of these impending moves, had reacted very strongly by freezing funds in order to halt trading. Since Japan drew on America for strategically vital steel and oil, imports of the latter amounting to sixty per cent of her total supply in 1940, this action had a profound effect: supplies already stockpiled could not be expected to last for more than two years.

American pressure was intended primarily to influence Japan's policy towards China. It failed because Japan's leaders, who felt that much blood had been spent on what they considered a morally justified crusade, refused to negotiate the withdrawal of an unbeaten army. At a series of liaison conferences from July to November 1941 it was decided to attack the territories of the United States, Britain and the Netherlands, should negotiations to reverse American actions fail. The principal reason for forcing the issue seems to have been the operational grounds that each day's delay brought a weakening in Japan's capacity to fight, particularly because of the drain on oil stocks. To a leadership unable to contemplate second or third class status for their country in the east Asian sphere, slow deterioration seemed as bad as capitulation through concessions in negotiation. Lieutenant-general Suzuki Teiichi, president of the planning board responsible for resources, put it this way on 5 November:

. . . since the probability of victory in the initial stages of the war is sufficiently high, I am convinced we should take advantage of this assured victory and turn the heightened morale of the people, who are determined to overcome the national crisis even at the cost of their lives, toward production as well as toward [reduced] consumption and other aspects of national life. In terms of maintaining and augmenting our national strength, this would be better than just sitting tight and waiting for the enemy to put pressure on us.[4]

The Pacific War

Two successive secret deadlines were set for successful conclusion of diplomatic negotiations with the American government. If negotiations were not successful, war would be declared. Action on the first deadline was prevented by Konoe's third and final resignation as prime minister in mid-October 1941. His successor was General Tōjō Hideki (1884–1948) whose narrowly military career and decisive character, contrasting with Konoe's civilian background and essentially non-belligerent approach, perhaps gives a false impression of drastic change in a critical period. In setting a second deadline to be met by the end of November the previous scene was re-enacted, but with less hesitation. Immediately after the deadline had been reached, surprise attacks were launched across the Pacific and in south-east Asia. Japan was at war with the United States and Britain.

Japan's success was immediate. The navy's carrier-based attack on Pearl Harbor on 7 December 1941 was the most important in a series of attacks on American installations on the islands of Wake, Guam, Midway and in the Philippines. Other operations took the army into the British colony of Hong Kong, and by sea from the island of Hainan to southern Thailand and north-eastern Malaya. As they headed southward men on the crowded troopships doubtless whiled away the hours studying the pamphlet 'Read This Alone—And The War Can Be Won',[5] with its fund of practical and heartening advice for surviving the sea voyage and the fighting ahead in unfamiliar tropical conditions. Perhaps they wondered how easy it would be, as they read:

Motor vehicles get through by determination. Force your way ahead, even if you have to carry the thing on your shoulders.

[4] Ike (ed.), *Japan's Decision for War—Records of the 1941 Policy Conferences*, p. 220.
[5] Tsuji, *Singapore—The Japanese Version*, contains a full translation by G. W. Sargent (pp. 295–349).

Westerners—being very superior people, very effeminate, and very cowardly—have an intense dislike of fighting in the rain or the mist, or at night. Night in particular (though it is excellent for dancing), they cannot conceive to be a proper time for war. In this, if we seize upon it, lies our great opportunity.

Within five months of the commencement of hostilities, Japan's armed forces had secured the whole of the Malay peninsula and the British fortress of Singapore, the Philippines (formerly under American control) and the Netherlands East Indies (now Indonesia). In addition, they overran Burma (under British rule) in the west and some British and Australian islands beyond Japan's own trust territories as far south as the Solomons in the south-west Pacific.[6]

The Japanese proved more successful in seizing territory from colonial powers than in transforming the rhetoric of their newly announced Greater East Asia Co-prosperity Sphere into a real partnership with the people of those lands. Patterns of organization developed in Japan, such as neighbourhood associations for local control, were enforced in occupied territories; established (Japanese) needs received priority, so that co-prosperity meant that oil, rubber, tin, nickel, bauxite, etc., were channelled from south-east Asia to Japan; while the moral cause proclaimed in Japan took little note of local aspirations until Japan's own position grew desperate.

In Indonesia, for example, a shortage of labour to perform essential works and discharge garrison duties brought suffering to many who were not properly cared for in the labour gangs, and privilege to a few in the new Peta Army. While some younger Indonesians enjoyed the warmth of fellowship in schools that taught co-existence and the Japanese language, older people were irritated at having to use Japanese local time (with a one and a half hour difference) and affronted, if they were Moslems, at having to bow in the direction of Tōkyō.

Yet, when all is said and done, Japan's victories and the public humiliation of erstwhile Western rulers, followed by Japan's own defeat, hastened the achievement of political independence by many colonial peoples. The regimes that Japanese forces fostered for their own ends in Burma and the Philippines, in Indonesia and Malaya, and in Indo-China when French authority was curtailed in 1945, became part of the early history of new nations.

Japan's greater empire, for such it can be called, extended over the widest area for about a year, from mid-1942 to mid-1943. This proved

[6] See map on back endpaper.

to be too short a time to utilize the resources of the entire area as sinews of war and so deny the Western Powers a prospect of victory. This tactic—the consolidation of east and south-east Asia into an impregnable *bloc* under Japanese control—had been Japan's basic strategy for the war. Early defeats for her navy, in the Coral Sea and near Midway in May and June 1942, revealed something of the force which could be brought to bear when America was fully committed to the fray. By 1943 the benefits secured by Japan's southward advance were being reduced as she lost command of the seas, particularly to American submarines. In 1942 the latter sank 4,074 tons and in the next year 388,016 tons of Japanese tanker shipping alone, a figure that doubled in 1944.[7] Added to this were losses to surface naval attack, mines and air attack, sustained at such a rate that Japan was incapable of replacing even half her total losses. In turn, the shortage of shipping and the hazards of long supply voyages gradually reduced the effectiveness of her scattered forces and, by cutting the flow of raw materials, the capacity of the homeland to defend itself against long-range air attack.

The strategy of the allied advance combined with Japanese shipping shortages left some islands and areas cut off and without supplies. Some idea of the hopeless situation in which troops in such areas found themselves can be gained from the experiences of a Japanese journalist sent to record the achievements of the Greater East Asia Co-prosperity Sphere in the New Guinea area in 1942. He recalls how disease, starvation and nervous disorders had reduced the army, driven back to the north coast of New Guinea by the allied advance, to a pitiful condition. Someone had used the words 'lost troops'.

> The words flashed into my mind and stuck there. Faced with unexpected, grave developments in the situation, the Imperial Headquarters had no longer any time to think of the troops they had sent out to New Guinea. Poor fellows . . . [they were] mostly non-career officers and men who had been called to the colours from among common people engaged in peaceful occupations. Were they not children of Japan just as any Japanese was?[8]

This desperate situation was reached as early as 1942 on the south-eastern perimeter of the newly conquered territories.

[7] Cohen, *Japan's Economy in War and Reconstruction*, p. 142.
[8] The person who spoke of lost troops was in fact Colonel Tsuji Masanobu who had played a major part in planning the conquest of Malaya and Singapore and who had just returned to Rabaul from Guadalcanal in a sober mood. See Okada Seizō, *Lost Troops*, from an unpublished translation by Seiichi Shiojiri, p. 45.

Japan's great victories at Singapore and in the Philippines during her quick drive south were to be outnumbered and overshadowed by actions in which her forces were defeated in 1943, 1944 and 1945 on the longer road to the end of the war: on Guadalcanal in the Solomons; on atolls in the Marshall Islands and Truk in the Carolines; near the Indian town of Imphal just across the border with Burma; on Saipan and other islands in the Marianas; and finally on Okinawa, in the southernmost prefecture of Japan. Each defeat shook those in authority in Tōkyō, with Saipan in mid-1944 and Okinawa in June 1945 bringing the resignation first of General Tōjō and then that of his successor as prime minister, General Koiso Kuniaki (1880–1950).[9]

The war effort had strained Japan's capacity from the beginning of the conflict in the Pacific, and it reduced the country to exhaustion. After all, as early as 1941 Japan had already been fighting in China for four years and was fielding an army of a million men. By early 1945, factories often stood idle or operated below capacity because of shortages of materials, even before allied bombing raids destroyed them. Labour shortages affected production in the countryside as well as in the cities, and incendiary raids inflicted death and homelessness on a people already suffering from food shortages. By the war's end, about a quarter of Japan's dwellings in the cities had been destroyed, and perhaps four million people had left Tōkyō. The situation was so bad that Prince Konoe urged those close to the throne to bring the war to an end for fear of a revolution.

---

[9] Official figures of war dead from July 1937 to August 1945 vary, but the accepted total is 3,100,000. The following figures can be found at Japan's equivalent of the tomb of the unknown soldier at Chidorigafuchi in Tōkyō.

Japan	102,900	Sumatra	3,200
Manchuria	46,700	Java	6,500
Russia	52,700	Borneo	18,000
China	455,700	Celebes	5,500
Philippines	498,600	Lesser Sundas	53,000
French Indo-China	12,400	New Guinea	127,000
Thailand	7,000	Mid Pacific	247,200
Burma	164,500	Solomons	88,200
Malaya-Singapore	11,400	Okinawa	89,400
		Taiwan	39,100

It is impossible to tell what proportion were killed in combat or by disease and starvation. It is equally difficult to balance an admiration for the bravery which the fighting armies showed with knowledge of the brutality with which prisoners were treated. Life had come to be regarded as expendable in areas where the campaigning was most grim.

The government was headed in the last stages of the war not by an army man but by Admiral Suzuki Kantaro (1867–1948) who had fought at the epic battle of Tsushima in the Russo-Japanese war and had narrowly survived the violence of the 1936 *coup*. It was he who brought the emperor to take the unprecedented step of declaring himself on an issue of vital national concern: whether or not to accept the unconditional surrender demanded by the allied Powers in the Potsdam Declaration of 26 July. Opinion among Japan's leaders was divided. The emperor's views, influencing military and civilian leaders alike, were solicited only in the final days of extreme peril, first on 9 and again on 14 August. Just previously, on 6 August, the first atomic bomb had been dropped on Hiroshima, and three days later Russia, having already denounced her neutrality pact with Japan, attacked in Manchuria. Russia's action ended an attempt to secure her good offices for a mediated peace.

In these circumstances the emperor favoured surrender on the terms proposed at Potsdam. Finally persuaded that unconditional surrender did not mean abolition of the imperial institution, the government's decision was made public in a radio broadcast by the emperor to the people on 15 August 1945. The uncertainty of success for the peace party lends the story of these last few months and days a dramatic intensity which did not seriously diminish until the peaceful nature of the foreign occupation of the country became clear to all. The crowning irony of Japan's peaceful surrender seems to be that the all-important authority of the emperor had been fostered by the military cliques which had taken the nation to war in 1941.

The Occupation

Despite the heroic stubbornness with which the Japanese had held out in Okinawa prefecture, there was no further armed resistance to the advancing allied forces elsewhere in the country once surrender had been proclaimed. Yet, though the victors did not have to use force directly, for six years and eight months (August–September 1945 to April 1952) they imposed a regime of indirect military rule, backed by a foreign army of occupation.

Following the allies, who were overwhelmingly American, came Japanese troops who were demobilized, and civilians and their families repatriated from the overseas empire where some of them had been living for as long as half a century. The scenes of devastation which greeted them in the cities, with wide stretches of ash studded with chimneys, safes, strong-rooms and the occasional gutted shell of a concrete building, matched the spiritless response of the populace as a whole. Tired out by the war effort, any energy that remained was spent in the search for work, for a roof or for food. In the countryside, with labour returning to the villages, people were better off. To prevent actual starvation, the army of occupation temporarily permitted the government of Japan to cope with such immediate problems as the food shortage.

The Occupation, which from the first had a civilian as well as a military character, was headed by General Douglas MacArthur (1880–1964), the Supreme Commander for the Allied Powers. Its role had been spelt out first in the Potsdam Declaration and then in the Initial Post Surrender Policy. The latter document made it plain that the elimination of a possible military threat in the future was the prime goal and that democratic tendencies were to be given every encouragement as a means of achieving this. It was expected that the Occupation would work through the Japanese government. This it proceeded to do, with increasing attention to detail.

The determination of the Occupation to succeed was embodied in the Purge. This was a bloodless attempt to eliminate important men from public life, and differed in both purpose and effect from the somewhat dubious arraignment of a few former leaders on a far more serious charge of war crimes, for which Tōjō Hideki and six others were executed. As a result of the Purge, professional military and naval men in particular, numbering about 167,000, were prevented from openly participating in politics since it was held that they were largely responsible for leading Japan into war. In all, about 200,000 people were purged with the wider aim of renewing the leadership of the country to protect a parliamentary democracy against the extreme right and, after 1950, the extreme left. Changes in American policy in east Asia brought communists (who had opposed the war) as well as ultra-nationalists within the scope of the Purge before it was ended.

In a more constructive fashion, General MacArthur's staff prompted the Japanese government between 1946 and 1950 to pass legislation reforming administration of the law, local government, the police, education, labor relations, rural land-holdings and big business. In many cases the intention was to restrict the powers of the central government in favour of local authority; in others the aim was a strengthening of the rights of individuals and associations under law. In every case, the Occupation personnel oversaw, where they did not initiate, the work of the Japanese government.

The speed with which the Initial Post Surrender Policy and other directives that flowed from the Potsdam Declaration were put into effect has lent a somewhat spurious unity to these undertakings. The Americans were largely ignorant of Japanese conditions and even of the Japanese language; and the success in putting so much legislation through the Diet depended on the willing co-operation of many Japanese. Though it was apparent that some people tried to please the Occupation authorities by anticipating their wishes, others grasped the opportunity to put previously held ideas into practice, and this factor mitigated the discontinuity between pre-war and post-war public life. Not that the Occupation's role in policy-making was restricted to implementing ideas long cherished in senior and reformist Japanese bureaucratic breasts; far from it; but to some degree this seems to have happened. Moreover, the Occupation wrought virtually no changes at all in the processes of government or the practicalities of administration.

It was in the realm of political rhetoric that the Occupation made its most signally original contribution. Fortified by victory in the field and strong personal conviction, the Supreme Commander himself spoke often of democracy, linking the emergence of a peaceful Japan with government based on 'the freely expressed will of the Japanese people'. The emperor, for his part, in a speech to the people at the new year in 1946, disavowed his mystical aura, but in words that did not borrow at all from the American store of democratic pronouncements. The latter had their most memorable Japanese expression in the new constitution of 1947, which was based squarely on ideas of popular sovereignty. Article 1 reads:

> The emperor shall be the symbol of the State and of the unity of the people, deriving his position from the will of the people in whom resides sovereign power.

But probably the most startling departure from existing constitutional theory and practice, not just in Japan but the world over, came in Article 9:

> Aspiring sincerely to an international peace based on justice and order, the Japanese people forever renounce war as a sovereign right of the nation and the threat or use of force as a means of settling international disputes.
>
> In order to accomplish the aim of the preceding paragraph, land, sea, and air forces, as well as other war potential, will never

be maintained. The right of belligerency of the state will not be recognized.

The will of General Douglas MacArthur as commander of the victorious armed forces was decisive in having these sentiments written into the constitution. Neither the war-weary masses nor the activists of the peace movement had much to do with it. The new constitution as a whole followed very closely a draft which had originated in the headquarters of the Occupation in February 1946. This fact, and the pressure placed on the Japanese government and Diet to adopt something close to the draft, accounts for language recalling not the Meiji constitution but the great documents of American political history. In conformity with the new rhetoric, the emperor's progress from his palace to the Diet building to promulgate the constitution in May 1947 contrasted with past practice. In the 1930s the authorities had tended to keep the emperor from public view. Now he could be photographed in an open horse-drawn carriage, arms upraised with a hat in his hand as he passed through the crowd in the plaza outside his palace.

By contrast with the rhetoric of the times and the constitution that expressed it, the Diet itself represented a considerable measure of continuity in political life. It is true that the old hereditary peerage was abolished not long after the war and that the upper house of the legislature became an elected House of Councillors. In the lower house, however, which had long been the real centre of parliamentary activity, methods of operation, party organization, and many party members themselves survived from pre-war days, at least for a time. Hatoyama Ichirō (1883–1959), the founder of the post-war Liberal Party, had been minister for education from 1931 to 1934. In 1946 he was purged from public life. His successor as head of the Liberal Party, Yoshida Shigeru (1878–1967) became the outstanding prime minister of the Occupation period. Although new to party politics, Yoshida represented another element of continuity because of a long and outstanding career as a professional diplomat.

To an even greater extent than in pre-war days, high-ranking bureaucrats now entered political life by joining parties before achieving cabinet office. Such men provided a leadership of safe and sensible conservatism. Their general philosophy was one of opposition to radicalism in either its Marxist or its ultra-nationalist form. Yet, in their own way, they were champions of modernism and willing to initiate pragmatic reform and administrative innovation.

Their distrust of idealistic extremism was matched by a cautious flexibility.

Given the fact that most changes in public life were effected by due process of law and without violence, the Occupation period seems to have been not so much revolutionary as reformist. A useful distinction can be made, however, between reforms which met the aims of officials or political movements in pre-war Japan, such as the enfranchisement of women and land reform, and those not previously sought, such as the reform of education.

In the case of land reform, the Japanese government redistributed almost four million acres of farmland before 1950 and thus converted most tenants into owner-cultivators. The experience of war-time controls on agriculture, the stiffening authority of the Occupation and the informed enthusiasm of officials and farmers all helped to provide a lasting solution to real problems.[10] A combination of inflation and administrative controls had already disposed landlords to accept redistribution with low compensation. Not until thirteen years after the end of the Occupation, in 1965, did the electoral strength of former landlords win them a larger measure of compensation from the government. There has been no attempt to undo the land reform itself.

In the case of education, the Japanese authorities acted at the insistence of the Occupation, cutting militarist and ultra-nationalist content from textbooks and purging teachers and officials. Then, from 1947, by one means or another students were encouraged to prolong their education beyond the secondary level in a vastly increased number of officially recognized colleges and universities. This development reflected American preconceptions about education and society, and ran counter to the pre-war Japanese idea of higher education for the few.

At the lower levels, in the nine year compulsory course secured by American pressure at a time of economic distress, a new subject called social studies was introduced. The American-derived syllabus expected the children themselves to confront social problems and attempt their solution in the classroom. It encouraged a critical attitude to the social order and a realization of the individual's role in society as an active one, capable of remaking the future. Great stress was laid on peace, democracy and culture as essential components of the new Japanese society to be built for the welfare of the people as a whole. This programme fitted well with the general rhetoric of the day, and

[10] Cf. Dore, *Land Reform in Japan.*

for teachers it provoked a searching reappraisal of the aims of education and a good deal of earnest group discussion.

Commentators, both Japanese and American, have subsequently
questioned the effectiveness of such far-reaching changes attempted
on a nation-wide scale. It is still not possible to give a final assessment
of Occupation policies on education. However, hasty expansion at the
tertiary level inevitably resulted in problems of low standards, poorly
paid staff and too many students, in the short term at any rate. As for
the social studies curriculum, this has lost much of the problem-
solving character that made it so radical in 1947. In its original form it
was found to be too difficult to teach and too neglectful of the country's
past achievements. But experiment with new educational ideas in an
unprecedented situation need not be written off as an attempt to please
the Occupation forces, and so persuade them to leave Japan sooner.

It took time, and the growing hostility of the United States to
communist countries, for the Occupation to promote the economic
recovery of Japan. Concern for demilitarization and democratization
had led to attempts to break up concentrations of economic power,
and the purging of some prominent businessmen. But just as the Purge
came to be extended in the new situation to left-wing political activists,
so positive attempts were made by the Occupation after 1948 to
strengthen Japan's capitalist economy as a counterweight to the
communists' success in China. Inflation, which had been rampant
since the end of the Pacific War, was steadied with American help,
and when the Korean war broke out in 1950 many large Japanese
firms were in a favourable position to accept orders to supply United
Nations forces. (Minor enterprises entertained them on leave.) The
situation was reminiscent of that in the first world war, and economic
recovery helped Japan to retrieve her political independence.

The ending of the Occupation was Yoshida Shigeru's greatest
achievement. It was foreshadowed in 1950 when permission was given
for the Japanese government to organize a para-military police force
to take over internal security from American troops. In fact, the latter
were no longer really concerned with the situation in Japan, but with
wider strategic considerations in east Asia. The agreement of
Yoshida's government to a military pact with the United States
allowed American troops to remain in Japan even after the signing of a
peace treaty in San Francisco in September 1951 and the formal
termination of the Occupation in April 1952.

Postscript

An observer of the scene in Tōkyō on May Day 1952, four days after the end of the Occupation, could be forgiven for having predicted a bleak future of political and social disorder for Japan. On that day, serious rioting outside the imperial palace left two dead and more than two thousand injured. Yet, seventeen years and nine months later, the legal judgment in the case brought against some of the rioters prompted no more than complaint at the ponderous ways of justice from people living under a remarkably stable constitutional order. In like manner, economists in 1952 doubted the viability and potential for growth of the Japanese economy. The latter had barely recovered from disaster only to be fortuitously stimulated by extraordinary American military expenditures in Korea. Yet, after two decades, the pessimists have proved to be wrong in economics as well as politics.

Predictions based on a study of Japan's more recent experience could be closer to the mark. Since 1952, Japanese society has produced more goods and services than in the past, and fewer people. The sustained yearly increase in the value of total production has exceeded by far that of any other country until, today, Japan ranks below only two nations, the United States and Russia, in national economic strength. In addition, the widespread use of contraceptives and legalized abortion have reduced the birth rate to one of the lowest in the world. Therefore, even though the population has grown from eighty-three millions in 1950 to over one hundred million in 1970, this increase reflects the predominantly youthful age structure at the end of the Pacific War, and is destined eventually to turn into a decrease. Already, Japan has an ageing population with serious shortages of labour. Such disadvantages are relatively trivial by comparison with the enormous boost given, in a capitalist and democratic society, to private *per capita* incomes by a combination of a marked drop in the birth rate with a spectacular growth in productivity. At no time in their history have individual Japanese been so well off as they are now, and this affluence will continue into the foreseeable future.

305

Economic success has been achieved by an intensification of certain important historical trends and social influences. Some of these go back to the Tokugawa period; for example, urbanization and a swelling tide of education and general dissemination of information. Others, notably industrialization which in post-war Japan has become increasingly dependent on oil as a source of power, are of rather more recent origin. Another important factor, a social ethic that stresses group loyalties and goals, can hardly be thought of as having been intensified since 1945. If anything, it has been less rigorous. Yet 'the Japanese family system' still exists and has been a constant element in the nation's modern history.

Urbanization and a falling birth rate have brought about a sharp decrease in the numbers of people living in the countryside, not only as a proportion of the total population (villagers are now well under twenty per cent of the total) but also in absolute terms. Rural outlying prefectures, away from heavily industrialized areas, have fewer inhabitants than they did twenty years ago. Partly because of this exodus, partly because of mechanization, and partly because of the increasing frequency with which members of farming households are able to get jobs in nearby towns, life is much easier for those who choose to go on living in the countryside than it was for their peasant fathers or grandfathers. Land reform, together with tariff protection and generous government subsidies for rice, has raised mass agricultural incomes handsomely above bare subsistence. Moreover, fiscal support and the greater availability of mechanical and scientific aids to farming have led to a situation in which fewer farmers are producing a super-abundance of rice. Japan continues to lead the rest of Asia by far in amount of rice harvested per acre and, even with a growth in population to one hundred million, the government's granaries contain two years' supply of the national staple. Such agricultural self-sufficiency has been unprecedented since mid-Meiji times, and is regarded as a mixed blessing by contemporary governments and (mainly urban) tax-payers.

Agricultural surpluses and the problem of what to do with them seem to be one of the 'merit badges' that the gods of economics insist on awarding to modern, developed societies. The same is true of pollution: it rises with the gross national product. Japan, relatively small, heavily industrialized and having its industry concentrated along a densely populated axis from northern Kyūshū to Tōkyō, is particularly susceptible to all forms of pollution—atmospheric, terrestrial and marine. The problem has only lately come to the forefront of the public and official minds, and no one can pretend that real solutions are in sight. Yet it is possible that, owing to the very urgency of the situation in Japan, and because of a convention of fruitful co-operation between government and business as well as the Japanese liking for setting and achieving fixed goals, Japanese society will be the first to tackle pollution successfully. Other of the universal and adverse concomitants of high living standards and industrialism to be found in present day Japan are accommodation and transport problems, especially in the big cities, and a slow but steady rise in prices.

Economic advance has been distinguished by more intensive use of capital and greater technological sophistication. The American bull-dozers that amazed crowds in the flattened cities at the war's end as they cleared building sites now have their Japanese counterparts. Land reclamation, which from the dawn of Japanese history usually signified new rice-fields, now makes possible the construction of oil refineries and petro-chemical works on flat land by deep berths for huge ocean going tankers bringing oil from the Persian gulf. The output of plastics and new synthetic fibres has opened a whole range of profitable and congenial occupations in the light industrial field, where the longer established but equally modern ceramic and photographic industries are also active. Meanwhile heavy industry has forged ahead, especially in the production of vehicles and other consumer durables. Much of the technology has been bought from American firms, but a two-way flow is developing with the Japanese contributions coming mainly from electronic and transport engineers.

Japanese architects quickly made up the lag in technology caused by military leaders' liking for aesthetic traditionalism and the interruptions of war itself. Those who had trained after the 1923 earthquake, when reinforced concrete proved its superiority over brick, were readily impressed by post-war edifices like the Tōkyō *Reader's Digest* building, which showed more recent skills in the handling of steel, glass and concrete. Again, ideas in public building technology and private home design have been exchanged across national frontiers: Le Corbusier (1887–1965) is a name to conjure with in Japan and Tange Kenzō (1913–) is well known abroad, especially for his Olympic gymnasia. It is less well known that modern architects like Tange have been employed in designing municipal offices and halls for music and entertainment, communal libraries and gymnasia, and that some of Japan's most distinguished modern buildings are to be found not only in the big cities but scattered among the smaller towns. They do not overawe the townscape as castles do, but serve the citizens of this secular age as temples and shrines once did, as focal points for community life. These community buildings point the way ahead, indicating social priorities much as the railway stations and banks of the Meiji era did in pre-war Japan.

Labour unrest has been a feature of the industrial scene since the end of the Pacific War. Trade union organization and activities were freely permitted by law for the first time by the Occupation; and many industrial disputes in the late 1940s and early 1950s were bitter. However, employer-employee relations have been much smoother since then, as a result of the Japanese worker's own diligence and productivity which have given him a constant increase in real income and living standards, and as a result of the innate cohesiveness of the family system. For example, most unions are 'house unions' consisting of the employees of only one concern, and their leaders prefer to negotiate with capitalists rather than fight them.

The continuing strength of the family or surrogate family as the basic social unit has also mitigated the problem of individual loneliness, or anomie, that comes with urbanization and the mass society. On the other hand, student activism, which has a long tradition in modern Japan and has recently permeated other advanced societies, continues to flourish in full revolutionary vigour. Its causes are manifold and its aims no clearer there than anywhere else. Nevertheless its virulence is but one indication that Japanese society, again like other comparable societies, should review its methods of education from the kindergarten to the post-graduate level. The seriousness with which both pre-war and post-war Japan regarded education has paid off handsomely in gross national product, for greater productivity has come about as a result of a spread of new skills fostered primarily by the nation's schools and colleges. But both Japanese and foreigners have expressed doubts with regard to the future, when continuous large rises in gross national product will presumably be no longer the dominant concern of society. At that juncture, will all that is required in this field be simply the training of more managers and technicians? Or should not the aims and organization of education be more oriented to individual needs rather than social demands?

Full modernization, with its real benefits as well as its undoubted drawbacks, has occurred under conservative political guidance. Since 1955 the government of Japan has been in the hands of a Liberal Democratic Party (*Jiyūminshutō*). This party represents a coalition of conservative social interests and political factions, and its central element has been the political following built up by that notable post-war politician Yoshida Shigeru. Since Yoshida's retirement in 1954, the two outstanding premierships have been those of Ikeda Hayato (1899–1965) and Satō Eisaku (1901–). The former took office in the middle of 1960, in a time of political crisis. He managed to calm the storms raised by his party's decision to enter into a ten year defence treaty with the United States. At the same time, Ikeda took the initiative in launching what then seemed an overly ambitious plan to double the national income by 1970. Satō Eisaku has been president of the *Jiyūminshutō* and so prime minister of Japan since Ikeda's untimely resignation due to illness in 1964. Having by now been prime minister for a longer period than anybody else in Japan's history as a constitutional State, that is, since 1890, Satō has been turned by the demands of his high office into a skilful and mature politician. He has exercised a stabilizing influence, unexpected but welcome, both on factions within his party and on national politics. His greatest single success has been the negotiations he conducted in Washington in 1969 for the gradual reversion of Okinawa prefecture from American military administration.

The Liberal Democrats have always favoured close military, political and economic ties with the United States. However, this dependence is not so marked as it once was; and Japan seems to be moving gradually to a multilateral, rather than bilateral, standpoint in its relations with the outside world. This latter position would be more in keeping with the nation's economic strength and its reliance on global markets and resources. This need for multilateral relations has led to active Japanese participation in such bodies as the United Nations Organization and the exclusive Organization for Economic Co-operation and Development.

Quite apart from this, Japan's diplomacy will be an increasingly important factor in super-power rivalries as the country approaches super-power status itself. Although no formal peace treaty has been signed with the Soviet Union to end the few weeks of hostilities in 1945, because of the Russians' obdurate refusal to discuss legitimate Japanese territorial claims in the Kurile Islands, Russo-Japanese relations are in fairly good shape. Ambassadors have been at their respective posts in Moscow and Tōkyō since the mid-1950s; more recently, regular air services between the two cities have been opened; and there are full scientific and cultural contacts. Russo-Japanese trade amounted to 821 million U.S. dollars worth of goods in 1970, and there is little doubt that if the territorial and associated fisheries problems could be amicably settled, this figure would swiftly grow.

In the case of China, post-1952 relations have largely been determined by the United States' strong international and ideological objections to the Peking Communist government. On the whole, Japan has been a faithful supporter of American policies with regard to the mainland, and has on its own account established close political and commercial ties with the rival Nationalist regime on Taiwan. At the same time, Japan has sufficiently departed from what was until recently a complete American embargo on commercial relations with mainland China to build up a substantial trade with that country. In 1970, Japan exported goods worth 572 million dollars to China, and imports amounted to 254 million dollars in value. Moreover, as President Nixon's America moves towards recognition of Peking, coupled with military withdrawal from Vietnam and the rest of Asia (including numerous bases in Japan and Okinawa), Japanese policies are bound to be modified. Full recognition of the Peking authorities as the lawful government of China will certainly come, but in time and on terms acceptable to the Japanese as well as the Chinese.

Another side of preparations for a new world situation in the 1970s is revealed by recently announced plans to increase significantly the strength of Japan's defences, especially at sea and in the air, despite constitutional barriers to rearmament. It is intended to make the existing Self Defence Forces capable of protecting the country and its strategically vital interests (e.g. the uninterrupted movement of cargoes across the world's oceans, and the stability of the present anti-communist state in south Korea with which Japan has had formally good relations since 1965) against 'conventional' attack. In common with the other countries of the 'West', Japan relies on American atomic might as a deterrent against threats of nuclear war.

The nation's sensitivity to the areas in north-east Asia closest to it is an obvious and continuing fact of political life; but the concern with China, Russia and Korea is not nearly so overwhelming now as it was before the Pacific War. Similarly Japan is specially tied by geography and the patterns of trade to south-east Asia and the Pacific area generally. Yet the country's economy is too big for it to be confined to one region, however vast; and since its interests are world-wide and peaceful, so should—and probably will—its aspirations be.

At home, the Liberal Democratic Party as a political organization appeals to elements of the moderate and parliamentary right: the bureaucracy, which is the single entity most responsible for Japan's success since 1952; big city business associations; small country town

Bibliography

A useful bibliography is included in a comprehensive general introduction to Japanese culture by John Whitney Hall and Richard K.
Beardsley, entitled *Twelve Doors to Japan*, New York, McGraw-Hill,
1965. This book's chapter headings are: A Geographic Profile of
Japan; Cultural Anthropology: Prehistoric and Contemporary
Aspects; The Historical Dimension; Language as an Expression of
Japanese Culture; Literature and Japanese Culture; The Visual Arts
and Japanese Culture; Religion and Philosophy; Personality Psycho-
logy; Education and Modern National Development; Japan's
Political System; Law in Modern Japan; Aspects of Japanese
Economic Development.

Works on Japan in Western languages generally are most fully
covered in *Catalogue of the K.B.S. Library*, Tokyo, 1965 produced by
Kokusai Bunka Shinkokai (The Society for International Cultural
Relations), while the best critical introduction to English language
books is by John Whitney Hall, in *Japanese History, New Dimensions of
Approach and Understanding*, the American Historical Association,
Washington, 1966, second edition.

Archaic Japan

Nowhere does Western scholarship on Japan lag more conspicuously
behind recent Japanese achievement than in work on Japan's earliest
period. J. Edward Kidder has helped to bridge the gap, so far as
material culture is concerned, with various publications including
Prehistoric Japanese Arts—Jōmon Pottery, Tokyo, Kodansha International, 1968. Other highly pictorial books adapted from Japanese
originals include Miki Fumio, *Haniwa—The Clay Sculptures of Proto-
historic Japan*, Tokyo, Tuttle, 1960. Tange Kenzo and Kawagoe
Noboru also offer interpretive comment in the first comprehensive
photographic record of the Ise Shrine, *Ise—Prototype of Japanese
Architecture*, Cambridge Mass., M.I.T., 1965. Japanese scholarship is
represented in the Kokusai Bunka Shinkokai series on Japanese Life
and Culture. See, for example, Komatsu Isao, *The Japanese People—
Origins of the People and the Language*, Tōkyō, K.B.S., 1962.

315

Quotations in the text from Japanese and Chinese have been taken from:

Aston, W. G. (translator) *Nihongi—Chronicles of Japan from the Earliest Times to A.D. 697*, London, Allen and Unwin, 1956.

Holtom, D. C. *The National Faith of Japan*, London, Kegan Paul, 1938.

Tsunoda, Ryūsaku and Goodrich, L. Carrington (translators and editors) *Japan in the Chinese Dynastic Histories—Later Han Through Ming Dynasties*, South Pasadena, P.D. and Ione Pekins, 1951.

Ancient Japan

G. B. Sansom, *Japan—A Short Cultural History*, revised edition, London, The Cresset Press, 1952 and the first volume of his fuller narrative history (George Sansom, *A History of Japan to 1334*, London, The Cresset Press, 1958) remain the best general works. John Whitney Hall, *Government and Local Power in Japan 500–1700—A Study Based on Bizen Province*, Princeton, Princeton University Press, 1966 is an excellent survey of local history set in a national context.

The most comprehensive selection of readings, covering the whole of Japanese history, has been compiled by Ryusaku Tsunoda, Wm. Theodore de Bary and Donald Keene, in *Sources of the Japanese Tradition*, New York, Columbia, 1958.

Additional books from which translations have been cited are:

Keene, Donald (editor) *Anthology of Japanese Literature from the Earliest Era to the Mid-nineteenth Century*, New York, Copyright 1955 by the Grove Press Inc.

Morris, Ivan (translator and editor) *The Pillow Book of Sei Shōnagon*, London, Oxford University Press, 1967.

Nippon Gakujutsu Shinkōkai *The Manyōshū—One Thousand Poems*, Tōkyō, Iwanami, 1940.

Reischauer, Edwin O. and Yamagiwa, Joseph K. *Translations from Early Japanese Literature*, Cambridge Mass., Harvard University Press, 1951.

Seidensticker, Edward (translator) *The Gossamer Years—The Diary of a Noblewoman of Heian Japan*, Tōkyō, Tuttle, 1964.

Soothill, W. E. *The Lotus of the Wonderful Law*, Oxford, Clarendon Press, 1930.

Vos, Frits *A Study of the Ise-Monogatari*, The Hague, Mouton, 1957, Vol. I.

Waley, Arthur (translator) *The Pillow-Book of Sei Shōnagon*, London, Allen and Unwin, 1928.

Waley, Arthur (translator) *The Tale of Genji—A Novel in Six Parts by Lady Murasaki*, London, Allen and Unwin, 1935.

Medieval Japan

By far the most useful general reading is to be found in the first volume of George Sansom's history and in the second *A History of Japan 1334–1615*, London, The Cresset Press, 1961. Again John Whitney Hall's *Government and Local Power in Japan 500–1700—A Study Based on Bizen Province* provides good supplementary reading. *Sources of the Japanese Tradition* is important for study of this period too.

Additional works cited in the text:

Coates, Harper Havelock and Ishizuka, Ryugaku *Hōnen the Buddhist Saint*, Kyōto, Sacred Books, 1949, Vol. II.

Keene, Donald (translator) *Essays in Idleness—The Tsurezuregusa of Kenkō*, New York, Columbia, 1967.

McCullough, Helen Craig (translator) *The Taiheiki—A Chronicle of Medieval Japan*, New York, Columbia, 1959.

McCullough, Helen Craig (translator) 'A Tale of Mutsu' in *Harvard Journal of Asiatic Studies*, Vol. 25, 1964–1965.

McCullough, William H. (translator) 'Shōkyūki—An Account of the Shōkyū War of 1221' in *Monumenta Nipponica*, Vol. XIX, 1964.

Murdoch, James *A History of Japan*, London, Kegan Paul, 1925, Vol. I.

Nippon Gakujutsu Shinkōkai *The Noh Drama—Ten Plays from the Japanese*, Tōkyō, Tuttle, 1955, Vol. I.

Sadler, A. L. (translator) 'The Heike Monogatari' in *Transactions of the Asiatic Society of Japan*, Vol. XLVI, Part II, 1918, and Vol. XLIX, Part I, 1921.

Sayers, Dorothy (translator) *The Song of Roland*, London, Penguin, 1957.

Early Modern Japan

Since no single book is sufficiently comprehensive, George Sansom's third volume, *A History of Japan 1615–1867*, London, The Cresset Press, 1964 is best read in conjunction with the narrative found in James Murdoch, *A History of Japan, Vol. III The Tokugawa Epoch 1652–1868*, London, Kegan Paul Trench Trubner, 1926; together with analytical and specialized work included in John W. Hall and Marius B. Jansen (editors) *Studies in the Institutional History of Early Modern*

Japan, Princeton, Princeton University Press, 1968; Thomas C. Smith, *The Agrarian Origins of Modern Japan*, Stanford, Stanford University Press, 1959 and Conrad D. Totman, *Politics in the Tokugawa Bakufu 1600–1843*, Cambridge Mass., Harvard University Press, 1967.

Additional works cited in the text:

Boxer, C. R. *The Great Ship From Amacon—Annals of Macao and the Old Japan Trade, 1555–1640*, Lisbon, Centre De Estudos Historicos Ultramarinos, 1959.

Cooper, Michael (editor) *They Came to Japan, An Anthology of Europèan Reports on Japan, 1543–1640*, London, Thames and Hudson, 1965.

Crawcour, E. S. 'The Japanese Economy on the Eve of Modernization' in *The Journal of the Oriental Society of Australia*, Vol. 2, No. 1, June 1963.

Crawcour, E. S. 'Some Observations on Merchants' in *Transactions of the Asiatic Society of Japan*, Third Series, Vol. 8.

Kaempfer, Engelbert *The History of Japan*, Glasgow, MacLehose, 1906, Vol. III.

Keene, Donald (translator) *Major Plays of Chikamatsu*, New York and London, Columbia University Press, 1961.

Sargent, G. W. (translator) *Ihara Saikaku—The Japanese Family Storehouse or The Millionaires' Gospel Modernised*, Cambridge, Cambridge University Press, 1959, by permission of the Faculty Board of Oriental Studies.

Yuasa, Nobuyuki (translator) *Bashō—The Narrow Road to the Deep North and other travel sketches*, Penguin, 1966.

Zolbrod, Leon M. 'The Vendetta of Mr. Fleacatcher Managorō, The Fifth' in *Monumenta Nipponica*, Vol. XX, Nos. 1–2, 1965.

Modern Japan

A number of general histories of modern Japan have been published, but the authors prefer W. G. Beasley, *The Modern History of Japan*, London, Weidenfeld and Nicolson, 1963. Beasley's chapters on the nineteenth century are particularly good. The large second volume of *A History of East Asian Civilization* written by John K. Fairbank, Edwin O. Reischauer and Albert M. Craig, entitled *East Asian The Modern Transformation*, Boston, Houghton Mifflin, 1965, gives the best overall coverage of modern Japan's history. Of more specialized works, apart from those listed below, two need special mention as outstandingly good: William W. Lockwood, *The Economic Development of Japan*

Growth and Structural Change 1868–1938, Princeton, Princeton University Press, 1954 and the six-volume series of articles under the general title of *Studies in the Modernization of Japan* published by Princeton University Press, with volumes edited by Marius B. Jansen, William W. Lockwood, Robert E. Ward and R. P. Dore (others will follow).

Additional works cited in the text:

Anderson, Joseph L. and Richie, Donald *The Japanese Film: Art and Industry*, Tōkyō, Tuttle, 1959.

Beckmann, George M. *The Making of the Meiji Constitution: The Oligarchs and the Constitutional Development of Japan, 1868–1891*, Lawrence, University of Kansas Press, 1957.

Caiger, John 'The Aims and Content of School Courses in Japanese History, 1872–1945' in E. Skrzypczak (ed.) *Japan's Modern Century*, Tuttle, Tōkyō, 1968.

——'Ienaga Saburo and the First Postwar Japanese History Textbook' in *Modern Asian Studies*, III, I, 1969.

Cohen, Jerome B. *Japan's Economy in War and Reconstruction*, Minneapolis, University of Minnesota Press, 1949.

Dore, R. P. 'Agricultural Improvement in Japan: 1870–1900' in *Economic Change and Cultural Development*, Vol. 9, No. 1, Pt. II.

Dore, R. P. *Land Reform in Japan*, London, Oxford University Press, 1959.

Hall, Robert King (editor) *Kokutai no Hongi—Cardinal Principles of the National Entity of Japan*, Cambridge Mass., Harvard University Press, 1949.

Ike, Nobutaka *Japan's Decision for War—Records of the 1941 Policy Conferences*, Stanford, Stanford University Press, 1967.

Itō, Hirobumi *Commentaries On The Constitution Of The Empire of Japan*, Tōkyō, Chūō Daigaku, 1931, 3rd edition.

Komiya, Toyotaka *Japanese Music and Drama In The Meiji Era* (trans. Edward G. Seidensticker and Donald Keene) Tōkyō, Ōbunsha, 1956.

McLaren, W. W. 'Japanese Government Documents' in *Transactions of the Asiatic Society of Japan*, Vol. XLII, 1914.

Maki, John M. *Conflict and Tension in the Far East—Key Documents 1894–1960*, Seattle, University of Washington Press, 1961.

Mason, R. H. P. *Japan's First General Election, 1890*, Cambridge, Faculty Board of Oriental Studies and Cambridge University Press, 1969.

Morley, James William *The Japanese Thrust into Siberia, 1918*, New York, Columbia University Press, 1957.

Okada, Seizō *Lost Troops—an unpublished translation by Seiichi Shiojiri*, Australian National War Memorial Library.

Pittau, Joseph *Political Thought in Early Meiji Japan 1868–1889*, Cambridge Mass., Harvard University Press, 1967.

Poole, Otis Manchester *The Death of Old Yokohama in the Great Japanese Earthquake of September 1, 1923*, London, Allen and Unwin, 1968.

Rosovsky, Henry 'Rumbles in the Ricefields: Professor Nakamura vs. the Official Statistics' in *Journal of Asian Studies*, Vol. XXVII, No. 2.

Totten, George O. *Democracy in Prewar Japan—Groundwork or Facade?*, Lexington, Mass., D. C. Heath and Company, 1965.

Tsuji, Colonel Masanobu *Singapore—The Japanese Version* (trans. M. E. Lake) Sydney, Ure Smith, 1960.

Ward, Robert E. and Rustow, Dankwart A. *Political Modernization in Japan and Turkey*, Princeton, Princeton University Press, 1964.

Postscript

Lawrence Olson has written an interesting appraisal of aspects of life in contemporary Japan in *Dimensions of Japan—A Collection of Reports Written for the American Universities Field Staff*, New York, A.U.F.S., 1963. The concerns of Japanese writers on the passing scene have found their way into English in the *Journal of Social and Political Ideas in Japan* (latterly called *The Japan Interpreter—a journal of social and political ideas*) and *The Japan Quarterly*. The latter also has good articles on traditional Japan.

Index

Abe family, 96
Africa, 275
agricultural incomes, 306
agricultural science, 190
agriculture, 15, 17, 155, 176–7, 226, 243, 275, 279; development in Edo period, 185–90; in Hokkaidō, 227; introduction of, 5; mechanization of, 306, 276; in medieval times, 117; in Meiji era, 233
Aichi prefecture, 215, 230
Aikokusha, 238, 240, 243
Ainu, 30, 47–8, 51, 169
Akashi bay, 62, 198–9
Akechi Mitsuhide (1528–82), 144.
Aki *han*, 215
Akiko (empress), 68
Akutagawa Ryūnosuke (1892–1927), 268
Alexander, 37
America/American, 155; *see also* Latin America and United States
Amida *bodhisattva*, 90, 190–6
Amidism, 128–32, 196
anarchism, 269, 272
Andō Hiroshige (1797–1858), 200
Anglo-Japanese alliance, 224
anti-American feeling, 293
anti-communism, 300, 304
Antoku (emperor) (1178–85), 101
Arai Hakuseki (1657–1725), 204
archaeology, 3–8, 10, 11, 21
architecture, 34, 85–9, 151–3, 307–8, 314
Arima *han*, 168
aristocracy, 8, 14, 31, 38–9, 50, 59, 65, 82, 85–6, 113, 157, 199, 236; displaced by military families, 95, 97, 137–8; local, 11, 28, 32, 51; and *shōen*, 53–4; and Taika reform, 26–8; see also *Kuge*
Ariwara no Narihira (825–80), 63–5
army, 230, 236, 245, 247–8, 250–2,

289; February 1936 mutiny, 286; general staff, 277, 282–3
artisans, 117, 180
arts, 81–2, 191, 207; *see also* architecture, music, painting, sculpture
Asahi newspaper, 267
Ashikaga family, 109–17, 143, 154; Takauji (1304–58), 110–11, 135; Yoshiaki (1537–97), 142–3, 146, 157; Yoshimasa (1436–90), 114–15, 118, 121; Yoshimitsu (1358–1408), 111–14, 118, 121; Yoshinori (1394–1441), 114
Ashio mine, 229
Asia, 3–5, 7, 14, 21, 35–6, 106, 253; pan-Asian leadership, 287
assassinations, 274, 279, 286; *see also* violence
astronomy, 205
atomic bomb, 299
atomic deterrent, 310
Australia/Australian, 170
Awa whirlpool, 63
Awaji island, 63

bakufu, see Kamakura *bakufu*, Muromachi *bakufu*, Edo *bakufu*
baku-han system, 161–6, 210, 246; and Meiji Restoration, 216–17
Bank of Japan, 230, 280
banking, 230–3
barley, 187
be, 14–15, 26–7
beer, 227
Belgium, 241
Benkei, 123–5
benshi, 265
Berlin, 241, 260
big business, 233–4
bills of exchange, 225
Biwa lake, 46, 144, 228
Blake, William, 137

321